ALASKA BY CRUISE SHIP

D0250324

THE COMPLETE GUIDE TO CRUISING ALASKA

ANNE VIPOND

THIRD EDITION

*YOUR PORTHOLE
COMPANION*

TM

**OCEAN
CRUISE
GUIDES**

Vancouver, Canada   San Clemente, USA

Published by:
Ocean Cruise Guides Ltd.
614 – 888 Beach Avenue
Vancouver, B.C.
V6Z 2P9

Third Edition.
Editors: Mel-Lynda Andersen, Diane Luckow
Contributing Editors: William Kelly, Michael Defreitas
Artwork by Alan H. Nakano.
Cartography: Reid Jopson, Doug Quiring, Cartesia, OCG.
Design: Ocean Cruise Guides Ltd
Printed and bound in Canada by Printcrafters Inc.
Publisher: William Kelly
Canadian Cataloguing in Publication Data

Vipond Anne, 1957 –
Alaska by cruise ship

ISSN 1482-9061

1. Cruise ships--Alaska--Guidebooks. 2. Cruise ships--British
Columbia--Pacific Coast--Guidebooks. 3. Alaska--Guidebooks. 4.
Pacific Coast (B.C.)--Guidebooks. I Title
F902.3.V56   917.9804'5   C98-301478-7

ISBN 09697991-5-2

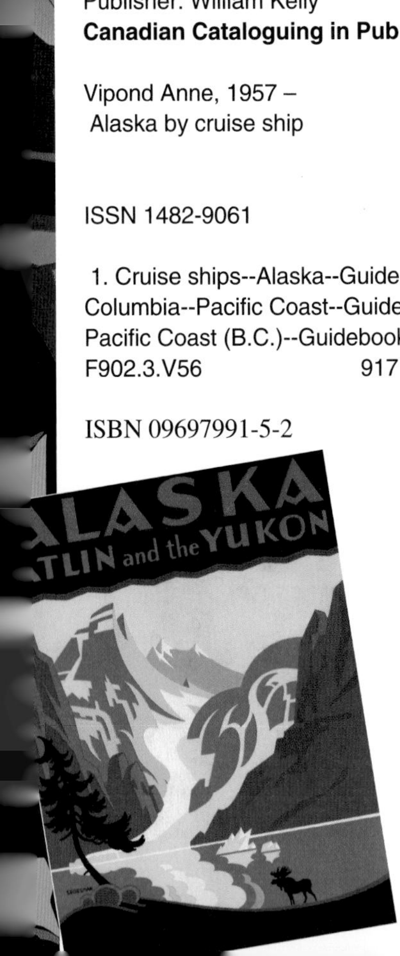

T he creators of this book wish to thank various people and organizations for their help and encouragement throughout this lengthy project. First, we would like to acknowledge the cruise lines that provided photographs and information. In particular, Helen Burford at Celebrity Cruises; Lawrence Dessler and Janis Goller at Holland America Line; Julie Benson and Denise Stanley at Princess Cruises; Rich Steck at Royal Caribbean International, and the public relations departments of Alaska Sightseeing Cruise West, Clipper Cruise Line, Norwegian Cruise Line and World Explorer Cruises. We also thank Cruise Lines International Association and the many travel and cruise agencies which have kindly provided information and suggestions in our efforts with this third edition. Also, a thank you to the various tourism officials at Alaska State Tourism, Tourism British Columbia, Tourism Vancouver, Tourism Yukon, Vancouver Port Corporation, Seattle-King County News Bureau and Port of Seattle.

The following individuals provided generous and invaluable assistance: Dr. David Stone, Geophysical Institute, University of Alaska; Jim Warren, former president of the Pacific Rim Cruise Association; Richard Thomson of the Canadian Hydrographic Service; Captain Terry Bennett of the Alaska Coastwise Pilots Association; Tim Stone at Sitka National Historical Park; and Ralph Bartholomew in the Borough of Ketchikan.

A special thank you to Joyce Kelly, Nan Vipond, Raymond Norris-Jones, Brenda De Jong, and Father Sergius and the Haakanson family in Old Harbor.

CONTENTS

Foreword..VIII

PART ONE

GENERAL INFORMATION

CHOOSING YOUR CRUISE 12

    The Inside Passage 14

    The Glacier Cruise 16

    Picking A Ship...17

    Land Tours 20

    Shore Excursions 24

PORTS OF CALL..30

PREPARING FOR YOUR CRUISE....................................32

THE CRUISE SHIP 38

HISTORY OF ALASKA AND THE PACIFIC NORTHWEST

    Alaska's Bumpy Beginnings 48

    First Arrivals 50

    European Explorers 51

    America's New Frontier 53

NATURAL PHENOMENA 57

WILDLIFE & HABITAT 68

NATIVE CULTURE 92

    Understanding Native Art 100

PART TWO

THE VOYAGE & THE PORTS

Chapter 1: VICTORIA & SEATTLE 108

Chapter 2: VANCOUVER 128

Chapter 3: CANADA'S INSIDE PASSAGE (PART I) 152

Chapter 4: CANADA'S INSIDE PASSAGE (PART II) 170

Chapter 5: KETCHIKAN 188

Chapter 6: PIONEER PORTS 206

Chapter 7: JUNEAU 218

Chapter 8: SKAGWAY..234

Chapter 9: GLACIER BAY NATIONAL PARK....................................252

Chapter 10: SITKA 268

Chapter 11: HUBBARD GLACIER & YAKUTAT BAY 284

Chapter 12: PRINCE WILLIAM SOUND 296

Chapter 13: ANCHORAGE / DENALI / FAIRBANKS.........................308

Chapter 14: EXPEDITION CRUISING 330

GLOSSARIES: NAUTICAL TERMS & CRUISE LINES 340

INDEX 346

COLOR PULL-OUT MAP 353
WITH PORT MAPS

Alaska – the Great Land – is best seen by ship. With close to 34,000 miles of shoreline, Alaska is very much a coastal state. For centuries its waterways were the natural routes for canoes, sailing vessels and steamships.

Modern cruise ships use the same waterways as travellers of bygone days and passengers are treated to the same, ongoing panorama of mountains, forests, glaciers and fjords. Much can be seen from the ship's rail: tree-clad islands, hanging waterfalls, glaciers dropping their ice straight into the sea.

Just as native villages once thrived along this coast, many of Alaska's towns are located on the water's edge – wedged between mountains and sea. Their pioneer history is kept alive by today's Alaskans – people who embody frontier hardiness and community spirit in a wilderness that cannot be tamed.

Whales still travel these waters, bears roam the land, eagles soar overhead, and schools of salmon swim homeward to the rivers that gave them life. The natural wonders are there for all to see, but there's more to Alaska than meets the eye. This book is designed to help you, the traveller, better appreciate the splendid scenery gliding past your porthole.

Perhaps no traveller loved Alaska more than John Muir. A naturalist, mountaineer and writer, Muir was a man of strong opinions who quickly lost patience with others who didn't show sufficient interest in the natural forces – glacial action in particular – which have shaped and are still shaping the landscapes of Alaska.

"Most people who travel look only at what they are directed to look at," he wrote in *Travels in Alaska*. "Great is the power of the guidebook maker, however ignorant."

As the maker of this particular guidebook, I can only hope that Mr. Muir – were he alive today – would not call me ignorant and that he might agree with some of the sentiments expressed here about his beloved Alaska.

As for you the traveller, I hope this book will help you see things that might otherwise go unnoticed as you cruise one of the most spectacular coastlines in the world.

– *Anne Vipond*

(Right) Port of Valdez

(Top) Glacier Bay
(Above) Ketchikan
(Left) Misty Fjords
(Bottom) Kodiak Island

PART I

General Information

Choosing Your Cruise

The Alaska cruise season is no longer confined to the summer months and now stretches from May to October. July and August remain the most popular months for cruising to Alaska, but the shoulder seasons of spring and fall offer more than just reduced fares.

Springtime brings heavy runoff from mountain snowfields, producing a multitude of cascading waterfalls along the steep channels and inlets of the cruise route. Also in spring, many of the Alaskan ports organize a variety of Mayfest celebrations.

June and July are the brightest months, with early dawns and daylight lasting well into the evening. During these months the plant life is at its height – leaves have budded, wildflowers are in full bloom, local parks and gardens are thriving. The summer months also bring feeding whales to Glacier Bay and Frederick Sound. In late summer and early fall salmon swim upstream along riverbeds and creeks, and passengers have numerous opportunities to witness the fascinating and heroic efforts of these sleek fish returning to their natal streams to spawn. Salmon lure other wildlife out of hiding when brown bears and bald eagles appear along shorelines and streams to feed on the weary fish.

The end of the season marks another change in the rhythms of nature. In September and October, pods of migrating humpback whales begin their journey south and are often sighted in the open ocean along the outer coast. This is also the time of year to see dolphins rejoice in their annual rite of fall – mating – and their acrobatics are a delight to watch. It is not uncommon to see dozens of these swift swimmers make a beeline for a large cruise ship to leap in the ship's bow wave.

City parks and gardens along Alaska's Inside Passage, nurtured by moisture and moderate temperatures, retain their splendor throughout the summer.

WHICH CRUISE?

Travellers to Alaska can take all kinds of voyages on all kinds of ships with most cruises departing from either Seward (near Anchorage) or Vancouver, Canada – home port of the Alaska fleet.

Your cruise can be on a large ship over 800 feet in length or on a small cruiser able to get close enough to a berg to plunk ice into your drink. A cruise can be as short as three days (with land tours usually added on) or as long as two weeks. Cruises can also include side trips and shipboard activities which are of specific interest to you. Some companies offer hobby or theme cruises, such as square dancing, big band music, financial planning, photography and nature classes complete with lecturing professors. And for passengers who want to see more of Alaska and Canada, extended land tours (described in the next section) are offered by most cruise lines.

The larger cruise ships trace two popular routes: the Inside Passage Cruise – a loop cruise from Vancouver to the top of the Panhandle and back – and the Glacier Cruise – a one-way cruise either to or from the Prince William Sound area. As mentioned, most ships use Vancouver as the home port, although a few cruises originate in Seattle or San Francisco.

The small ships (under 300 feet) which service these routes call at the major ports and some of the smaller ones, and offer imaginative itineraries into less-travelled areas of the coast. Passage along these routes can also be gained on the British Columbia and Alaska ferry systems. The ferries travel the same channels as the luxury liners but do not make sightseeing detours into glacier-fed inlets.

The Alaska fleet is one of the newest in the world with most ships less than ten years of age.

The Inside Passage to Alaska is so named because it lies 'inside' a long chain of coastal islands which act as a protective buffer from the rough seas of the North Pacific Ocean. Rugged capes, cliffs and fjords define this coast and each hour of cruising brings another spectacular scene into view. This route remains extremely popular for very good reasons: it offers an endless supply of dramatic scenery, friendly Alaskan ports that welcome cruise visitors, numerous port-of-call attractions, and a mild, maritime climate.

The Inside Passage cruise is an excellent introduction to Alaska. About seven days in duration, this round trip will whisk you through 2,000 miles of intricate channels, passes, straits and islands. This is the cruise to take if you are prone to sea sickness. Almost the entire trip is on flat, calm water and there is virtually no motion aboard the ship. Starting and ending in Vancouver, the halfway point is Skagway (or Sitka) – at the very top of the Inside Passage – where (if pre-arranged) you can disembark for a land tour to Anchorage and a flight home.

The twisting channels and passes which evoke rave reviews from cruise passengers are also exciting waterways for the ship's officers up on the bridge. One major pass that raises the neck hairs of ship's pilots is Seymour Narrows, located about 100 miles north of Vancouver. It's a thrill to watch your ship thread its way through the S-turn of this tight pass which used to contain a treacherous, mid-channel obstacle called Ripple Rock until it was blown up in 1958.

There are many beautiful sights along the Canadian portion of the Inside Passage, but Grenville Channel is exceptional. Ship captains have to be very careful navigating this narrow channel where steep, towering mountains and numerous cascading waterfalls are a delight for passengers to view.

Large ships follow the main routes through Southeast Alaska (the Panhandle) while the small ships and ferries traverse the narrower channels and pull into some of the smaller ports.

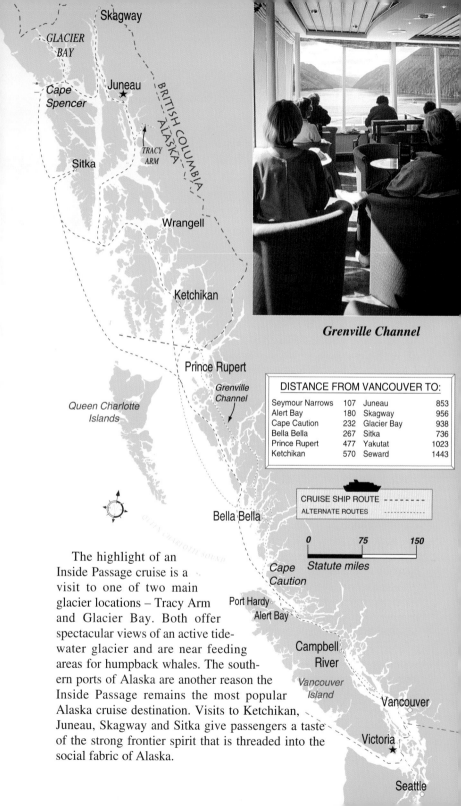

Skagway

GLACIER BAY

Cape Spencer

Juneau ★

BRITISH COLUMBIA

ALASKA

TRACY ARM

Sitka

Wrangell

Ketchikan

Grenville Channel

Prince Rupert

Grenville Channel

Queen Charlotte Islands

DISTANCE FROM VANCOUVER TO:			
Seymour Narrows	107	Juneau	853
Alert Bay	180	Skagway	956
Cape Caution	232	Glacier Bay	938
Bella Bella	267	Sitka	736
Prince Rupert	477	Yakutat	1023
Ketchikan	570	Seward	1443

CRUISE SHIP ROUTE - - - - - -
ALTERNATE ROUTES ················

0   75   150

Statute miles

Bella Bella

Cape Caution

Port Hardy
Alert Bay

Campbell River

Vancouver Island

Vancouver

Victoria ★

Seattle

The highlight of an Inside Passage cruise is a visit to one of two main glacier locations – Tracy Arm and Glacier Bay. Both offer spectacular views of an active tide-water glacier and are near feeding areas for humpback whales. The southern ports of Alaska are another reason the Inside Passage remains the most popular Alaska cruise destination. Visits to Ketchikan, Juneau, Skagway and Sitka give passengers a taste of the strong frontier spirit that is threaded into the social fabric of Alaska.

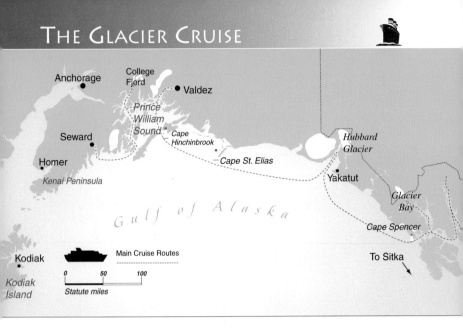

T he cruise lines introduced glacier cruises to Prince William Sound
in the mid-to-late 1980s to provide new destinations for their many
repeat passengers. These are straight-line or one-way cruises which,
when northbound, start in Vancouver and end in Seward, a two-hour
drive to the bright city lights of Anchorage. Seven to 10-day voyages,
these cruises take you past some of Alaska's largest and most active
tidewater glaciers. The following details a northbound trip; simply
reverse the order if you are on a southbound ship.

The voyage normally consists of four or five days travelling the
Inside Passage, stopping at three or four ports and a glacier or two. The
ship then proceeds into the Gulf of Alaska and heads north.

The Gulf of Alaska, part of the North Pacific Ocean, shallows
abruptly about 50 miles offshore. This causes ocean swells to 'bunch
up' near the coast, which translates into a gentle rolling or pitching
motion on board a ship. Unless strong winds are blowing, this motion is
short-lived and localized around Cape Spencer and Cape St. Elias.

You may be able to spot Cape Spencer if you keep a lookout on the
starboard side of the ship (port side if southbound). Within an hour of
passing Cape Spencer, you'll see the only tidewater glacier that discharges its ice directly into the Pacific Ocean. Cruise lines don't often
refer to it in their brochures, but this is the LaPerouse Glacier and it is
stunning. (See Chapter 9 for further information.) Once your ship
leaves the protection of the Inside Passage (or Prince William Sound if
southbound), you will be at sea for about 24 hours. Some ships pull into
spectacular Yakutat Bay to see massive Hubbard Glacier. Those ships
continuing to Prince William Sound will soon pass dramatic Cape St.
Elias – a haunting, lonely cape that juts into the Gulf. After rounding
this cape, cruise ships set a course for Hinchinbrook Entrance and enter

A ship visiting College Fjord nudges close to a glacier's snout where chunks of ice will drop with a thunderous crash into the sea. Often, half a dozen pieces will calve in the space of an hour.

the peaceful waters of Prince William Sound. Major attractions here are the active Columbia Glacier and the many glaciers of College Fjord.

Some ships visit the local ports of Valdez and Whittier, while others proceed to Seward in Resurrection Bay, or cruise the length of the Kenai Peninsula to Anchorage. All cruise ships will, however, be passing within a few miles of Bligh Reef where the *Exxon Valdez* ran aground in March 1989. Cruise companies were just starting to venture into this area when the oil spill occurred and several cruise lines donated substantial funds to assist with cleanup efforts. There is little evidence today of the spill, although ongoing studies continue in coves and bays where salmon streams were effected. (For more detail, see Chapter 12.)

PICKING A SHIP

Once you've decided which areas of coastal Alaska you want to see, the next step is deciding which cruise line to book with. This is not a simple decision but the cruise companies make it a pleasant exercise with handsome brochures containing information on their ships and itineraries. The on-board experience is fairly consistent throughout each cruise line's fleet, and a good cruise agent will be able to explain the individual style of each cruise line. Let your travel agent know what you're looking for in terms of atmosphere and activities, i.e. a casual, family oriented vacation versus a quieter, more refined ambience.

While small ships have the ability to cruise closer to the scenery, large ships have more on-board facilities.

All ships are given ratings by independent travel organizations, and these are based not on the seaworthiness of a ship (safety codes are strictly enforced by marine insurers) but on its level of accommodations, service, cuisine and upkeep.

The cost of a cruise can range from less than $200 a day (per person) on the lower-rated ships to $1,000 a day (including air fare) on the highest rated ships. This price includes all shipboard meals and entertainment. Your choice of stateroom (ranging from an inside cabin to an outside deluxe suite with balcony) is another factor in the cost of a cruise, as is the season in which you travel. The small ships generally fall in the mid-to-high price range when compared to the large ships.

The ferries are your most economical option, especially if you travel as a foot passenger and sleep on deck. There are staterooms available on the ferries and you can take a vehicle if you book ahead, all of which adds to the basic cost of a ferry trip. Another option is to purchase an Alaska Pass which includes train, bus and ferry transportation.

Cruise ships have been compared to floating hotels or resorts, with the large ships offering an astounding array of onboard facilities and entertainment. The small expedition ships offer more intimacy and closer proximity to the scenery. They also tend to be more casual than the large ships which retain traditions from the golden age of ocean liners, such as a

Cruise ships are well known for providing passengers with impeccable service and excellent cuisine.

Captain's Gala and dress codes for dinner, although optional casual dining is becoming a standard feature on the large ships.

When choosing a travel agent, there are a few things to keep in mind. A growing number of travel agents now specialize in cruise holidays and are affiliated with Cruise Lines International Association (CLIA) – an independent marketing and training organization for the North American cruise industry. CLIA offers a course for travel agents which, upon completion, earns them Cruise Counselor Certification and provides them with a high level of expertise in cruise travel. The veteran cruise agents have gained their expertise through years of practical experience.

Cruise lines reward people who book early with lavish discounts, prizes, gifts and, if the opportunity arises, free upgrades. If you know when you want to take your cruise holiday, book early and purchase cancellation insurance.

Ships operating in Alaska are generally well maintained and operated by experienced companies. Holland America Westours and Princess Cruises both offer complete integration of tour and cruise operations, thus assuring a consistent level of quality should you decide to extend your cruise with a land tour or take optional shore excursions while in port. Other cruise lines offer tours through independent operators or through the tour services of Princess or Holland America.

LAND TOURS

There is a sense of excitement during an Alaska cruise when the ship arrives at and departs each port of call. There is, however, a distinct change of atmosphere when it comes time to disembark at the end of the voyage. As passengers bid farewell to one another, many wish their holiday were just beginning instead of ending. The lucky ones, mind you, planned ahead and booked themselves a land tour – which extends their cruise vacation.

Most cruise lines offer land tours which are taken before or after the cruise and must be confirmed when you book your cruise. Ranging from a week to 10 days in duration, these land tours cover hundreds of scenic miles by road, rail and river. They are not be to confused with 'shore excursions', which will be explained in the next section.

Just as the rugged scenery of coastal Alaska is best enjoyed from the decks of a cruise ship, so too are the inland sights best viewed from a spacious motorcoach, private railcar and paddle-wheeled riverboat. Sightings of whales, seals and otters are replaced with glimpses of bear, moose and caribou.

These land tours, organized by the cruise company, include driver-guides who explain the sights and provide entertaining anecdotes about the various areas you are visiting. If you prefer a bit more flexibility, independent tours are offered in which your accommodations and transportation are arranged, and a tour company representative is on hand to answer questions, but you are free to do whatever you like at each stop.

Glacier cruises to and from Seward include an opportunity to visit Denali National Park. (Left) The view from near Mt. McKinley Princess Lodge.

The rail journey to Denali National Park is an increasingly popular land tour option for passengers booking a 'glacier cruise'.

Because there is no end to the combinations of cruisetours available, the best approach might be to decide which parts of interior Alaska and/or Western Canada interest you the most. One popular approach is to take a northbound cruise followed by a land tour of Alaska, then fly back from Anchorage. In reverse, you could fly to Anchorage, embark on a land tour, then board your ship and cruise south to Vancouver. This gives you the best of both coastal Alaska and its scenic interior.

Among the array of land tours available to cruise passengers, an enduring favorite is the trip by road or rail to Western Canada's Rocky Mountains. Famous worldwide for their beauty, the national parks of Banff and Jasper, along with Yoho and Kootenay, encompass 7,800 square miles and three mountain ranges.

The challenging terrain of these parks was opened up to tourists a century ago with the construction of railroads. In 1883, some railway workers chanced upon the Cave and Basin hotsprings. The area was set aside as park reserve and, in 1887, Canada's first national park was established. Initially called Rocky Mountains Park, the name was later changed to Banff National Park.

Jasper National Park was established in 1907 when a second, more northerly transcontinental railway was built. The townsites of Banff and Jasper quickly became service centers for railway workers and park visitors. Both towns contain lovely stone churches, log buildings and gracious hotel resorts. Banff's most famous man-made landmark is the baronial Banff Springs Hotel. Resembling a Scottish castle, this magnificent hotel was built by the Canadian Pacific Railway and has hosted European and Hollywood royalty.

A regal sight, the famous Banff Springs Hotel stands on the slopes of the Bow River Valley in the Canadian Rockies.

Nature, however, receives top billing and today's movie stars must follow much stricter guidelines than did Robert Mitchum and Marilyn Monroe when *The River of No Return* was filmed in Jasper National Park in 1953. No one objected then to their chopping down a huge pine in one of the movie's scenes, but when filming takes place today a park warden is always on hand to ensure park rules are followed.

The parks' natural habitat ranges from sub-alpine meadows filled with wildflowers to valley slopes covered with stands of Douglas fir. The parks are home to 56 species of wildlife. Moose, elk, mountain goats, bighorn sheep and deer are often seen by park visitors – most frequently in the early morning or evening. Less frequently sighted are the bears, cougars and timber wolves that roam the parks.

Summer weather in the Rockies is pleasantly warm with occasional hot spells. On any given day throughout the summer, the parking lot at Lake Louise in Banff National Park is filled with cars bearing license plates from across North America. Described by some people as "the most beautiful place on earth," turquoise-hued Lake Louise is a soothing sight. Lawns and flowers border the lakefront, in genteel contrast to the rugged mountain backdrop which is dominated by the impressive Victoria Glacier. Chateau Lake Louise, resembling a European villa, offers its visitors a picture-window view of the lake's alpine setting.

The highway connecting Banff and Jasper is called the Icefields Parkway, and it snakes through the highest, most rugged mountains in the Canadian Rockies. They form the Great Divide – the continent's backbone – and contain the Columbia Icefield which covers 125 square miles, including the Athabasca Glacier which terminates right beside the Parkway. Snowcoach tours prompt many travellers to pause in their journey and take a ride on a glacier.

The townsite of Jasper is smaller than Banff, but the park itself is larger. It too contains a famous railway-built resort called the Jasper Park Lodge which overlooks Lac Beauvert and glacier-clad Mount Edith Cavell. The highway west of Jasper National Park affords eastbound travellers a spectacular view of Mount Robson – highest peak in the Rockies. If you're heading west, be sure to look back at its dramatic face. A tour to the Rockies will include the interior of British Columbia with scenery ranging from arid ranchland to lush valleys dotted with freshwater lakes, fruit orchards and golf courses.

Whistler Resort, a scenic two-hour drive from Vancouver, is an appealing alpine retreat.

Near Vancouver is another alpine retreat called Whistler. Popular as a day trip from Vancouver or as an overnight destination, this village is a world-class ski resort in winter and is transformed each summer into a haven for golfers, hikers and for those who simply appreciate beautiful mountain scenery. The village streets – open to pedestrian traffic only – are lined with charming shops and sidewalk cafes.

Other pre-and post-cruise tours out of Vancouver and Seattle include ferry rides through the lovely Gulf and San Juan Islands to the British-flavored city of Victoria and the world-famous Butchart Gardens. (See Chapter 1 for more details.)

If the gold rush history fascinates you, then a tour of the Yukon should be part of your cruise itinerary. Some passengers begin or end their Yukon tour at the Alaskan port of Skagway. By rail or road, they are whisked over the Chilkoot Mountains to retrace the gold rush Trail of '98 to Dawson City. (See Chapter 8 for more details on the Klondike.)

A Klondike land tour usually includes a riverboat ride in a paddle-wheeler and a visit to an Athapaskan native village. Kluane National Park and the Yukon Wildlife Preserve are also featured in some cruise-tour itineraries. Overnight stops include Fairbanks where the University of Alaska is based, and where the Alaska Highway terminates. (See Chapter 13 for information on the Alaska Highway.) Passengers also get to see the Trans-Alaska Oil Pipeline, and those who take an extended tour to the pipeline's source at Prudhoe Bay will come face to face with the Beaufort Sea.

Lying between Fairbanks and Anchorage, largest city in Alaska, is Denali National Park, home of the tallest mountain in North America – Mount McKinley. The rail journey that connects these two cities offers passengers some breathtaking views of the Alaska Range as they ride in private cars of either the McKinley Explorer (operated by Holland America Westours) or the Midnight Sun Express (operated by Princess Tours). An overnight stay in the Park provides plenty of opportunities to see wildlife and perhaps embark on a flightseeing expedition, a horseback ride or a relaxing nature walk. (See Chapter 13 for details.)

Other tours include flights from Anchorage to the Land of the Midnight Sun. You will cross the Arctic Circle when you visit the Eskimo village of Kotzebue on the Bering Sea Coast. You will also land at Nome – a town rich in gold rush history and the location of the

MAASDAM

finish line for the famous Iditarod Trail Dog Sled Race which is held each March, starting at Anchorage.

A few of the cruise lines now offer tours to Russia's Far East. Flights out of Anchorage land at Khabarovsk, cultural centre of Russia's Far East, and the tour includes a journey on the Trans-Siberian Railway.

Whether you start or end your Alaska cruise with a land tour, it is sure to enhance your appreciation of this vast and varied country.

Passengers can board a float-plane from a temporary dock moored right beside their ship.

SHORE EXCURSIONS

A cruise to Alaska contains many 'highlights' and shore excursions often top the list. These port-of-call activities are purely optional but usually worth the additional expense. The following is an overview of the shore excursions being offered in Alaska. (For detail on a port's attractions, turn to the chapter covering that port of call.)

Captivating as the ports themselves are, their outlying wilderness areas are what many people envision when they think of Alaska. And there's no better way to see a large wilderness area in a short time than from a floatplane. These usually take off right beside the ship or a short distance from where it's docked.

Weather checks are made every hour and if your flight is cancelled, you will receive a full refund. However, planes still fly in cloudy weather – when the crystal blue ice of a glacier looks even bluer and the fjords are said to be their most beautiful, with mist rising from the water. Headsets are provided with commentary to keep you informed while in flight, but such narration is secondary to the incredible land-scapes passing beneath the plane's wings.

Glaciers come in many forms and from the air you'll gain a different perspective of them. You'll see entire valleys filled with ice and thick sheets of snow blanketing mountainsides. You'll also see blue ice hanging from valley walls, and row upon row of icy pinnacles frozen in a downhill march. If you choose a helicopter tour, your pilot will land the plane right on a glacier and in the moon boots provided you will

Although expensive, a helicopter flight to a glacier is one of the most exciting shore excursions offered on a cruise.

A kayaking excursion heads up Ketchikan Creek.

walk on the surface of a glacier and peer down its deep crevasses.

Flightseeing trips are not the only adventures offered while in port. Water-borne excursions abound: river rafting, lake canoeing, kayaking, sportfishing, wildlife watching and boat trips to nearby attractions. Even seemingly sedate tours by coach are informative, entertaining and a good way to get an overview of a port before setting off by yourself on foot. These tours also give you an opportunity to meet the people who live and work in Alaska, and to ask them a few questions.

Each port has excursions unique to its area and these are detailed at the end of each chapter. For instance, Ketchikan is the flightseeing base for the Misty Fjords – a post-Ice Age landscape of forests, fjords and pristine mountain lakes, upon which your floatplane will land for a few idyllic minutes. Other popular excursions in Ketchikan are the guided nature hikes and the native culture tours to Saxman Village and Totem Bight Park. Sportfishing trips, mountain lake canoeing and kayaking expeditions are also offered in Ketchikan.

Juneau is the main port for taking flights over the massive Juneau Icefield with its many glaciers. Landing on a glacier in a helicopter is a thrilling experience, as is flying over the icefield to Taku Inlet for a salmon bake at a rustic wilderness lodge. Coach tours take passengers to Mendenhall Glacier – Alaska's "drive-in" glacier – and the Mendenhall River is where gentle whitewater rafting can be enjoyed. Golfing, gold panning and sportfishing are also offered in Juneau, as are full day tours to the glacier-lined fjords of Tracy Arm and Lynn Canal.

Skagway, at the head of Lynn Canal, is another port of call offering unique shore excursions. This is where thousands of gold rush prospectors began their trek to the Klondike, and Skagway's tours reflect this colorful past. Most impressive is a ride on the narrow-gauge railway across gorges and through tunnels to the White Pass Summit – one of the gruelling routes taken by stampeders and their pack animals when following the Trail of '98. The Chilkat Bald Eagle Preserve at nearby Haines is also worth seeing.

More wildlife watching is offered at Sitka where sea otters are often sighted. Sitka's Russian and native history is highlighted in city tours which include the totem-lined paths of Sitka Historical Park.

For passengers choosing a glacier cruise to Prince William Sound, excursions include a boat trip across Portage Lake to view the Portage Glacier, and local boat rides past the dramatic sea arches and glaciers of the Kenai Fjords. City tours of Anchorage are also available.

Your cruise line will enclose, with your ticket, information on their shore excursions. These are usually grouped by port of call with their activities described and their prices indicated. Some cruise lines offer advance booking, and once you're on board the ship you can usually book (or cancel) your excursions right up to the evening before you pull into that port. At least one cruise company offers discount packages – a good buy if you're interested in the three excursions (one per port) contained in the package.

At the beginning of your cruise, the ship's Shore Excursion Manager will no doubt present a slideshow talk on the tours being offered. Throughout the cruise additional presentations on upcoming ports will likely be presented, as well as lectures on each area's wildlife and habitat by the ship's naturalist. If you have any additional questions, you can stop by the ship's Shore Excursion Office. There are limited capacities on some shore excursions (you will be told which ones) and these are sold on a first-come/first-served basis.

Your cruise agent or the ship's shore excursion staff can help you co-ordinate your excursions if you decide to take two while in a port and are concerned about a conflict in timing. If you book your shore excursions through the cruise line, there's no need to worry about getting back to the ship on time – the shore excursion staff will make sure everyone's back on board before the ship departs.

You can write ahead for information and book your excursions directly with local tour operators. Should you decide to do this, bear in mind that you're responsible for getting yourself back to the ship on time. Also, the cruise lines maintain a high level of quality control on the excursions they offer their passengers, so if you book independently be prepared to take your chances.

Travellers to Alaska should adopt a bit of pioneer spirit if they are going to get the most out of their port visits. This means preparing for the changeable weather by dressing in layers to stay warm and dry (shirt, sweater, jacket, rain poncho). But also bring your sunglasses – the sun may shine and even in cloudy weather there will be glare off an icefield and off the water. A few of the day-long excursions depend on evening light for return flights and may not be offered late in the season, but most run throughout the entire cruise season in all types of weather.

When booking your shore excursions, try to leave time for a leisurely stroll at each port of call so you can soak up your own impressions.

(Top) Ships departing Vancouver's scenic harbour pass beneath the Lions Gate Bridge. (Middle) The Empress hotel overlooks Victoria's famous Inner Harbour. (Below) Ketchikan's colorful Creek Street.

(Top) Governor's Mansion, Juneau. (Middle) Alaska's Russian heritage is showcased in Sitka. (Below) The gold rush era has been preserved in Skagway.

(Above) Seward is the northern base port for Alaska cruises.
(Right) Kayakers enjoy the breathtaking scenery near Valdez in Prince William Sound.
(Below) Anchorage's Town Square is filled with flowers in summer.

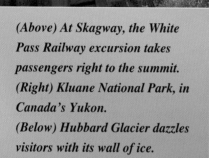

(Above) At Skagway, the White Pass Railway excursion takes passengers right to the summit.
(Right) Kluane National Park, in Canada's Yukon.
(Below) Hubbard Glacier dazzles visitors with its wall of ice.

T he wonderful thing about preparing for a cruise is the lack of effort required. You must pack of course, and you will want to read up on the ports of call you'll be visiting. But as soon as you step on board the ship, your work is done.

For the duration of the cruise you will be treated like a privileged guest. Your luggage will be brought to your cabin by a smiling steward. Your meals will be served by friendly waiters in a sumptuous dining room. Your cabin will be kept spotless by a steward who moves in mysterious ways – never disturbing you but there when needed. Your time will be your own to do as you please, yet the days will fly by. So, to ensure you make the best use of your time aboard, here are some tips on what to take and what to expect.

DOCUMENTATION & CURRENCY

While a valid passport is the best proof of citizenship a traveller can carry, American citizens do not need a passport or visa to enter Canada but must carry proof of U.S. citizenship, such as a birth certificate or voter's registration card. If you're a non-U.S. citizen residing in America, a passport or Alien Registration Receipt Card is required. Canadians do not need a passport to enter Alaska but must carry proof of Canadian citizenship.

From the ship's rail, a pair of binoculars will give you a close look at the snow-covered mountains and tidewater glaciers of Alaska.

In addition to sharing the longest undefended border in the world, Canada and the United States also share time zones. Most of British Columbia and the Yukon are part of the Pacific Time Zone. Alaska has its own time zone which is one hour behind Pacific Time.

American currency is accepted by most Canadian businesses but you'll receive the best rate of exchange at a bank or currency exchange service (there are several at the Vancouver International Airport). Canadian bills are color coded, with coins for denominations up to $2.

Automatic tellers in Canada are often connected to major ATM networks in the U.S. Most American credit cards are accepted in Canada, as are telephone calling cards. Long distance calls can be made between Canada and the U.S. without dialing a country code.

Canada uses the metric system of measurement – distances are measured in kilometres (1 mile = 1.6 kilometres), temperatures are in Celsius (18° Celsius = 65° Fahrenheit; 24° Celsius = 75° Fahrenheit) and liquids are in litres (1 U.S. gallon = 3.8 litres).

WHAT TO PACK

Most passengers fly to the port where their cruise is originating and are therefore limited to two suitcases and one carry-on bag per person by the airline. This same restriction usually applies to cruise passengers who are taking a land tour before or after their cruise. With a bit of planning, everything you need for a one-to-two-week cruise or cruisetour will fit into two suitcases. Keep any valuables (jewelry, travellers cheques, camera, etc.) in your carry-on luggage as well as all documentation (tickets, passport, etc.), prescription medicines and eyeglasses.

Bring casual attire for daytime wear – both on board the ship and in port. The weather in Alaska can change rapidly, so dress in layers. Start with slacks and a light shirt, a sweater, and a light jacket or windbreaker. Also take an umbrella or rain poncho and wide brimmed hat, in case you get caught in a downpour. If the sun shines, you can peel off a couple of layers, and if the sky suddenly clouds over, you won't be cold. On sunny summer days, it will be warm enough to sunbathe by the swimming pool, so bring some resort wear.

Footwear is also important. Your shoes should be comfortable and leather is preferable to canvas in wet conditions. Give your shoes a good spray of all-weather protector before packing them and bring along a second pair in case your first pair gets soaked and needs time to dry. A warm hat is also recommended for those brisk days at sea or when your ship is approaching a tidewater glacier, where air temperatures can be cool. Sunglasses are another must. There is always some glare off the water, even on overcast days. If you're heading inland on a cruisetour, pack some insect repellent or a bottle of Skin So Soft – an Avon product used by sweet-smelling loggers to keep the bugs away.

Your evening wear should include something suitable for the one or two formal nights held on board the large ships. Women wear gowns or cocktail dresses on these occasions and men favor dark suits or tuxedos. For informal evenings, women wear dresses, skirts or slacks, and men wear a shirt and tie or a sports jacket with an open-necked shirt. Should you not feel like sitting down to a formal meal, you can usually order room service or enjoy the casual dining available in other restaurants on most ships.

Check with your travel agent regarding your ship's on-board facilities, such as whether there will be a hair dryer in your cabin, and whether the ship has coin-operated laundrettes with irons and ironing boards. Those that don't will provide a laundering service and hand washing can be done in your cabin.

Sea sickness is not a widespread or prolonged problem on Alaska cruises, especially in the protected waters of the Inside Passage. Modern ships also use stabilizers to reduce any rolling motion when in open seas. However, if you're susceptible to motion sickness, there are a number of remedies. One is to wear special wrist bands, the balls of which rest on an acupressure point. Over-the-counter medications include Dramamine or Gravol pills, which should be taken ahead of time, before you start to feel nauseous. Another option is to chew Meclizine tablets (usually available at the ship's infirmary). Check first with your doctor before taking any medication. Natural remedies include taking ginger in capsule form or sipping on ginger ale and nibbling on dry crackers. Fresh air is another antidote.

Consider bringing a pair of binoculars for viewing wildlife and the passing sights, and don't forget to leave some space in one of your suitcases for souvenirs, gifts and other purchases.

Staterooms can be as modest or luxurious as your budget allows.

YOUR STATEROOM

Modern cruise ships provide the average passenger with a larger stateroom than did ocean liners of the past when there were separate public areas for each class of passenger. Now we are all fortunate enough to not only travel first class and dine, dance and mingle together in luxury, but our sleeping accommodations have also become more spacious.

Depending on what grade of cabin you booked, you will find your stateroom to be, at the very least, clean and comfortable. It will no doubt have a telephone so that you can call room service, fellow passengers or your steward. Long-distance calls can be made from the ship via satellite telephones, but these are expensive and you might want to wait until you're in port before calling home. Telexes and facsimiles can also be sent from the ship's radio room via satellite transmission.

Televisions are another feature of modern staterooms, with which you can watch movies, documentaries and shipboard shows. But most people, after unpacking, are eager to start touring the ship. Valuables can be left in your stateroom safe or placed in a safety deposit box at the Front Office. Security, however, is rarely a problem on board a ship and passengers can feel totally at ease in any of the ship's public areas at any time of night or day.

THINGS TO DO

There are so many things to do on a modern cruise ship, you would have to spend a few months on board to participate in every activity and enjoy all of the ship's facilities.

A daily newsletter, slipped under your door, will keep you informed of all the ship's happenings. If exercise is a priority, you can swim in the pool, work out in the gym, jog around the promenade deck, join the aerobics and dance classes or the pingpong and volleyball tournaments. Perhaps you just want to soak in the jacuzzi, relax in the sauna or treat yourself to a massage and facial.

Stop by the library if you're looking for a good book, a board game or an informal hand of bridge with your fellow passengers. Check your newsletter to see which films are scheduled for the movie theater or just settle into a lounge chair and gaze at the beautiful scenery gliding past the large windows.

Your days on the ship can be as busy or as unstructured as you want. You can play the slot machines in the casino or relax in a deck chair, breathing in the fresh sea air. You can stay up late every night, enjoying the varied entertainment in the ship's lounges, or you can retire early and rise at dawn to watch the ship pull into port.

There are usually two sittings for dinner on the large ships. Early sitting is about 6:00 p.m., late sitting about 8:00 p.m. You should indicate your preference when you book your cruise. If you're on a special diet, your needs can probably be accommodated. For those

There are many activities for all ages on board a cruise ship.

who are simply watching their calories, each night's menu will contain a number of low-calorie dishes in addition to the usual fare, all of which is excellent. There's no shortage of fresh fruit, salads and other healthy cuisine served on board, only a shortage of will power when confronted with so many delicacies.

Children are welcome on most cruises and special activities are often planned for them as well as for any teenagers on board. Honeymooners also get special treatment, and get-togethers for singles are a regular event.

SHOPPING

Basic toiletries are available on most ships, and luxury goods are often sold (tax and duty free) at the onboard shops. But if Alaskan handcrafted items are what you're looking for, the ports of call are where you will be doing most of your shopping.

The shopping districts at most Alaskan ports are located within easy walking distance of the cruise ship or tender docks. In fact, the shops themselves are often housed in or stand among the town's historic buildings and are part of a walking tour – so you can mix sightseeing with shopping.

If you're looking for 'authentic' Alaskan souvenirs, be sure the item carries one of two symbols: the Silver Hand on genuine native crafts or the Made in Alaska polar bears on merchandise made by Alaskans.

Alaskan native crafts include engraved silver jewelry, wood and soapstone carvings, silkscreen prints, ceremonial masks and beaded moccasins. Different native groups spe-

Look for the authentic logo on Alaska souvenirs.

cialize in different art forms and use a variety of materials. (See the Native Art section on page 100 for more detail.) If you buy an ivory carving, the U.S. Fish & Wildlife Service requires that you buy an export/transit permit unless you choose to mail it home. In Canada, whalebone and walrus ivory are both banned imports and offenders can be fined for illegally importing these animal parts.

Gold nugget jewelry is another popular Alaskan souvenir. These nuggets are sold in their natural shape – unaltered and mounted with prongs onto pendants. Each nugget is unique and has a gold content of 70 to 95 percent (compared to 41 percent in 10 karat gold and 58.5 percent in 14 karat gold). The nuggets are weighed by troy ounce, which is slightly heavier than a standard ounce. Local gems include jade (in a variety of colors) and blue topaz – also called 'glacier ice.'

Smoked salmon comes vacuum packed and is handsomely packaged for take-home gifts. Popular children's gifts are the stuffed bears, sled dogs and baby seals, as well as the Eskimo dolls. Russian stacking dolls, lacquer boxes and hand-painted icons are available in Sitka and Juneau. Local bookstores at the various ports offer books on Alaska as well as calendars and prints featuring the work of local wildlife artists and photographers.

VACATION PHOTOS

There is much to photograph during a trip to Alaska and photography buffs will certainly enjoy the challenge of capturing on film the region's unique landscapes, seascapes and wildlife.

A zoom lens is mandatory for shooting wildlife but a large supply of patience is even more critical. Professional photographers spend days, even weeks, waiting to get a good shot of a whale breaching or an eagle plucking a salmon from the water. Count yourself lucky if you get a good action shot of a wild animal. Natural lighting is also unpredictable because of Alaska's changeable weather, but northern skies – especially around sunrise and sunset – often provide dramatic lighting conditions.

If you're a point-and-shoot photographer with an automatic camera, 200-ASA print film is probably your best choice for all-around conditions. And remember to have fun with your picture taking. Be spontaneous and creative rather than analytical when framing a shot. Pack plenty of film and be sure to take your camera to the dining room for the Captain's Dinner – often the last formal-dress night of your cruise.

EXTRA EXPENSES

There are very few additional expenses once you board a cruise ship. Your cabin and all your meals (including 24-hour room service) are completely paid for, as are any stage shows, lectures, movies, lounge acts, exercise classes and other activities held in the ship's public areas.

If you make use of the personal services offered on board – such as dry cleaning or a beauty treatment – these are not covered in the basic price of a cruise. Neither are any drinks you might order in a lounge (although you can certainly sit there and enjoy the ambience without ordering a drink). You will also be charged for any wine or alcoholic beverages you order with your meals.

Tipping is extra, with each cruise line providing its own guidelines on how much each crewmember should be tipped. On some cruise lines tipping is a personal choice while on others it is expected. A general amount for gratuities (in US dollars) is $3.50 per day per passenger for both your cabin steward and dining room steward, half that amount for your bus boy, and 10 to 15 percent of your total wine bill for the wine steward. Tips for these staff are usually given the last night at sea and preferably in American cash. Tipping of lounge or bar staff should be done at the time of service.

The romance of a cruise ship derives from many sources: a change of routine, meeting new people, and returning to a part of our past when travel was slower and more intimate. Literature, movies and television have all contributed to the allure of ships. Even the language of the sea is exotic.

The complexities of safely operating an ocean-going vessel prompted mariners to develop their own nomenclature, its conciseness transcending the descriptive power of landlocked words and phrases. A colorful vocabulary, it has been adapted with lyrical precision to describe each task. As quoted in Smythe's Sailor's Word-Book, "How could the whereabouts of an aching tooth be better pointed out to an operative dentist than Jack's, 'Tis the aftermost grinder aloft, on the starboard quarter.'" Should you wish to question a ship's officer in the vernacular, there is a nautical glossary located at the stern of this book.

Ships evolved as a result of economic need. During the 15th century, when commerce with distant lands became increasingly profitable, trading countries began investing in improvements in ship design. This resulted in stronger, faster ships with better sailing characteristics. Chartmaking was also improved, as were navigational instruments, all of which resulted in Western influences eventually spreading around the world. It is this legacy of exploration, combined with tales of character and courage, that has endowed shipboard travel with an aura of adventure and mystique.

Cruise ships have plied the waters of the Inside Passage to Alaska for well over 100 years. The noted writer and naturalist John Muir first arrived in Alaska by steamship in 1879 and his writings about Glacier Bay sparked tremendous interest in the area. Soon more ships were bringing travellers to view this unique area.

*P&O's **Arcadia** was one of the first large liners to cruise Alaska's Inside Passage in the late 1960s. Built in 1954, she was 30,000 tons and carried 647 first class and 735 tourist class passengers.*

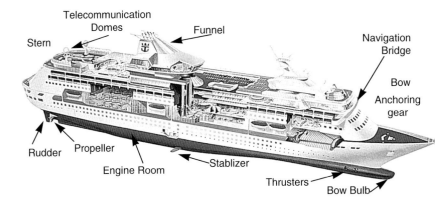

Although a number of companies offered Alaskan voyages through the early part of this century, notably Canadian Pacific, it wasn't until 1957 that Alaskan cruises came into their own. In that year, Westours bought two 110-passenger steamships from Union Steamships Ltd. of Vancouver and with these two ships, the Coquitlam and Camosun, Westours (now part of Holland America) became the first dedicated Alaska cruise ship operator. In 1969, Westours was joined by P&O's Princess Cruises and the cruise business grew into an industry now employing thousands of people.

How Ships Move

Ships of all types and sizes have many things in common. For example, all have a pointed end at the front – the bow – and a stern at the back where one or more propellers drive the vessel. All ships are steered from a high vantage point overlooking the bow, which is referred to as the bridge. A wheel, called the helm, controls the ship's rudder, which is usually situated just behind or aft of the propellers.

A propeller, often referred to as a screw, is the most efficient method of moving a large ship. The blades of a propeller are angled to push water away as the propeller shaft turns. This forces the boat to go in the opposite direction of the repelled water – either forward or backward. (Purists will argue that a propeller actually "flies" through the water, generating high and low pressure areas behind and ahead of the prop.) Props can be 15 to 20 feet in diameter on large cruise ships.

When a ship is being propelled through the water, it can be turned by moving the rudder to the right – starboard – or to the left – port. Turning a ship with a rudder can be compared to turning a canoe with a paddle. The person seated in the rear of a canoe can turn it to left or right by dipping a paddle in the water and holding it there at an angle.

Almost all the cruise ships currently sailing Alaskan waters were built in the last two decades and most in the last ten years – a testament to the booming cruise industry. These new ships have been dubbed 'floating resorts' for their extensive onboard facilities, from swimming pools and health spas to show lounges and casinos. Cabins, formerly equipped with portholes, now are fitted with picture windows or sliding glass doors that open onto private verandas.

Modern cruise ships are quite different from those of the "Golden Era" of ocean liners, which ended on a high note with the launch of the SS France (now the Norway) in 1960 and the Queen Elizabeth II in 1969. These ships were designed for the rigors of regular year-round ocean crossings and some of the worst weather imaginable. Constructed with heavy riveted plating, their design features included a deep draft (more stability in rough seas) and a low profile (less windage, more maneuverability in storms).

Ships built today are generally taller, shallower, lighter and powered with smaller more compact engines. And although their steel hulls are thinner and welded together in numerous sections, modern ships are considered as strong as the older ocean liners because of advances in construction technology and metallurgy. However, some cruise aficionados say that these new ships do not "take the weather" as well as older ships. In stormy conditions, newer ships shudder and pound more but they roll less than older, deeper draft ships. Almost all cruise ships today also have stabilizers – a modern design feature described further in this section – which dampen most of this rolling motion.

Fortunately, an Alaskan cruise is mainly along protected coastal waters and rough conditions are uncommon. There are, however, some regular challenges a crew faces when navigating a modern cruise ship

An anxious moment on the starboard bridge wing as the ship's officers and pilot try to maneuver their vessel away from Ketchikan's cruise terminal in gusty winds. Tugs are sometimes used to assist.

through coastal waters. The first occurs when a large ship is executing a tight turn around one of the many islands of the Inside Passage. You will observe, if you stand near the bow or stern, that the officers begin the turn well ahead of time and the stern – because of the ship's flat bottom – seems to slide across the water for some distance before it gains way or speed in the new direction.

The second situation to watch will be during docking. In strong winds the ship's bow and stern thrusters may be inadequate for maneuvering a high-windage vessel, and tugs will be called upon to help. Ketchikan especially can experience strong afternoon westerly winds. If your ship is trying to leave the dock in such conditions, be sure to watch the action taking place on the bridge wings.

THE ENGINE ROOM

The heart of the ship is without doubt the engine room. Located many decks down from the bridge, the engine room is a labyrinth of tunnels, catwalks and bulkheads connecting and supporting the machinery that generates the vast amount of power needed to operate a ship. A large, proficient crew keeps everything running smoothly, but its size is a far cry from the hundreds of men once needed to operate the coal-burning steam engines that were used before the advent of diesel fuel.

Gauges, meters and control panels monitor the various systems which keep hot and cold water flowing to your cabin, the lights working, the radio and television playing, the heating and air conditioning functioning. All is controlled by the engine room where an incessant and cacophonous racket is punctuated regularly by shrill, insistent

An engineer inspects the fuel lines on one of two 7-cyclinder diesel engines which propel a modern cruise ship and provide enough electrical power for a city of 20,000 people.

alarms. "Just something wanting attention," one engineer drolly explained to some passengers touring the engine room.

The letters in front of a vessel's name indicate the type of engines running the ship. Cruise ships have either SS, MS or MV before their name. SS designates a steam ship – which uses diesel fuel to boil water, forcing steam through turbine blades that drive the prop shaft. A motor ship (MS) and motor vessel (MV) employ large diesel engines to turn the prop shaft. Some cruise aficionados say the older steam ships have less vibration, but today's diesel engines are well dampened to eliminate most of this problem. Diesel-electric engines (which use a diesel engine to generate power for running the electric motors which turn the propellers) are also very smooth running. Almost all ships on the Alaska run are diesel or diesel-electric powered with just a few exception such as World Explorer Cruises' steam powered *Universe Explorer* (formerly the *Enchanted Seas*).

Power needs vary from one-to two horsepower per measured ton, depending on the use, size and age of the ship. On large diesel-powered cruise ships, the engines are three to four storeys in height with pistons two to three feet in diameter. The engines are slow turning, generally under 250 revolutions per minute.

Many cruise ships use variable pitch propellers, which means the blade angle of the propellers can be changed, allowing the officers to increase or decrease the speed of the ship while the engine speed is kept constant. This also means the ship can go from forward to reverse without changing gears and, if necessary, stop quickly. Diesel-electric engines also have the ability to apply reverse power quickly.

Three recent technical advancements below the ship's waterline are the bow bulb, stabilizers and thrusters. The *bow bulb* is just below the waterline and displaces the same amount of water that would be pushed out of the way by the ship's bow. This virtually eliminates a bow wave, resulting in some fuel saving as less energy is needed to push the ship forward. *Stabilizers* are small, wing-like appendages that protrude amidships below the waterline and act to dampen the ship's roll in beam seas. These are normally not needed during an Alaskan cruise. *Thrusters* are port-like openings with small propellers at the bow and sometimes also at the stern, located just below the waterline. They push the front or rear of the ship as it is approaching or leaving a dock and greatly reduce the need for tug assistance.

THE BRIDGE

If the engine room is the heart of the ship, the bridge is the head. The bridge, as its name implies, is an elevated, enclosed platform bridging (or crossing) the width of the ship with an unobstructed view ahead and to either side. The bridge is usually located at the bow (front) of a cruise ship. It is from the ship's bridge that the highest-ranking officer, the captain, oversees the safe operation of the ship during moments requir-

The captain is responsible for the running of the ship and all people on board. (Above) The captain keeps an eye on the shore as his ship glides through the difficult Snow Passage just north of Ketchikan.

ing important navigational or safety decisions. Many cruise lines offer tours of the bridge which, to anyone with an interest in ships, offers a fascinating insight to the navigation of these large vessels.

An array of instrumentation provides the captain with pertinent information. The electronic positioning instruments use a system of satellite signals to indicate where the ship is – often to within a few feet of its exact location. This position is displayed in a series of numbers indicating the latitude and longitude which is then compared with a chart to determine the ship's location. These electronic instruments are functional in any weather and can be used anytime.

Radar is used most intensely in foggy conditions or at night. Radar's electronic signals can survey the ocean for many miles, and anything solid – such as land or other boats – appears on its screen. Radar is also used for plotting the course of other ships and for alerting the crew of a potential collision situation. Depth sounders and plotters track the bottom of the seabed to make sure the ship's course agrees with the depth of water indicated on the official chart.

Other instruments monitor engine speed, power, angle of list, speed through water, speed over ground (which is affected by the numerous currents encountered in the Inside Passage) and time arrival estimations. About the only thing a modern ship doesn't have is a transporter beam to transfer passengers ashore.

During the Inside Passage cruise, large ships must have a pilot on board to give navigational commands to the ship's officers. For exam-

From the bridge of a large cruise ship, the officer on watch scans the horizon while the quartermaster steers a compass course and the pilot closely monitors the ship's route.

ple, a ship departing Vancouver has two Canadian pilots on board. They alternate six-hour shifts up the Inside Passage to Dixon Entrance where they disembark near Prince Rupert, south of the Canada/Alaska border. A few miles north of the border, their American counterparts climb on board to handle the ship's pilotage through Alaskan waters.

When a ship travels in open waters, a pilot is not required. But within coastal waters, the pilot is in charge of the ship's navigation and is there because of government requirements. A captain overrides a pilot at his own and the company's risk. It is a very uncommon occurrence but it can happen if, for example, a captain decides the ship is not responding the way the pilot expects. The pilot knows every back eddy, stray current and dangerous reef in his or her territory and earns a living helping to thread the big ships through the narrow passes and channels which make Alaska cruises so thrilling.

On the bridge, in addition to the pilot, will be the watch officer, one or two assistant officers and the quartermaster or helmsperson. The officers (ranked 1st to 4th) stand four-hour watches with various duties such as recording all course changes, keeping lookout and making sure the junior officers keep a fresh pot of coffee going. A qualified officer is on bridge duty at all times – even when the ship is in port. The captain does not usually have a set watch but will be on the bridge while entering or leaving port, during poor weather, or when there are numerous vessels in the area.

The streamlined look of a modern cruise ship includes such innovations as fully enclosed bridge wings, as shown here on the Maasdam, launched in 1993. Note the lack of a bow wave.

The helm on modern ships is a surprisingly small wheel. An automatic telemotor transmission connects the wheel to the steering mechanism at the stern of the ship. Ships also use an 'autopilot' which works through an electronic compass to steer a set course and is generally used only when the ship is in open water.

There are many navigational challenges encountered on an Alaskan cruise. Those commonly cited by pilots and officers include: Seymour Narrows (fast currents), Cape Caution (lumpy seas, reefs and occasional poor visibility), Grenville Channel (very narrow and often clogged with working fish boats), Snow Passage (fast currents, shallow and twisting passage), Cape Decision (choppy seas and often poor visibility combined with a blind corner), Cape Spencer (steep seas and contrary currents), Cape St. Elias (occasional storms, lumpy seas, poor visibility), and Hinchinbrook Entrance (currents, occasional poor visibility and the most menacing cliffs you're likely to see anywhere!). On the positive side, icebergs are generally not a safety factor (with the exception of the entrance area to the Columbia Glacier) because those breaking off of glaciers usually melt before they drift into the shipping lanes.

BOAT SAFETY

On most bridges, a large area of instrumentation is devoted to the monitoring of numerous fire alarms placed throughout the ship. If an alarm sounds, it rings on the bridge and is illuminated on a ship's diagram so that its location is immediately known. If a serious fire exists, the officers will enact a safety procedure which promptly secures the area and prevents the blaze from spreading. After ship navigation, the threat of a fire is the most serious concern for the ship's officers and the crew practise fire safety drills religiously.

The cruise lines place safety as a top priority. Fire and life boat drills are just part of the higher standards introduced over the last 20 years by the International Maritime Organization. These also include regular ship inspections for cleanliness and seaworthiness in order to obtain insurance and stay in business.

Cruise ships must adhere to a law requiring that a lifeboat drill take place within 24 hours of embarkation, and many ships schedule this drill just before leaving port. You will be asked to don one of the life-jackets kept in your cabin and proceed to your lifeboat station (directions will be displayed somewhere in your cabin). Your steward and other ship's staff will be on hand to guide you through the safety drill but it's wise to pay attention so you know what to do in the unlikely event of an emergency. These safety drills are similar to that experienced on aircraft and passengers shouldn't become apprehensive – cruise ships are one of the safest modes of travel.

HOTEL STAFF

The Purser's Office/Front Desk is the pleasure center of the ship. And since a cruise is meant to be an extremely enjoyable experience, it is fitting the Hotel Manager's rank is second only to that of the Captain.

In terms of staff, the Hotel Manager has by far the largest. It is his responsibility to make sure beds are made, meals are served, wines are poured, entertainment is provided and tour buses arrive on time – all the while keeping a smile on his face. His management staff includes a Purser, Food Service Manager, Beverage Manager, Chief Housekeeper, Cruise Director and Shore Excursion Manager.

Hotel managers generally have many years experience on ships before rising to this position. Often they train in either the hotel or food industries, where they learn the logistics of feeding hundreds of people at a sitting.

A ship's hotel manager will plan on four to five meals a day per passenger and three per day for each crew member. This amounts to an astounding quantity of food consumed in a seven-day cruise. A 1,200-passenger ship, for example, would go through 5,000 pounds of beef, 4,000 pounds of chicken, 4,500 pounds of fish and 24 pounds of caviar.

The uniforms of hotel staff, like those of the ship's officers and engineers, will vary depending on their role. Even if a hotel officer doesn't recognize a crew member, he will know at a glance that person's duties by the color of his uniform or the distinguishing bars on his sleeve. The hotel staff on ships often come from Southeast Asia, Europe or the countries of the Caribbean.

The Alaska cruise fleet has one of the lowest passenger-to-crew ratios in the world, averaging just over two passengers per crew mem-

A ship's Hotel Manager oversees a large staff that works around the clock to transform an ocean liner into a floating resort.

ber. This means generally good service, depending on the crew's training and how well they are treated by the cruise company.

ADDITIONAL INFORMATION

Most ships serving Alaska have very advanced communications systems. If you roam around the upper decks you will see large domes which contain the ship's telecommunications equipment. These enable the crew or any passenger to telephone home at any time during the voyage.

Fresh water on Alaska cruise ships is normally obtained from various ports of call. This is cheaper for the cruise companies than making their own by desalinating ocean water. Fuel is taken on in Seattle, Vancouver or one of the Alaskan ports every third or fourth trip. The fuel used for the Alaska run is a higher grade than normal, producing less smoke and pollution. No ship can discard any garbage along Canadian or U.S. coastal waters and all ships have some recycling program in place to minimize the size of refuse pile at the end of a cruise.

Large ships generally travel at a speed of 15 to 18 knots on Alaskan cruises, while smaller ships may cruise in the 10-to-12 knot range. Using the distance table at the back of this book, you can calculate your ship's average speed based on the hours of travel between each port.

For a complete listing of ships serving the Alaska cruise run, see the Cruise Lines Glossary at the back of the book.

ALASKA'S BUMPY BEGINNINGS

Alaska, were it rated by Hollywood censors, would receive an "R" for violence. A battle scene on a planetary scale is occurring along the west coast of North America where sections of the earth's crust – called tectonic plates – are colliding. For geology students, this is exciting stuff.

As the Pacific plate rams into the North American plate, dramatic action is taking place along the Gulf of Alaska coastline. Here some of the world's tallest coastal mountains, caught between these two plates, are being shoved upwards. Others are slipping into the sea as they are dragged under along the collision zone. Something's got to give with this constant pushing and pulling going on, and that something is the occasional earthquake or volcanic eruption. Mountains twist, shake and heave tons of snow and rock from their slopes, or spew from their cores a fiery ash that turns day into night.

The tectonic tug of war that eventually formed Alaska, started when the earth's crust began dividing into plates – a process which seems to have started shortly after the crust was formed. As these large plates rubbed against each other, pieces chipped off and became terranes. These fragments could move more freely than the large plates and the earth's crust became a sort of jigsaw puzzle as pieces slowly moved from one location to another. An island, perhaps where the Philippines are today, gradually made its way across the Pacific Ocean to lie off Canada's West Coast and become part of Vancouver Island.

Alaska's dramatic Gulf of Alaska coastline was formed by terranes – pieces of the earth's crust – being jammed between two major plates.

While this rearranging of pieces was going on, the continental plates joined together to form the supercontinent Pangaea, which then broke apart again into continents much as we know them today. Ocean basins opened and faults (fractures in the earth's crust) formed. It was during the middle period of this era – the Mesozoic – that dinosaurs roamed the earth, only to reappear in the Hollywood film Jurassic Park.

Over the last few hundred million years, terranes off the Pacific Plate have been pushed, as if on a conveyor belt, up the west side of the North American Plate where they docked against ancestral Alaska, and against one another, at the top of the Gulf of Alaska. These terranes are still moving today, with the Yakutat terrane riding on the Pacific plate but also docking against the earlier arrivals. If the terrane upon which Los Angeles sits continues moving north at it's rate of two inches per year, it will reach the northern Gulf of Alaska.in 76 million years.

The current era – the Cenozoic – began 65 million years ago. It began with volcanism and huge slices of crustal rocks stacking one upon the other to form the Rockies and other mountain ranges. Early whales appeared, as did the hardwoods and redwoods of North America. Then the warm, humid climate cooled and fur-bearing animals such as the bear, seal and raccoon came into being. As the climate continued to cool about five million years ago, the widespread giant ape evolved into a manlike ape and the earliest human artifacts date from this era which ended about two million years ago.

The Pleistocene era – the age of glaciers – came next and it contained four or five separate periods of major glacial advance and retreat. These rumbling fields of ice eroded rock and transported huge deposits of clay, sand and gravel across large sections of North America.

When the glaciers staged their most recent retreat 10,000 years ago, the landscaping they left behind included lakes, valleys and fjords. Channels of the Inside Passage mark the location of inactive faults, their weakened rock eroded by glaciers to form U-shaped valleys that were eventually flooded by rising sea levels. Some mammals (such as the sabertooth tiger) didn't survive the Great Ice Age but homo sapiens did.

New Eddystone Rock, situated in the East Behm Canal within Misty Fjords National Monument, is a 234-foot shaft of rock called a 'stack' by geologists.

THE FIRST ARRIVALS

Ice covered much of Alaska during the age of glaciers, extending across the northern Gulf of Alaska. Sea levels were also lower, and an ice-free corridor of land connected Alaska with Siberia via the Bering Land bridge – now referred to as Beringia. About 30,000 years ago, humans began to migrate from Asia to North America, where they established hunting camps in Alaska's interior and Canada's Yukon. About 10,000 years ago, following the retreat of the glaciers, some of these nomadic peoples may have migrated south along a coastal plain before the melting glaciers flooded this corridor. Sea levels finally stabilized about 5,000 years ago, and the Inside Passage as we now know it became permanently inhabited by people. The maritime climate was mild, the rivers were filled with salmon and the lush forests of cedar and spruce provided an endless supply of building material.

The Aleuts wore ceremonial cloaks made from the skins of hundreds of tufted puffins.

Prime waterfront locations were snapped up as bands established summer and winter villages, and fishing and hunting territories. These highly organized societies thrived along the entire Inside Passage, from Puget Sound to the top of the Alaskan Panhandle. The rest of Alaska's coastline was inhabited by Eskimos and Aleuts, while Athapaskans – the region's first inhabitants – lived in the interior.

Each of these native groups was affected in different ways when European explorers arrived at their shores and engaged them in the fur trade. The Aleuts were traumatized by the Russian promyshlenniki (frontier men) who enslaved them as hunters, but the coastal Indians initially profited from the fur trade – exchanging their furs for metal and tools. Eventually, rum and firearms became popular items of exchange and native social structures began to unravel. The deadliest European import was disease, and whole villages were wiped out by smallpox and other epidemics.

EUROPEAN EXPLORERS

The 18th century was an era of great naval exploration. Russian explorers – led by the Danish sea captain Vitus Bering – set off from the shores of Siberia to discover what lay to the east. Spanish, French and British ships also ventured into the Pacific's northern waters in search of the elusive Northwest Passage. During this Age of Enlightenment, naval commanders such as Britain's Cook, France's La Perouse and Spain's Malaspina all led scientific expeditions to the New World.

Sitka Sound was already a popular port of call for British and American merchant ships when Russian fur traders built a fort here in 1799.

The logbooks of these and other commanders provide a wealth of information on the native cultures that thrived at this time of First Contact. Some natives, upon initially seeing these strangely clad, pale-skinned men, fled into the forest. Others, overcome with curiosity, ran their hands across their visitors' faces to see if darker skin lay beneath a layer of white paint.

Captain Cook speculated that cannibalism was practiced by North Coast natives, but this rumor was dispelled by Captain Vancouver when he wrote that his men, while camped on shore, offered venison to some natives who mistook it for human flesh and made their aversion quite clear, refusing to eat any of it until the British sailors produced a deer carcass to prove that they were not cannibals.

The natives were duly impressed with the white-winged sailing ships that magically appeared on the horizon. Captains were honored guests at the homes of village chiefs and, in a show of reciprocal hospi-

A wooden cross at Three Saints Bay on Kodiak Island marks the location of Alaska's first permanent European settlement established here by the Russians in 1784.

tality, ship's tours were often held for high-ranking village members. The ships and their nautical instruments fascinated the natives. One chief, when shown how a telescope worked, asked a naval officer if he could see around a bend in a channel with it and watch for approaching enemy tribes.

The Spanish explored much of the Pacific Northwest in the mid-to-late 1700s but were secretive about their discoveries. When the journals of Captain Cook's final voyage were published in America and Europe in 1783-84, merchant ships began flocking to these northern waters in pursuit of sea otter pelts. Dubbed 'soft gold,' these luxuriant pelts fetched a phenomenal price in China.

As more merchant ships (from Europe and America) frequented the coast, inevitable misunderstandings erupted in bloodshed. The natives became increasingly wary of white fur traders and, at times, openly hostile. Captain Vancouver's men reported incidents in which they were approached in their open survey boats by canoes filled with weapon-bearing natives. A few shots fired over their heads, however, would prompt the natives to unstring their bow-and-arrows and offer them in trade.

Settlers eventually followed the fur traders, and their arrival changed the coastal landscape. The natives' territorial boundaries became obsolete as homesteaders farmed, logged and mined the land, while Spain, Britain, Russia and America disputed borders and trade monopolies. Spain withdrew from the North Pacific in the late 1700s, after a political showdown with Britain over territorial rights. The dispute centered around control of Nootka Sound – a strategic harbor on the west coast of Vancouver Island.

In 1867, Russia withdrew from the North Pacific by selling Alaska to the United States for what now seems like a fire sale price of $7.2 million – about two cents an acre. At the time, however, the lucrative fur trade had dwindled and the American people showed little enthusiasm for this large tract of distant land their government had just acquired.

Britain's **HMS Plumper** *lies at anchor in Port Harvey on Johnstone Strait during a 19th century survey expedition.*

AMERICA'S NEW FRONTIER

The man who masterminded the purchase, U.S. Secretary of State William H. Seward, was ridiculed for his efforts with quips about "Seward's folly." Alaska was dubbed "Seward's icebox" and, for the most part, was neglected by its new owner. The American army and navy were sent to police this vast territory but no civil government was established until 1884 – at the urging of Reverend Sheldon Jackson. A Presbyterian missionary, Jackson travelled throughout Alaska establishing missions to educate the natives and assimilate them into the American way of life. Jackson also supported prohibition in Alaska, to protect the natives from the influence of rum. Liquor licensing was introduced in 1899, however, when the Klondike gold rush proved too much of a match for the prohibitionists.

Gold changed many Americans' perception of Alaska. The first strikes saw prospectors hurry to Wrangell and Sitka in 1872. Juneau was founded almost overnight when gold was discovered in the area in 1880. More strikes followed at Forty Mile River, Yakutat Bay, Lituya Bay, Mastodon Creek and the Kenai Peninsula. Then came the really big one – the Klondike strike on Bonanza Creek in Canada's Yukon. Men and women flocked by the thousands to Skagway for a chance to get rich in the Klondike. The gold fever ended as quickly as it began, with many rushing to Nome to try and cash in on yet another strike.

Bush pilots opened up Alaska, covering vast distances relatively quickly, and floatplanes remain a major mode of transport for isolated coastal communities.

The 20th century brought continuing social changes to Alaska. Bush planes opened up the rugged interior – formerly the domain of riverboats, pack animals and dogsleds. The first flight up the Inside Passage, from Seattle to Ketchikan, was made in 1922, and 10 years later the first plane to land on an Alaskan glacier touched down on Mount McKinley's Muldrow Glacier.

In 1942, during World War II, the U.S. Army Corps of Engineers built the Alaska Highway – a supply route safe from the hazards of wartime shipping. In just eight months they constructed a 1,500-mile road from Dawson Creek, in northern British Columbia, through Canada's Yukon to Fairbanks. Alaska was now joined to "the Outside" and the next step was statehood – achieved in 1959, making Alaska the 49th State of the Union.

The discovery of North Slope oil and natural gas deposits in 1968 transformed Alaska's economy. A pipeline was built from Prudhoe Bay on the Beaufort Sea to Valdez on Prince William Sound. Completed in 1977, this 800-mile-long pipeline is half underground and half above-ground where it's supported in a flexible, zigzag pattern to withstand earthquakes.

The city of Anchorage, economic center of the state, now has a population of a quarter of a million, but Alaska (with a median age of 27 years) continues to attract people of pioneer spirit. America's two largest fishing fleets are stationed at Dutch Harbor in the Aleutians and at Kodiak Island. In the early 1980s, a sudden population boom of king crab in the Bering Sea, coupled with a strong demand for this product in Japan and the U.S., turned fishermen not yet out of their twenties into instant millionaires.

The money madness made for some interesting stories. One year, during a protracted strike, hundreds of boats sat moored in Dutch Harbor waiting for a settlement. When the word came, fishermen

Commercial fishing in Alaska is a billion-dollar industry ranking high above any other American state, both in volume and in value of fish landed.

dashed to their vessels and, during this chaotic mass departure, boats were rammed and skippers accidentally left behind. One frenzied crew forgot to untie the docking lines and had to cut themselves loose.

The end came as quickly and mysteriously as it arrived. Old myths die hard though, and each summer college kids flock to Alaska's legendary fishing ports, drawn by tales of lucrative deckhand jobs. The greenhorns often have trouble getting hired as crew and have to settle for work in the canneries.

When the Exxon oil spill of March 1989 threatened the fisheries of Prince William Sound and Kodiak Island, entire fishing fleets stayed home that year to help with clean-up operations. Ironically, this environmental disaster focused world attention on the natural beauty of Prince William Sound. Oil tankers now share these waters each summer with increasing numbers of cruise ships and tour boats bringing people to view the area's beautiful fjords and tidewater glaciers.

Although petroleum taxes and royalties currently produce about 85 percent of Alaska's general revenue, the state's greatest resource may prove to be its spectacular scenery. America's 49th state is enjoying a tourism boom right now and, unlike the rush for furs, gold and other natural resources, this one looks like it will last. Mankind cannot deplete the mountains and fjords which took millions of years to create. All we can do is gaze at them in wonder.

A WORD ABOUT PLACE NAMES

Thousands of place names have, over the centuries, been bestowed on the islands, channels and mountains of the Inside Passage and Gulf of Alaska coastline. The natives who first inhabited the coast had their own names in place when European sailing ships began appearing on the horizon in the mid-1700s.

Survey expeditions continued in the 1800s. In Canadian waters these were conducted by the British Royal Navy, while the United States surveyed Alaskan waters after purchasing the territory from Russia in 1867. The Bostonian William Dall was a member of various American survey expeditions from 1865 to 1899, and his name now graces an island in Southeast Alaska, not far from Annette Island which he named for his wife. Dall's romantic streak is further evidenced in his naming Marmiom Island to commemorate a poem by Sir Walter Scott.

Then there was Captain Pender of the British Royal Navy who, while surveying the Canadian Inside Passage in 1864, named a point of land Connis after his Skye Terrier. Alma maters, winning racehorses and wives, mothers and sisters have all been honored with place names along this coastline.

The rules for naming landmarks were never cut and dried. The natives often had more than one name for certain places and when explorers from various countries were busy surveying this coast, it was anyone's guess which name would endure. Some names are misnomers, such as British Columbia's Gulf Islands – named when the Strait of Georgia was incorrectly called the Gulf of Georgia. Others, such as the city of Seattle and the country of Canada, are derivatives of native names. Alaska's name comes from the Aleut word Alyeska, meaning The Great Land.

The last word on place names goes to John Muir, an explorer who harbored a healthy skepticism about the relevance of place names. "People look at what they are told to look at or what has been named," he wrote in Travels in Alaska. "Nameless things, however fine, go unnoticed."

GLACIERS

G laciers are rivers of ice, always in movement. Fed by layers of compacted snow at higher elevations, they flow at varying speeds, depending on a variety factors such as the height and slope of the mountain collecting the snow. The causes of glacier movement are complex and unique to each glacier, with the center and surface of a glacier moving more rapidly than the sides and bottom which encounter friction. Decreased snow accumulation or increased melting results in a retreating (or shrinking) glacier. Those still advancing (or expanding) move at speeds varying from several feet daily to sudden surges of up to 300 feet per day. A stationary glacier is one in which its rate of advance and rate of melting are the same.

Yalik Glacier has retreated in the last century, but its ice flows steadily seaward from the crest of the central Kenai Mountains.

Most glaciers stopped advancing in the mid-1700s and have been retreating ever since. A few are re-advancing and this is often due to a slight change in the local climate – either a drop in temperature or an increase in snowfall. Regardless of whether a glacier is retreating, advancing or stationary, its ice always flows in a downhill direction (due to gravity).

Glaciers carve deep valleys and when valley glaciers flow together at the base of a mountain, they become a fan-shaped piedmont glacier. An icefield forms when numerous alpine glaciers join together and cover a large land mass with solid ice and snow. A tidewater glacier is a valley glacier that flows right down to the sea and lies at the head of the fjord or inlet it carved while retreating.

When chunks of ice fall from the snout of a tidewater glacier and crash into the sea, the glacier is said to be calving. The causes of glacial calving are still being studied and debated, but one known factor involves ice melting faster when in contact with water versus air. This results in an erosive undercutting of a glacier's snout below the high water mark. Each time the tide drops, an eroded section of the snout loses the water's support and this weakening of the ice may hasten its collapse. Blue ice at the face of a glacier means it's actively calving. The water near a glacier often appears milky turquoise because of fine sediments carried by glacier meltwater.

Although Alaska's glaciers are millions of years old, they flush their ice fairly rapidly, and the chunks we see dropping off the face of a tidewater glacier are usually a few hundred years old. These bergs are

GLACIER GLOSSARY

BERGY SELTZER – Also called 'ice sizzle', in reference to the crackling or sizzling sound emitted when a melting iceberg is relieved of the intense pressures that formed it and trapped air bubbles are released.

CALVING – The breaking away of ice from the terminus (or snout) of a tidewater glacier.

CIRQUE – A valley head shaped like an amphitheater, its vertical walls eroded by a mountain glacier's source.

CREVASSE – Deep, elongate cracks that form in a glacier's brittle surface due to tensions caused by the glacier's movements. A snowbridge is a layer of snow concealing a crevasse.

DRIFT – The sedimentary deposits of a glacier, including till – which is unsorted drift deposited directly by a glacier.

FIRN – The intermediate stage in the transformation of snow to glacier ice. The compression of snow into dense firn takes about one summer.

MORAINE – Unsorted glacier deposit of rock and gravel that collects, through erosion, along the sides and snout of a glacier.

NEVE – The upper end, or source, of a glacier covered with perennial snow.

SURGING – A sudden rapid movement (up to 300 feet per day) of a glacier, that may or may not involve an advance of the glacier's terminus. Factors causing a surge include the build-up of water pressure beneath the ice. Famous surges include those of Hubbard, a tidewater glacier that advanced hundreds of feet within a few weeks during the summer of 1986, and Bering Glacier, which advanced six miles between October 1993 and July 1994, stopping within five miles of the Gulf of Alaska coast.

TERMINUS – Also called the snout or toe, this lower extremity of a glacier can be rounded in shape or form a sheer wall of ice. In the case of tidewater glaciers, the terminus is often several hundred feet in height with much of it submerged in water.

(Above) Icebergs are slippery and can suddenly roll, but some people can't resist climbing aboard for a quick ride.

much smaller than those discharged from the polar ice caps and they melt quickly in the relatively warm Alaskan waters. One of the largest bergs ever recorded in Alaska was about 300 square feet and a hundred feet above the water. It was discovered in May 1977 floating in Icy Bay, which is located on the Gulf of Alaska at the base of the massive Bering Glacier complex.

An iceberg's blue color is the result of compressed ice absorbing light's short wave colors (reds) and reflecting the long wave colors (blues). If a piece of ice is relieved of pressure, air bubbles form and create a porous surface which is rough (like snow) and doesn't allow any light to penetrate, with light coming back as white. When afloat, about five-sixths of a berg is usually submerged. This ratio can vary, depending on the iceberg's shape and the amount of rock debris it might be carrying.

EARTHQUAKES

The coastal belt of the Pacific Ocean is one of the world's most active earthquake zones. This is due to the earth's surface being divided into crustal plates, some of which meet along the edges of the Pacific Ocean. Blocks of rock move along these plate boundaries, passing one another along fault lines (fractures in the earth's crust). Their relative movements can be vertical, horizontal or oblique and are usually mea- sured in inches per year, except when a sudden release of stress along a fault triggers an earthquake.

An earthquake begins with tremors, followed by more violent shocks which gradually diminish. The origin (focus) of a quake is underground or underwater, and the epicenter is a point on the surface directly above the focus. The magnitude and intensity of an earthquake is determined by the Richter scale, which measures the ground motion to determine the amount of energy released at the quake's origin.

A reading of 4.5 on the Richter scale indicates an earthquake causing slight damage; a reading of 8.5 indicates an earthquake of devastating force. The energy of a quake measuring 8 on the Richter scale is equal to that of a 250-megaton thermo-nuclear bomb. (The atom bomb dropped on Hiroshima in 1945 was .02 megatons.)

The January 1994 earthquake in Los Angeles measured 6.6 on the Richter scale and among its casualties were the personal diaries and home movies of Charles Richter, co-founder of the Richter Scale, who died in 1985. His scientific materials, however, were safely stored at the California Institute of Technology in Pasadena when fire gutted the Granada Hills home of Richter's nephew, who had possession of his famous uncle's memorabilia.

The Good Friday earthquake which hit Alaska in 1964 measured between 8.4 and 8.6 on the Richter scale and is the strongest recorded earthquake ever to hit North America. Its epicenter was in northern Prince William Sound and the damage was widespread. A block of the

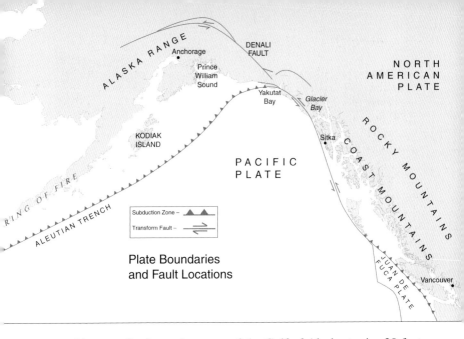

**Plate Boundaries
and Fault Locations**

earth's crust tilted, causing parts of the Gulf of Alaska to rise 30 feet and coastal land to sink as much as 10 feet.

TSUNAMIS (TIDAL WAVES)

A tsunami – meaning harbor wave in Japanese – is often referred to as a tidal wave. However, tsunamis are not caused by tidal action (although a high tide can increase their onshore damage) but by sea floor earthquakes or underwater landslides. Such seismic disturbances rarely trigger tsunamis, but when they do – watch out.

Up to 100 miles in length but with heights of only a few feet, tsunamis can travel thousands of miles across the open ocean at speeds exceeding 500 miles per hour. Their movement is undetected by ships at sea, but when they approach a shelving coastline they build into a series of waves of disastrous proportion. Anywhere from 10 to 40 minutes can pass between crests and the highest wave may occur several hours after the first wave. The sudden withdrawal of water from a shoreline could be the trough of an approaching tsunami, so people who venture onto these newly exposed beaches risk being engulfed by the wave's huge crest.

A tsunami warning system is in place for the Pacific Ocean (where almost two-thirds of all tsunamis occur). Countries with gauge stations include the United States, Canada, Japan, Chile, New Zealand and the Philippines. Should any of the stations record a drastic change in water elevation, direct telephone contact is made with the warning center located in Honolulu.

The 1964 Alaska earthquake was of such intensity that it sent a series of tsunamis to the far reaches of the Pacific. Waves over 20 feet high swept ashore in Oregon and California, killing 15 people. The

Downtown Anchorage, built on glacial silt deposits, was devastated by the 1964 earthquake when sections of streets collapsed.

Gulf of Alaska ports were hardest hit, with 107 people losing their lives. In 1946, an earthquake in the Aleutians sent 100-foot waves sweeping onto Unimak Island where the lighthouse was destroyed and five people perished.

Tsunamis of such magnitude are extremely rare. However, the Alaska Tsunami Warning Center – established at Palmer in 1967 – now provides timely warnings to prevent further loss of life from an approaching tsunami.

Star marks the 1964 earthquake's epicenter in Prince William Sound. Shaded area shows crustal uplift (+) and subsidence (-). Curved lines show leading edge of resultant tsunami, generated at 7:36 p.m.

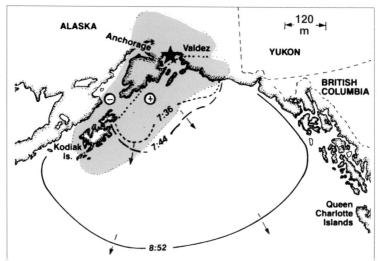

AURORA BOREALIS (NORTHERN LIGHTS)

A poet would describe the Northern Lights as curtains of shimmering light that flutter across the sky. A scientist would say they are high-speed particles from the sun colliding with the earth's air molecules. Both descriptions are correct.

When charged electrons and protons – released during sunspot activity – drift toward the earth, they are magnetically pulled to the planet's northern and southern latitudes. These charged particles strike gases in the earth's upper atmosphere and turn luminous – ranging from silvery white through the colors of the rainbow. The shimmering effect is caused by the differing intensities of light.

The aurora borealis is most prevalent over the Arctic Circle but can occur throughout the northern latitudes. (Those which occur over the Antarctic Circle and southern latitudes are called the aurora australias.) The northern lights appear most often during the spring and fall equinoxes, when the sun crosses the equator and night and day are of equal length. Northern lights can also occur on dark winter nights and during increased sunspot activity, which happens in cycles. The last phase of intense sunspot activity was during the late 1950s.

VOLCANOES

There are about 500 active volcanoes on our planet, with more than 70 of these located in Alaska. They are part of the Ring of Fire that encircles the Pacific Ocean basin and marks the collision zone of various tectonic plates which comprise the earth's crust. Volcanoes also exist beneath the ocean's surface and are called seamounts. About 100 of these extend from the Gulf of Alaska to the Oregon Coast.

Volcanoes form around an aperture in the earth's crust, through which gases, lava (molten rock) and solid fragments are ejected. A dormant volcano quickly loses its conical shape to erosion, so any mountain that is cone-shaped can be considered a potentially active volcano.

A volcano's crater is formed when the cone collapses during an eruption. Steam vents often cover a crater floor or the collapsed summit may fill with glacial meltwater. The crater lake atop Mount Katmai on the Alaska Peninsula is a unique robins-egg blue, due to glacial silt and sulphur in the water which remains ice-free for most of the year because of volcanic heat.

The Alaska Peninsula contains 15 active volcanoes, its most famous being Mount Katmai which erupted in June 1912 through a vent in its base. One of the greatest volcanic eruptions in recorded history, it was twice the size of Krakatoa, which killed 35,000 Indonesians in 1883, and ten times the force of Washington State's Mount Saint Helens which erupted twice in 1981 and killed 60 people. Because of Katmai's remote location, no people were killed, but the residents of Kodiak (90 miles away) were rained with ash so thick that for two days a person couldn't see a lit lantern held at arm's length. Acid rain fell 2,000 miles away in Vancouver, Canada, where laundry hanging on clotheslines disintegrated. An entire valley was filled with burning ash which spewed from Mount Katmai. In total, the volcanic eruption blanketed 40 square miles with ash that was 700 feet deep in places. The 1992 eruption of Mount Spurr, near Anchorage, was merely a hiccup in comparison, dusting Prince William Sound with a quarter inch of fine volcanic ash.

Mount Katmai is one in a chain of volcanoes extending westward along the Alaska Peninsula and Aleutian Islands. Pavlof Volcano, near the tip of the Peninsula, erupted in 1996, and Makushin Volcano, on the Aleutian Island of Unalaska, erupted in 1994. The Aleutians, a string of volcanic islands, stand on the edge of the Aleutian Trench. This ocean trench is a subduction zone in which the Pacific plate is descending beneath the North American plate, and the waters along this trench are thousands of feet deeper than the nearby ocean bottom.

Far away from the Aleutian Trench is Mount Edgecumbe – a solitary volcano located near Sitka on the Alaska Panhandle. This volcano has been inactive for the last 200 years, although in 1974 the residents of Sitka wondered if another eruption was imminent when black smoke was seen rising from the volcano's caldera. The smoke, however, was coming from a pile of burning tires placed there by an April Fool's Day prankster.

Volcanic ash from Mount Katmai's 1912 eruption still lies on the nearby mountains of Geographic Harbor.

(Top) An upthrust rock formation at the entrance to Taku Harbor in Stephens Passage is evidence of a now inactive fault of the earth's crust. (Middle) A pleasure boat steams past a chunk of glacial ice at the entrance to Tracy Arm. (Bottom) The aurora borealis lights up the northern skies of Alaska.

Bishop Bay, along the Canadian Inside Passage, has a bathhouse fed by a natural hotspring.

HOTSPRINGS

The hot water flowing from a natural spring is the result of ground water seeping to great depths through faults in the earth's crust, where it is heated and recirculated back up to the surface. A soak in a steaming mineral bath is considered by many to be one of the most therapeutic pastimes imaginable.

Alaskans are fortunate to have about 80 such thermal springs scattered throughout their state. Half of these are located along the volcanic Alaska Peninsula and Aleutian chain, with another concentration of hotsprings in southeastern Alaska.

Some of these natural springs are developed, with bath houses built over tubs which collect the flow of spring water. The village of Tenakee Springs on Chichagof Island grew up around its hotsprings. Enclosed by a cement bathhouse with bathing hours for men and women posted on the door, the springs at Tenakee attract plenty of visitors seeking relaxation, including state legislators from Juneau. The Alaska ferry calls at Tenakee Springs, as do fishermen and pleasure boaters looking for a good soak in a hot bath – compliments of Mother Earth's ingenious plumbing system.

MARINE WEATHER

Alaska encompasses a number of climatic zones: maritime along its southern coastlines; continental in its vast interior; arctic along its northern shores. The cruise ship routes remain within the moderate maritime zone, which is dominated by the Pacific Ocean.

Weather systems flow in an easterly direction in the northern hemisphere, so the west coast of North America enjoys the moderating effects of the Pacific Ocean throughout the year. Winters on the west coast are less severe than those on the east coast, which is affected by cold, continental air masses. Wet and windy weather prevails along the Pacific coast in winter as storms originating offshore flow into the Gulf of Alaska where its mountain-rimmed coastline acts as a catch basin. Precipitation that falls as snow in low lying coastal areas rarely remains on the ground longer than a few weeks.

Summer weather in the North Pacific is dominated by a subtropical high which brings reduced precipitation and increased sunshine. Autumn is a transition season as the North Pacific High gradually shrinks and the relatively light breezes of summer are replaced with winter storms generated by the Aleutian Low. At any time of year, winds along the sheltered Inside Passage are less intense than those on the open Pacific. Coastal weather and sea conditions are highly localized due to the rugged terrain.

Ocean currents also flow eastward across the Pacific from Asian waters, but the warm Japan Current never reaches the shores of Alaska. This slow-moving current joins the North Pacific Current (a broad, slow, easterly drift), which eventually veers south somewhere off the Oregon or California coast. The Subarctic Current runs parallel with the North Pacific Current and it gradually splits as it approaches the Washington/British Columbia coast, with one branch veering south to become the California Current, and the other veering north to become the Alaska Current. This current flows in a counter-clockwise direction along the Gulf of Alaska coastline and keeps it free of winter ice, except in protected waters.

It can take two to five years for a parcel of water carried by the Subarctic Current to cross the North Pacific. Along the way its temperature is determined not by the current's origin but by the surface water's constant heat exchange with the atmosphere.

This archival shot of Kodiak's harbor, taken before a breakwater was built, shows the smoking waters of a winter storm as it sweeps onshore from the Gulf of Alaska.

A cruise to Alaska offers passengers a chance to see wildlife in their natural habitat. This section profiles some of the species most frequently sighted.

WHALES

Called cetaceans and found in all the world's oceans, whales vary greatly in size, with the smaller ones also known as dolphins and porpoises. These aquatic mammals, which never leave the water at any stage in their lives, are warm blooded, breathe air and produce milk for their young. Their skin is nearly hairless and an insulating layer of blubber keeps their internal body temperatures high. Their nostrils (blowholes) are located on top of their heads to allow breathing while swimming, with the nostril valves closing and lungs compressing during dives. Most whales must surface every 3 to 20 minutes to breathe, although some can remain submerged for up to an hour. Although their eyes are small (to withstand great pressures), whales have good eyesight and excellent hearing, often navigating via echolocation. Their flattened tails with horizontal flukes propel them through the water.

Whales are broken into two major groups: toothed and baleen. Those with teeth, such as the killer whale (orca), eat salmon and other marine mammals. Baleen whales are filter feeders who eat schooling fish, plankton and other small organisms, which they catch by swimming with their mouths wide open. When the whale closes its mouth, it raises its tongue to force the scooped water out the sides where the bristles of its baleen plates trap the food.

HUMPBACK WHALE

The humpback whale, a filter feeder, is frequently sighted in Alaskan waters. Almost one quarter of the world's 8,000 to 10,000 humpback whales feed in Alaskan waters each summer. In winter, they migrate south to Hawaii and Mexico to breed and calve in tropical waters. December and January are the birthing months, following a 12-month gestation period. Cows give birth to a single calf weighing about a ton and measuring 12 to 15 feet in length. Calves are born without a blubber layer and nurse on their mother's milk which contains 50 percent butter fat.

WHALE WATCHING:

Good areas to sight humpback whales include Frederick Sound and Stephens Passage (south of Juneau), off Point Adolphus (opposite the entrance to Glacier Bay), and in western Prince William Sound. Whales, dolphins and porpoises can all be sighted along the Inside Passage, but this requires a patient lookout from the ship's rail. One telltale sign to watch for is the appearance of a plume of mist in the distance, which could indicate a pod of whales surfacing.

(Opposite) A humpback whale breaches in the temperate waters of Southern Alaska. (Far left) Humpbacks blow air bubbles in a column to collect krill.

Adult humpbacks are, on average, 45 feet long and weigh about 40 tons. Their large flippers provide maneuverability and the pleats on the sides of their mouths can create a pouch large enough to hold six adult humans. When feeding, they blow bubbles beneath schools of fish to create a concentrated cloud which they then lunge at with their mouths wide open. Sea birds, attracted by the water disturbance, feed on shrimplike krill and herring which swim to the surface.

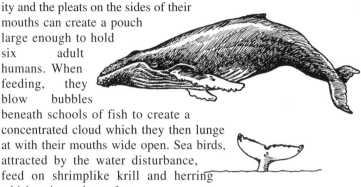

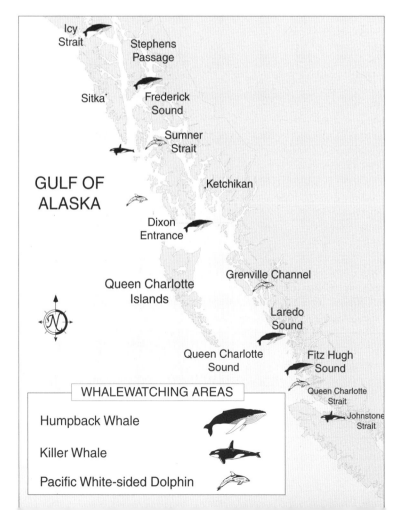

Icy Strait

Stephens Passage

Sitka

Frederick Sound

Sumner Strait

GULF OF ALASKA

Ketchikan

Dixon Entrance

Grenville Channel

Queen Charlotte Islands

N

Laredo Sound

Queen Charlotte Sound

Fitz Hugh Sound

Queen Charlotte Strait

Johnstone Strait

WHALEWATCHING AREAS

Humpback Whale

Killer Whale

Pacific White-sided Dolphin

Humpbacks travel in threesomes – a female, her calf and a male escort. The male earns his position as escort. He serenades the female by performing a repeated pattern of sounds (called a song) at depths of 60 feet or more. If this doesn't win her, the male will confront her current escort by smacking him with his fluked tail which packs 8,000 pounds of muscle and, studded with barnacles, is a humpback's most powerful weapon.

Only the males sing and they rarely do this while feeding in Alaska. They do, however, perform their usual acrobatics such as breaching (heaving themselves out of the water), lobtailing and flippering (smacking the water's surface with their tail or flippers). No two humpback tails are alike and scientists identify each whale by the pattern on its flukes which are visible when the whale raises its tail high out of the water before making a deep dive.

KILLER WHALE (ORCA)

Killer whales belong to the dolphin family of toothed whales and for decades they were much feared by humans because of their swift, ferocious attacks on seals and other prey, their mouths holding more than four dozen sharp teeth. Today the social habits of this handsome species are a source of fascination for both scientists and enthusiastic whale watchers.

dorsal fin

saddle patch

Male Orca

Female Orca

There are two types of killer whales – resident and transient. Resident orcas feed mainly on fish, such as salmon, while transient orcas will pursue other marine mammals. Resident pods remain near established salmon runs along inshore waters; transient pods traverse the entire coast from Alaska to Washington State in search of food. Every killer whale belongs to a pod – the family group into which it was born – and resident pods, with a dozen or more members, are usually larger than transient pods.

Males, which can reach 30 feet in length, live for about 50 years while females, who average 20 feet in length, can top 100. The male is distinguished from the female by his taller, straighter dorsal fin (up to six feet high on mature males). Each sub-group within a pod consists of a mature cow and her progeny of all ages. Females give birth to single calves following a gestation period of one year. Mature males likely mate with females of other pods, but they always return to their own pod and remain with it until death. Pod structures change very slowly, many lasting the lifetime of the cow.

Resident pods communicate with squeaking sounds that can be heard on hydrophones (underwater microphones), and each pod has its

A killer whale's most distinguishing features are its prominent dorsal fin and the white marking just behind it, called a saddle patch.

own dialect. Transient pods remain silent, so as not to alert potential prey (such as harbor seals) of their presence. Scientists who observe killer whales are developing a data base in which regularly sighted pods and their members – identified by individual markings – are given reference names. **Killer whales are frequently sighted in Johnstone Strait (feeding on salmon) and in the waters off Victoria, but can appear anywhere along the Inside Passage, Prince William Sound and Gulf of Alaska. Their distribution is worldwide.**

OTHER WHALES

The smallest baleen whale to frequent Alaskan waters is the minke which reaches lengths of 33 feet. The blue whale, the largest known animal ever to have lived (reaching 100 feet in length), is sometimes sighted during July and August in eastern and northern areas of the Gulf

The beluga, a northern whale, can often be sighted close to shore in Turnagain Arm south of Anchorage.

of Alaska. This whale came close to extinction about 50 years ago, but the species has fought back and, although still endangered, estimates of its population run as high as 17,000. Blues are protected worldwide.

The gray whale is another large, baleen whale, about 40-45 feet in length and weighing up to 40 tonnes. Strongly migratory but a relatively slow swimmer, the grey whale travels near shore on its twice-yearly migration between Mexico and the Beaufort Sea.

The beluga (or white whale) is a small, toothed whale. Reaching lengths of 19 feet, the beluga is sometimes called a 'sea canary' for the variety of noises it makes. Travelling in large groups, belugas winter in the Arctic Ocean and in summer enter northern rivers and inlets, such as Turnagain Arm, south of Anchorage in Cook Inlet.

The legendary sperm whale, largest of the toothed whales, is usually blue-black in color and has a blunt snout containing up to a ton of sperm oil (a liquid wax). Males can grow to over 70 feet and their range extends from the Bering Sea to Antarctica. Females, which grow to 30 feet, remain closer to the tropics. Herman Melville based his novel Moby Dick on the 1822 ramming and sinking off South America of a Nantucket whaling ship by an albino sperm whale.

DALL PORPOISE

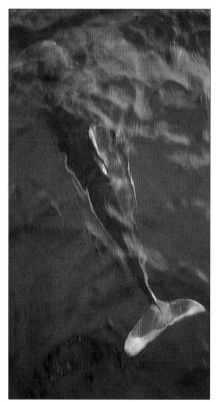

These speedy mammals are sometimes confused with killer whales because their black-and-white coloring is similar. However, Dall porpoises are much shorter (about seven feet long) and stockier in shape, and their dorsal fin is topped with white. They are the world's fastest marine mammals, reaching speeds of 30 miles per hour. Travelling in groups of a half dozen or more, they swim just beneath the surface of the water, kicking up splashes called rooster tails when they leap partially out of the water.

Dall porpoises skim the water's surface at speeds reaching 30 miles per hour.

These sociable creatures love to ride the bow wave of a moving vessel and will perform dazzling, crisscross patterns as two pairs race toward the front of the bow, one from either side, only to veer off at the last moment to prevent a collision. Their split-second reflexes and swift speed allow them to dart through the water and turn quickly. They range from the Bering Sea to Baja California.

PACIFIC WHITE-SIDED DOLPHIN

Playful and sociable, these high-spirited dolphins travel in large groups (115 members on average) and are, like the Dall porpoise, attracted to the bow waves of moving vessels. The larger and faster the vessel, the better the surfing as far as a Pacific white-sided dolphin is concerned.

Slightly longer than the Dall porpoise, these dolphins are black with a white belly and a hooked dorsal fin. During the fall mating season, they go crazy with acrobatics – leaping with total abandon in front of large fish boats and cruise ships. Passengers watching from a forward lounge are often treated to the sight of hundreds of dolphins leaping and somersaulting in front of the ship.

Fall sightings can occur in Sumner Strait, Dixon Entrance, Grenville Channel and Queen Charlotte Sound.

Pacific white-sided dolphins are playful and sociable, often seen leaping in the bow wave of a moving vessel.

A female harbor seal and her pup rest on a small piece of glacier ice which affords some security from predators.

SEAL & SEA LION

These fin-footed marine mammals have a thick layer of fat beneath their outer, hair-covered skin and spend much of their time in the water. They do, however, leave the water to rest, breed and give birth, but they always remain close to the water's edge. They haul out onto rocky islets, sandbars and ice floes where land predators cannot reach their pups. Sea lions gather in colonies to breed, with mature males assembling harems. Seals and sea lions live for about 30 years and feed on fish.

Harbor seals are commonly seen throughout the Inside Passage and Prince William Sound, often poking their large-eyed faces above the water to take a look around. They fear the transient killer whale and will quickly climb onto the closest rock or shoreline if such a pod is in the area. In one instance, a seal that was being circled by killer whales leaped into a whalewatching vessel to escape its predators.

Steller sea lions are larger than seals, with the males reaching 13 feet in length and weighing up to 2,000 pounds. Seals and sea lions will steal fish from fishermen's nets, and sea lions have been known to pull fishermen into the water from docks and skiffs, but it's illegal to shoot them under the 1972 Marine Mammal Protection Act. The Steller sea lion has, in recent years, suffered a dramatic decline in population – due possibly to an unexplained shortage of forage fish.

Two popular haul-out and pupping sites for seals and sea lions are Benjamin Island in Lynn Canal and Seal Rocks at the entrance to Prince William Sound.

Sea lions haul out on rocky outcroppings to breed and tend their young. Sea lion populations have declined sharply in recent years.

Sea Otter

The largest member of the weasel family, a sea otter can reach five feet in length and weigh close to 100 pounds. Although an aquatic mammal, the sea otter is kept warm not by blubber, like other marine mammals, but by its extremely thick fur coat – the most dense of any mammal at 675,000 hairs per square inch.

Sea otters congregate in large groups where they play together in pairs, hugging each other while they roll and perform somersaults in the water. A young otter will ride on its mother's stomach as she floats on her back. Sea otters also eat urchins and other shellfish on their chests, which they break apart with a rock. They're a crowd pleaser with their playful personalities and round, whiskered faces.

Sea otters once ranged from the Aleutians to Baja Calfornia, their population about 150,000. Russian fur traders, realizing how quickly these animals were being decimated for their valuable pelts, eventually set quotas to limit harvests, and by the mid-1800s the species was recovering. However, when the U.S. purchased Alaska in 1867, unlimited hunting was again allowed and the total sea otter population was reduced to about 2,000. In 1911 sea otters were given complete protection and they have now returned to numbers approaching their original population.

Sea otters are often sighted along the northern and western shores of Chichagof Island and on sightseeing expeditions out of Sitka. They are also a common sight in Prince William Sound, near Seward in Resurrection Bay, and around Kodiak Island.

Sea otters spend much of their time floating on their backs – grooming, eating and nursing their young.

RIVER OTTER

River otters, like sea otters, belong to the weasel family. With webbed feet, they are agile both on land and in the water. They run humpbacked because of their long bodies and relatively short legs. Males reach four feet in length and weigh up to 25 pounds. River otters are very sociable and playful. They like to slide headfirst on their bellies down mud banks into the water.

FISH

SALMON

Salmon are at the top of the fish evolutionary ladder and, with a very streamlined body and a powerful tail fin, they are fast, agile swimmers. The meat on all species of salmon is rich in protein, providing an important food source for humans and animals. Many coastal towns and cities owe their existence to this fish, which every year returns in large schools to natal spawning streams along the Pacific coast.

There are five species of Pacific salmon caught in Alaskan waters: king (chinook) is the largest; silver (coho) is prized by sportsfishermen; red (sockeye) with its rich red meat, is the highly-valued commercial salmon; pink (humpy) is the most common and an important commercial fish for the canneries; and chum (dog) salmon, when smoked, is a tasty delicacy.

Salmon spawn in fresh water, usually streams, where they spend varying lengths of time depending on the species, before heading out to sea. Some juveniles migrate directly to saltwater while others linger in

Coho (silver) salmon, a favorite of sportfishermen, has become seriously depleted in southern waters of the Inside Passage.

river estuaries where they grow and adapt to the mix of fresh- and salt-water habitats. Depending on the species, salmon will spend one to seven years in the open ocean before returning to their natal streams to spawn.

Salmon struggle against incredible odds to return to the stream of their birth. If a fish makes it past the sport and commercial fisheries, there will be other predators – such as bears and eagles – waiting along stream banks to make a meal of these weary fish. Salmon often have to leap up waterfalls and swim against rushing currents to return to their spawning grounds. Once there, the females dig nests in the gravel and lay their eggs while their male partners release milt which fertilizes the eggs. All Pacific salmon spawn only once – in late summer or fall – then die.

Salmon stocks are suffering serious depletions in some areas of the Pacific Northwest. A complex combination of factors is likely to blame, including overfishing and destruction of stream habitat. Salmon are also extremely sensitive to temperature fluctuations and a recent increase in ocean temperatures, possibly due to global warming, is another likely culprit. Each salmon stock, which is grouped according to its stream of origin, has a specific genetic make-up which has evolved over tens of thousands of years. Sudden environmental changes, whether natural or man made, threaten a specific stock's ability to adapt and survive.

HALIBUT

While salmon are generally found within 100 feet of the ocean's surface, halibut are always found near the bottom. Salmon is a pink or red meat; halibut is white. This fish is highly valued in Alaska, and around the world, for its delicate taste and texture. Few fish dishes can surpass fresh halibut served with a light lemon sauce. Pacific halibut can grow to over eight feet and weigh over 800 pounds. Halibut fishing is generally good near Sitka and Seward.

KING CRAB

In 1976, a sudden and inexplicable explosion in the number of harvestable king crab occurred in the Bering Sea. Within months hundreds of young men rushed to cash in on a boom which lasted almost eight years. Some came away millionaires, but many ended up with only memories of exciting years in the tough waters off Kodiak and in the Bering Sea. King crab can weigh up to 15 pounds and measure six feet across from claw to claw. Although the king crab population has declined since the mid-1980s, a large number of crab boats still operate out of Dutch Harbor and Kodiak.

BIRDS

There are many opportunities to spot birds on an Alaskan cruise. Gulls follow ships looking for scraps, cormorants and sea ducks can be seen near the docks at port, and eagles seem to be almost everywhere – perched on telephone poles and tree branches. It's interesting to look closely at the great variety of birdlife and discover how each species has adapted to survive. Over 400 species of birds have been documented in Alaska and British Columbia, many of which are rare elsewhere in the world.

Birds differ dramatically in size, shape and plumage but wing shape is an indication of a bird's survival strategies. Some, like gulls and shearwaters, have long tapered wings suitable for gliding long distances over water with little effort. Others, like auklets and murres, have short and less efficient wings more suitable for propelling themselves underwater. And some, like eagles and ospreys, have long wide wings to provide additional payload capacity for such maneuvers as snatching salmon out of the water.

The flight of any bird is a marvel to behold. It derives both forward power and upward lift from its wings. As a bird propels itself forward from the motion of wing flapping, a slight vacuum or low pressure area is created above the wing, lifting the body. As the bird picks up speed, the wing and tail feathers fold in to streamline the bird's shape and provide greater flying efficiency. A bird can turn very quickly using elements of its body, such as tilting the head, fanning the wings' secondary feathers, or subtly angling the tail feathers.

Most birds are opportunistic – always on the lookout for a meal. Gull, crows and ravens will suddenly appear near your fish and chips on a park bench, eagles perch on the tallest tree near a salmon stream, and oystercatchers in Ketchikan are always out on the beach at low tide. If you are interested in birds, it's well worth bringing a pair of binoculars and a field pocketbook to identify birds along your cruise.

For an Alaska-bound traveller one of the best locations to see birdlife is Vancouver's Stanley Park. Walk along the park's seawall and you will spot many species of ducks – goldeneye and bufflehead are quite common. If you walk to Lost Lagoon or Beaver Lake you will see a stunning array of bird species. Trumpeter and mute swans, wood ducks, American wigeons, teals, geese and bald eagles all frequent this 1,000-acre park. Along the Inside Passage you'll likely see cormorants (often perched on pilings and buoys with their wings outstretched), gulls, herons, sea ducks and bald eagles. In the Gulf of Alaska, shearwaters and albatross can be identified by the keen birder, and near Seward you're likely to see large colonies of puffins. Mendenhall Valley is another popular location to spot many species of birds. Loons, mergansers, sea ducks, herons and eagles are common visitors to the marsh-like conditions of this protected area.

(Above) Bald eagles use their talons to grab at salmon swimming near the surface.
(Left) Bald eagle's nest is the largest of any bird in North America, built five to eight feet in diameter and two to 10 feet in depth.

The following is a sampling of birds to watch for on your cruise.

BALD EAGLE

Without a doubt, the bald eagle is one of the most magnificent sights of an Alaskan cruise. With a wingspan of between six and eight feet and, weighing 15 pounds or more, the bald eagle is the largest member of the hawk family. The bald eagle gets its name from its distinctive snow-white head. Its bill is yellow and it has a thin, chittering call.

A high soaring eagle can spot a fish from over a mile away and can dive from the sky at 100 miles per hour. Eagles mate while somersaulting through the air with their talons locked. The female lays one to three eggs in late April and the young birds leave the nest in early fall. Their mortality rate is high, with over 90 per cent failing to survive the first few years of life. Juvenile eagles retain their ragged plumage until the age of five, when they attain the distinctive markings of a mature bald eagle.

Eagles usually build their nests in the tallest tree of their nesting territory (a range of one to five miles) and close to the water. Since eagles mate for life, the couple will return to their nest each year and do minor upgrading, renovations, and the occasional expansion. One excellent opportunity to see a nest is the Eagle Tree on the ground floor of the Alaska State Museum in Juneau. This exhibit includes the nest, eggs and mounted specimens of juvenile and adult eagles.

Although protected now, the bald eagle was once the target of bounty hunters, with over 100,000 killed before the predator control program was repealed in 1952. Today, of North America's total bald eagle population of 75,000, about 35,000 to 45,000 reside year round in Alaska, where they congregate near salmon streams during the summer spawning season.

PUFFIN

Horned and tufted puffins thrive by the thousands near the western end of Prince William Sound, along the Kenai Peninsula and around Kodiak Island. A day trip from Seward will take you to some of the largest nesting colonies in the area at the entrance to Resurrection Bay. Puffins, like murres and auklets, are alcids (seabirds) and are able to swim underwater to great depths using their

Horned puffins, when gathering food for their young, can hold three or four small fish at a time in their large bills.

wings. These birds are not great flyers, however, and are often seen bouncing off wavetops trying to take off. Puffins come ashore only to breed and nest.

RAVEN

Ravens and crows use their sense of curiosity as a survival technique. Anything dropped or odd in shape or color will be quickly spotted by these black birds which promptly swoop down to investigate. Ravens are larger than crows and have thicker bills. They are very intelligent, capable of making various diverse sounds, and are highly respected in most native cultures.

CANADA GOOSE

Sometimes referred to as the "Vancouver" Canada Goose, this is the largest of several subspecies in Alaska and is easily recognized by its incessant honking. Canada geese are common thoughout Southeast Alaska, particularly at the Mendenhall Wetlands near Juneau. However, if you want to see them in their home setting, take a walk due west from the cruise ship terminal in Vancouver and within minutes you'll spot plenty near Stanley Park.

Geese have a social hierarchy which places mated pairs with families at the top, followed by couples without goslings. At the bottom are singles and yearlings. Geese, like eagles, are thought to mate for life.

Barrow's Goldeneye, a common sea duck, is seen near shore along the Inside Passage.

SEA DUCK

Sea ducks eat intertidal invertebrates (mussels, hermit crabs, snails) and dominate the bird populations in many coastal areas of Alaska. They are robust, noisy and have colorful summer plumage, most notably the Harlequin duck. Sea ducks can be observed near shore while in port, often parading past in single file.

MERGANSER

Mergansers are fish-eating, diving ducks and are distinguished from sea ducks by their long, thin serrated bills. Hooded and red-breasted mergansers can be seen along quiet foreshores. During late spring and early summer in Vancouver or Ketchikan, you may spot one of nature's most beautiful displays of maternal care when a red-breasted merganser swims by with a brood of chicks on her back.

GULL

Gulls are one of nature's runaway successes because of their well-developed scavenging abilities. Most common are white and light grey glaucous-winged gulls, herring gulls (with black-tipped wings) and mew gulls – smaller birds with cries similar to a child's. Another member of the gull family is the kittiwake, flocks of which feed on tiny krill near tidewater glaciers.

ALBATROSS

Glacier cruise passengers, while traversing the Gulf of Alaska between Yakutat Bay and Prince William Sound, may be fortunate to spot the black-footed albatross. These beautiful gliders spend most of their lives at sea and, for survival, have special adaptations. To meet their freshwater needs, they drink seawater which is filtered and secreted through enlarged nasal glands to remove the salt. These birds, along with shearwaters and petrels, are called "tube-nosed swimmers" because their nostrils are situated in raised tubes on their bill. This gives them a sense of smell so acute they are believed to track fish and squid underwater.

At kittiwake nesting colonies, such as this one in Glacier Bay, each chick can recognize its parents' voices from among hundreds of others through minute differences in pitch.

LAND MAMMALS

BEAR

Of all the land mammals in Alaska, none excite the imagination quite like bears – most particularly the brown bear (Ursus arctos) and the grizzly, a sub-species of the brown bear. The brown bears that inhabit the Alaska coast are especially large because they have an advantage over interior (grizzly) bears – namely large numbers of available salmon spawning in shallow streams. This protein-rich diet combined with a mild climate produces bears that are between eight and nine feet tall (when standing upright) and weigh well over 1,000 pounds. In 1969 a brown bear measuring over ten feet was recorded on Kodiak Island.

This brown bear is one of many who arrive at the McNeil River each summer to feed on spawning salmon.

Brown bears are solitary animals, usually avoiding one another, but will exhibit a site-specific tolerance for one another at particularly abundant salmon feeding streams, such as Pack Creek on Admiralty Island (28 air miles south of Juneau) and the McNeil River on Cook Inlet (200 air miles southwest of Anchorage), a site that draws photographers from around the world. Brown bears may also be spotted on the foreshore from ships or ferries travelling through Peril Strait or along Lynn Canal.

The black bear (Ursus americanus) is the most widespread and numerous of North American bears. Although smaller and seemingly more docile than the brown bear, it can still pose a serious threat when hungry, startled or injured. Black bears forage mainly on berries and occasionally on salmon along the coast. Adult male black bears weigh an average of 500 pounds, are 6 feet long and vary in color from blonde to black, including the rare blue (or glacier) bear, which is found in the Yakutat Bay area along the Gulf of Alaska. Black bears have been known to spend their entire lives within five miles of their birthplace, and a transplanted black bear will travel many miles to return to its home range.

The polar bear (Ursus maritimus) is rarely sighted by the casual traveller to Alaska, for this large white bear (adult males can reach 9 feet in length and weigh up to 1600 pounds) lives mainly on the drifting pack ice. Its hair is extremely dense and its paws have hairy soles for gripping the ice. A fearless and wily hunter, the polar bear will stalk any prey, including humans. Well aware that its black nose gives it away, a polar bear stalking seals will often hold a paw in front of its nose to conceal it.

Bears have an excellent sense of smell and hearing, and can run with bursts of speed reaching 35 mph. Black bears are also good tree climbers and polar bears are exceptional swimmers, crossing 30 miles of water at a time. Bears sleep through most of the winter in dens made in caves or holes in the ground but they do not truly hibernate, for their metabolism remains normal and they may even awake and emerge during warm spells. Polar bears wander all winter, except for pregnant females who dig dens in the snow. Cubs are born in pairs during the winter and remain with their mothers for about a year.

WOLF

Close to extinction in the Lower 48, the gray wolf (also called timber wolf) is thriving in Alaska where it enjoys a high reproductive rate and is protected by strict trapping and hunting regulations (aerial sporthunting of wolves has been banned since 1972). Resembling a German Shepherd dog, the gray wolf stands three feet at the shoulder and weighs about 100 pounds. Wolves usually travel in a pack (family group) which averages five to eight members and they hunt just about everything from moose to mice, wearing down even the swiftest of prey with their ability to run at about 20 mph for many hours. The wolf is of the genus Canis and can be bred with dogs to produce hardy animals for pulling sleds.

The coyote is a small, swift wolf and resembles a medium-sized dog. Its cry – mournful high-pitched yelps – is heard early in the evening.

SLED DOGS

Dogs in the north have always been highly valued, both as working animals and as man's best friend. The early gold prospectors relied on dogs for winter transportation, and stealing someone's dog was a serious crime leading to arrest. The Alaskan malamute is one of the oldest arctic sled

Sled dogs are part of the northern lifestyle.

dogs and is often referred to as a 'husky', although this term actually applies to the purebred Siberian husky. The snowmobile threatened to replace the working dog-sled team, but dog mushing has made a come-back and was named Alaska's official state sport in 1972, with races held in various locales throughout the winter. Each March, the state's famous Iditarod Trail Sled Dog Race is run between Anchorage and Nome. The race, first held in 1973, follows an old dog-team mail route blazed in 1910. Strictly a winter trail of frozen muskeg and river ice, over 1,000 miles in length, it was made famous in 1925 when teams of mushers relayed a life-saving diphtheria serum to epidemic-threatened Nome.

MOUNTAIN GOAT

This agile animal inhabits mainland mountains, alongside Dall sheep, and is often spotted on windswept ridges and the steep slopes of fjords and inlets. With a body designed for balance (short legs and heavy shoulders), the mountain goat climbs steep rocky terrain on spreadable, padded hoofs. Its double coat of long coarse outer hair over a thick layer of cashmere-quality wool insulates the mountain goat from winter winds as it battles sub-zero temperatures and snow-covered slopes in search of exposed forage. The mountain goat's ability to survive in steep terrain is its main protection from predators who no doubt get dizzy just looking up at a mountain goat's precarious perch atop sheer cliffs and narrow rock ledges.

Mountain goats can scramble up steep mountainsides on spreadable hooves cushioned with skid-proof pads.

DALL SHEEP

A white, wild sheep, this animal inhabits Alaska's mountain ranges and alpine meadows. Its current population is about 50,000. Dall sheep graze on grasses and other plants, and climb above the timberline in summer in pursuit of succulent new growth. The ram's horns are heavy and curled, and their growth rings determine the sheep's age.

A dall sheep and her young.

SITKA BLACKTAIL DEER

This beautiful creature – smallest of the blacktail deer – is native to the Inside Passage and has been successfully transplanted to Yakutat Bay, Prince William Sound and Kodiak Island. Its coat is reddish-brown in summer, turning dark gray in winter, and the black top of its tail contrasts with its white bottom. Fawns eventually lose their white spots, and bucks grow velvety antlers. Their only serious predators are wolves and, occasionally, bears.

In June and July they move up the mountainsides, eating new growth that appears as the snow melts, and they remain in alpine areas until fall. From fall through spring these deer live in the forests. At southern latitudes they thrive in second-growth forests, but farther north – in areas of high snowfall – their rate of survival is better in old-growth forests where browse plants grow around toppled trees and the forest's canopy prevents snow from covering the ground.

CARIBOU

A member of the deer family, both the male and female caribou grow antlers. On a mature bull, the antlers extend four feet from base to tips. Caribou number more than 300,000 statewide. They often travel in large herds and have been called 'nomads of the north' because they are always on the move in search of food – and thus hard to track. Alaska's interior and the Alaska Peninsula are where these elusive animals roam.

MOOSE

The largest member of the deer family, with mature males standing as high as 7 1/2 feet high at the shoulder and weighing up to 1,800 pounds, the moose inhabits mixed woods and wetlands, its range extending from the Alaska Panhandle to the Arctic. The spread of a bull moose's antlers can measure six feet and males become very aggressive during the fall mating season. In winter, to avoid deep snow, moose often travel at night along highways where they present a serious traffic hazard.

The barren-ground caribou of Alaska's tundra regions have broad hooves which provide support on boggy or snow-covered ground.

Moose are a frequent summertime sight in Denali National Park. In winter, when snow cover restricts their grazing range, they often show up in downtown Anchorage in search of food.

A WALK IN A RAINFOREST

Alaska's coastal rainforests flourish during the long, warm days of summer. Fronted by shoreline meadows of tall grass and leafy alders, these forests contain towering evergreens that can grow over 200 feet tall and live for hundreds of years.

The two common species of conifer found in Southeast Alaska are the Sitka spruce (Alaska's official tree) and the Western hemlock. The Sitka spruce grows quickly (up to three feet per year), reaches an average height of 160 feet and is three to five feet in diameter. Its branches project at an upward angle from its straight trunk, giving the tree a conical crown, and its spiky green needles are a deep green. The tree's strong, lightweight timber is used for boatbuilding, piano sounding boards and, in the early days of aviation, for aircraft construction.

Skunk cabbage, as its name implies, has a pungent odour.

The Sitka spruce grows in pure stands or alongside the Western hemlock – a tall, slender tree with branches that droop slightly and with twigs containing two rows of needles that are flat and soft. At an average height of 100 to 150 feet and a diameter of two to four feet, the Western hemlock covers 75 percent of Southeast Alaska's forested area. This tree is tolerant of shade and often sprouts up among the faster-growing Sitka Spruce. Western Hemlock is a major source of pulpwood and lumber.

Another member of the pine family that thrives along the Pacific Northwest coast is the Western red cedar – the giant of the forest with a massive trunk (two to eight feet in diameter) and an average height of 100 to 175 feet. Its shiny needles grow in splayed clusters from the cedar's drooping branches and its aromatic wood is straight grained, durable and resistant to decay – the perfect material for dugout canoes and totem poles, as well as for panels, posts and other outdoor objects. The Western red cedar grows throughout the southern half of the Panhandle and along Canada's Inside Passage.

Carpeting the forest floor are ferns, mosses and flowering plants. In an old-growth forest, toppled trees are reclaimed by mosses and become "nurse" logs to evergreen seedlings. Skunk cabbage is found in wet areas of the forest, near streams and bogs, and is easy to spot with its yellow, tulip-shaped inner leaf and large outer leaves. These leaves are eaten by deer and geese, and were tradtionally used by natives to wrap salmon for baking.

Blueberry and salmonberry bushes are plentiful and are a major food source for bears. Blue lupine, its tall spires thick with pod-like flowers, is a common sight, and brilliant fireweed grows in dense stands on recently-cleared land, its bright rosy pink petals blooming on stalks that grow four feet high.

Other plants to look for include devil's club, a big, prickly, maple-leafed plant that belongs to the ginseng family, its medicinal properties long ago applied by the natives who would make a tea brewed from the root to cure colds and other ailments. The plant's tough, prickly spines can inflict bad scratches on bare-legged hikers. However, if you stay on park trails maintained by the Forestry Service, you will have to watch out for nothing more than the odd slug lying on the path. Slugs feed at night on roots and plants and they grow to grand proportions in Alaska, earning such labels as Banana Slug.

Slime mold is a fungus that grows under the damp leaves and rotting logs of a rainforest. Coral slime looks much like frost covering a log, and scrambled-egg slime resembles an unappetizing helping of powdered eggs fried sunny side up. A conk is a type of bracket fungus that grows on dead tree trunks. When conks become hard and dry, Alaskans like to snap them off and turn them into decorative ornaments.

A variety of birds and animals live in the forest, including bears, porcupines, bald eagles, Steller's jays and blue grouse. The chattering of squirrels and clucking of ravens is commonly heard. Streams abound and open areas of muskeg contain low shrubs and natural bonsai (dwarf trees).

A recommended rainforest walk is the one at Sitka National Historical Park where groomed trails are signposted and easy to hike.

Sunlight filters through the canopy of this northern rainforest.

Thousands of years ago, when the inhabitants of our planet lived in isolated pockets, few locations were more remote than the Aleutian Islands. A string of barren, volcanic islands, the Aleutians dot the open waters west of Alaska where the North Pacific meets the Bering Sea. The Aleuts who lived here were highly skilled at open-ocean hunting. They set out to sea in baidarkas (kayaks made of animal skin) and they used harpoons with poisoned tips to kill whales many times the size of their tiny vessels. Their waterproof clothing was made from strips of sea lion intestine stitched together and their boots were made from sea otter flippers.

When winter came and the hunting season ended, the Aleuts spent much of their time feasting and dancing. They lived in pit dwellings with sod roofs, and their villages extended throughout the Aleutians and along the Alaska Peninsula to the Shumagin Islands.

Sharing many of the Aleut customs, such as matrilineal descent and a similar language, were the Southern Eskimos whose territory bordered the Bering Sea and Gulf of Alaska coastlines, including Kodiak Island and Prince William Sound. They too hunted individually from kayaks and wore wooden visors to protect their eyes from both rain and ocean glare.

Kodiak Island is covered not with forests but tall grasses, and the Koniag Eskimos who first lived here resided in semi-subterranean sod houses. The Chugach Eskimos, living on the forested shores of Prince William Sound, built planked wooden houses.

Alaska's Northern Eskimos, living along the Arctic coastline, built homes to withstand the freezing temperatures of winter. An underground entrance tunnel, which trapped any cold air coming in from outside, led into a semi-subterranean dwelling where seal-oil lamps were used for light and warmth. For clothing, they wore two layers of fur-lined garments. The Northern Eskimos hunted for whale and walrus from umiaks (large open skin boats) but also used kayaks and, on land, sleds. They often saved Yankee whalers when their ships became trapped in Arctic ice.

The Aleuts and Eskimos believed in reincarnation and in maintaining a positive relationship with animal spirits through special rites performed at the beginning of each hunting season. The blanket toss, in which a person is bounced high in the air off a trampoline made of seal skins and held taut by a circle of onlookers, was traditionally held after a successful whale hunt. Shamans – who could cure illness and foretell the future – were important members of all native groups.

The Athapaskans, who lived in the interior of Alaska and Northern Canada, were nomadic tribes who lived by hunting and fishing. Their clothing was often made of moose and caribou hides, and their homes were of various forms – from semi-subterranean log dwellings to dome-shaped tents made of animal skins. In the 18th century, the Athapaskans increased their hunting and trapping of furbearing animals to supply the flourishing fur trade.

NATIVE GROUPS OF ALASKA AND BRITISH COLUMBIA

NORTHERN ESKIMO

ATHAPASCAN

Anchorage

Prince William Sound

SOUTHERN ESKIMO

Kodiak Island

ALEUT

TLINGIT

Sitka

HAIDA

TSIMSHIAN

KWAGIUTL

COAST SALISH

NOOTKA

Ocean going canoes were carved from huge cedar logs, then steamed to soften the wood and allow the sides to be spread. Separate prow and stern pieces were added and the hull torched to harden the wood before sanding it smooth with dogfish skin.

The natives who inhabited the Inside Passage enjoyed a mild climate in a region where rivers teemed with salmon and foreshores were covered with shellfish. These reliable food sources supported a thriving population who had free time to develop sophisticated art forms. Their ancient civilizations are today recognized as complex social structures that produced monumental works of art.

The pyramids of Egypt were being constructed when permanent settlement of the Inside Passage began about 5,000 years ago. People had already been inhabiting this region for four or five thousand years, following the last retreat of the glaciers, but wild fluctuations in sea levels kept forcing them to relocate. When sea levels finally stabilized, the area's inhabitants began establishing permanent coastal villages. But their building materials, unlike those of the Egyptians, were not of stone but of wood.

Thick stands of cedar, spruce and hemlock provided an abundance of building materials but, just as uncut conifers eventually topple to the ground and slowly rot, so too did the natives' wooden dwellings and monuments. What did survive, however, were their kitchen middens.

A midden is a prehistoric refuse dump of shells and bones. At first glimpse it appears to be a natural beach of crushed shell, when in fact it is an archaeological site containing clues to a lost civilization. The shell, neutralizing the acid in the soil, has preserved ancient tools and artifacts such as antler carvings and stone bowls, engraved with human

The massive corner posts and cross beams of this Kwagiutl long house formed a permanent support for cedar planks that could be removed and transported between the clan's winter village and summer fishing camps.

Today's visitors to the Inside Passage can enjoy (but not disturb) the area's numerous shell beaches which are prehistoric kitchen middens from native societies.

and animal figures. Weapons for hunting and warfare have also been found in middens, as well as skeletal remains and the caches of warrior chiefs.

Middens were formed from empty clam and mussel shells tossed into heaps which, over time, were crushed and compressed into beaches several yards deep. These white beaches were easily spotted by villagers returning after dark in their canoes. Another feature marking ancient village sites is a fish trap – stone barriers designed to trap salmon near shore at low tide. The fish could swim across the trap at high water, but as the tide dropped they could not get past the row of stones blocking their way seaward.

While the Athenians of Ancient Greece were erecting the Parthenon on the Acropolis some 2,500 years ago, a complex and artistically productive civilization was also thriving in the Pacific Northwest. Archaeological digs reveal a society that produced masters at weaving, woodworking and sculpturing. Personal adornments were miniature works of art depicting human, animal and supernatural figures carved from stone, bone, antler and tooth. Petroglyphs were cut into foreshore stones, and pictographs were drawn on rock walls. These images were possibly inspired by shamanism – a belief in supernatural powers – or some may have had a more pragmatic purpose, such as marking a good fishing hole or a territorial boundary.

As the feudal knights of medieval Europe rode off to battle, chiefs and warriors of the Northwest Coast also engaged in warfare, paddling their canoes hundreds of miles into enemy territories. The northern tribes often headed south to raid villages and capture slaves – the lowest rank in a social hierarchy consisting of nobility, commoners and slaves. During this period, mortuary practices shifted from burying the dead in middens to placing their remains in boxes hung from trees or inside small mortuary houses behind the village.

Ancient petroglyphs, such as this one at Port Neville on Johnstone Strait, are found throughout the Inside Passage.

The Renaissance introduced new ideas to European civilization, and this flowering of artistic and scholarly accomplishments was followed by the 18th century's Age of Enlightenment, in which the pursuit of knowledge prompted numerous scientific expeditions. Europe's maritime nations sent their explorers on voyages of discovery, and the inevitable exploration of the North Pacific marked the end of prehistory for its inhabitants.

When European explorers first landed on the Northwest Coast, they encountered various native groups who shared some general traits but spoke different languages and displayed regional differences in their architecture, art and social customs. Coastal Indians ranged from the top of the Alaska Panhandle to the lower reaches of the Inside Passage.

The three northern groups – the Tlingit, Tsimshian and Haida – were highly respected as warriors and artisans. The Haida's cedar dugout canoes were considered top-of-the-line and the Haida would often tow a newly carved canoe across Hecate Strait to the mainland where they would trade it to the Tsimshians for candlefish oil. The Haida, skilled mariners, travelled as far away as present-day San Francisco in these seaworthy craft.

Although their languages were unrelated, the northern groups' social structures were similar. The Tlingit and Haida were divided into two sub-groups (called moieties by anthropologists) which were symbolized by the Eagle and the Raven. The Tsimshian were divided into four sub-groups, termed phratries. Sub-groups were further divided into kinship clans represented by crests (totems) depicting the Frog, Beaver, Wolf, Grizzly Bear and Killer Whale. Each clan was further subdivided into family households.

Descent was through the female line and a person was not allowed to marry someone from the same moiety or phratry. This intermarriage among sub-groups forged alliances between village chiefs and their heirs. Etiquette and ceremony were fundamental to these structured societies in which power and wealth were manifested in potlatch celebrations of feasting, dancing and gift giving. Custom dictated that invited guests would repay the host chief's hospitality with a reciprocal potlatch, preparations for which could take years. Totem poles were often raised at a potlatch.

The post-and-beam houses of the northern groups were solidly built. Massive corner posts and cross beams – which sometimes took 300 men to raise – supported the roof and sides made of cedar planking. The main frontal pole and interior poles, elaborately carved, displayed the clan and moiety crests. Sometimes a portal was carved in the lowest figure of a frontal pole to serve as the entrance. Freestanding poles were raised in front of the houses to commemorate an important event, such as a birth, marriage or, most importantly, a death. When a high-ranking chief died, his cremated remains were eventually placed in a niche at the back of a mortuary pole that was raised – with much ceremony – in his honor.

The architecture of the Wakashan groups to the south was slightly different from that of the northern groups. House planks were not permanently attached to the post-and-beam framework, allowing them to be dismantled and towed by canoe to a summer village during the salmon season. The earthen floors were also simpler than the recessed levels of northern homes, but common activities included burning indoor fires and hanging salmon to dry.

Wakashan is a linguistic term and the people of this language group consist of the Kwagiutl, who inhabit much of British Columbia's central coast, and the Nootka, who live on the west coast of Vancouver

The Beaver Clan House at Saxman Village near Ketchikan is an example of Tlingit art and architecture.

Island. Because the natives' traditional languages were oral and not written, there is often a variation in the spelling of their words and names. Early explorers, attempting to phonetically record what they were hearing, gave certain groups erroneous names. For instance, the Nootka were called such by Captain Cook, but they prefer to be known as the Nuu-chah-nulth or simply the West Coast peoples. The Southern Kwagiutl have proposed they be called Kwakwaka'wakw – "those who speak Kwakwala".

The societies of the Wakashan peoples were, like the northern groups, based on kinship. Each clan bore its own hereditary crests such as the killer whale and thunderbird. Ancestral privileges among these groups were more often inherited through the male line than the female, and the right to display certain crests and perform certain songs and dances was passed down through the generations.

Kwagiutl potlatch festivities were the most flamboyant of all the groups, their theatrical dances performed with elaborate props and costumes, especially masks. They often painted themselves and even altered the shape of their heads by binding them in infancy to make them elongated and thus more beautiful. The West Coast (Nootka) natives were skilled mariners who hunted whales and other sea mammals in the open waters of the Pacific.

The southernmost group is the Coast Salish, their territory encompassing the modern cities of Vancouver and Seattle. The Coast Salish inhabited flat-roofed houses that were often built in long rows under a common roof and divided by plank partitions, which could be removed for social and ceremonial occasions. At the time of European contact, their social structure was less rigid than the Wakashans or the northern groups, and class distinctions were less evident. Their winter festivities were more contemplative, less devoted to feasting and dancing than to personal acquisition of spirit power. To acquire a guardian spirit meant success at hunting and fishing. Those with the ability to foretell events and cure sickness became shamans and their supernatural powers were highly respected.

Also respected were the souls of other living creatures. In mythic times, it was believed that animals had the ability to transform themselves into humans. Elaborate rituals were conducted at the beginning of each fishing and hunting season to pay homage to the various species which were sought for food and clothing.

Native legends were passed orally from generation to generation. These traditional stories, set in a timeless past, are an expression of the universe's creation and the evolution of humanity. In native mythology, the Raven plays a major role as a supernatural trickster and transformer. The Raven represents curiosity and he continually alters the world provided by the Creator. While stealing, he accidentally released the sun and stars, and when he opened a clamshell he released the first humans.

UNDERSTANDING NATIVE ART

At the time of first contact by European explorers, Northwest native communities were filled with skilled artisans. The explorers engaged in a healthy trade with the natives, acquiring artifacts that were sometimes handcrafted on the spot. In exchange, the natives received European tools which enhanced their woodworking and carving. Glass beads were also a coveted trade item, especially with the Athapaskans who used them to decorate their leather garments.

Basket weaving was a skill shared by all the native groups. The women of the coastal Indian tribes wove watertight hats and baskets out of spruce roots and cedar bark. The Athapaskans used willow root, and the Southern Eskimos and Aleuts used beach ryegrass.

Another product of native craftsmanship was the bentwood box – made from a single cedar plank that was steamed until soft enough to bend at ninety-degree angles. Three of the corners were, as a result, perfectly smooth while the fourth corner was skillfully joined with pegs or spruce root stitches. These boxes held all sorts of items and were often decorated with ornate carvings.

Totem poles, made from the trunks of massive red cedars, were the most monumental of all native art. As the chosen cedar was felled, the cutters looked away while its spirit departed. Master carvers were commissioned to sculpture the pole and, upon its completion, they performed a dance around the base of the pole while it was being raised. A freestanding totem pole survived for about 60 years before the elements took their toll and the weathered pole toppled to the ground. When this happened, its spirit would depart and the fallen pole was left to return to nature.

Throughout the early years of the fur trade, native groups flourished and their art continued to evolve. But when white missionaries and schoolteachers moved into these regions, native customs were discouraged

The sculptured figures of Tlingit totem poles can be viewed at Saxman Village, including works in progress in the carving shed.

Haida dancers re-enact native myths, which were passed orally from generation to generation at potlatch celebrations.

and a unique art form was all but abandoned. Its rebirth came in the late 1960s and gained momentum in the '70s when native artists discovered a new medium – the silkscreen print. The ensuing mass production of native art prompted the general public to take an interest in both its form and the culture it represents.

Each group has its own artistic style but they share basic components. The form line defines the shape of the figure being portrayed. Its flowing outline varies in thickness and is usually painted black, with the figure's secondary features in red.

Black and red are the traditional colors of native art. Red was made from ochre (a clay-like mineral) ground to a powder and turned into a paste with the addition of a binding agent such as the oil from salmon eggs. Black came from charcoal, graphite or lignite. With the introduction of commercial paints, artists began experimenting with non-traditional colors; however, much of their work is still done in the original colors. The Kwagiutl traditionally used more colors than the northern artists, adding green, white and yellow to their palettes.

Another basic component is the ovoid – an oval that is pushed out of shape to fit inside the form lines. An ovoid can represent a face, eyes, major joints or simply fill in empty spaces. The U form is used to help contour the figure, fill in spaces or represent features such as feathers. The S form is also used in a variety of ways, such as joining elements, filling in space or representing part of a leg or arm. The four basic design elements – form lines, ovoids, U forms and S forms – are closely assembled to create other shapes in the spaces between them.

Split figures (mirror images) are also widely used, as are transformation figures (i.e. half human/half animal). The basic elements of a figure are sometimes dismantled and rearranged to fit inside a given shape, such as a blanket, hat or spoon. The key to recognizing the figures portrayed in native art is to learn a few of their dominant features.

For example, a raven has a long, straight beak whereas an eagle has a shorter, hooked beak. The legendary Thunderbird – a crest used only by the most powerful and prestigious chiefs – is always portrayed with outstretched wings and a sharply recurved upper beak. A bear will have flared nostrils, clawed paws and sharp teeth, sometimes with its tongue hanging out. The beaver has two large front teeth and a cross-hatched tail. The wolf is often shown standing on all four legs whereas the bear and beaver are usually sitting upright.

One of the easiest motifs to recognize is the killer whale, frequently portrayed in an arched position with a tall dorsal fin protruding from its back and two saw-like rows of teeth in its mouth. The moon, an exclusive crest of high-ranking Haida chiefs, is round with a face in the centre. The sun is similar to the moon but with long rays projecting from the outer circle. Human figures are also part of native art and those wearing high-crowned hats atop a totem pole are watchmen who can see others approaching. In Kwagiutl art, the eyes of supernatural beings are hollow and those of animals and people protrude.

Haida drawings and sculptures embody Northwest native art's classical purity. The trademarks of Haida art are a fluid, stylized use of well-defined form lines and a complex intertwining of figures. Poles and other objects are minimally altered by shallow carvings that blend with the basic shape. Heads are often large (especially those portrayed on totem poles) and in print works the blank spaces are seldom left unadorned. Tlingit art is similar to Haida, although the figures on a Tlingit totem pole are more isolated and sculptured. The Tlingit are well known for their Chilkat blankets – woven of goat hair and decorated with clan crests – and for their button blankets on which intricate crests are outlined with thousands of buttons. Tsimshian artists imple-

This 19th century Haida drawing by Johnnie Kit-Elswa represents the Raven in the belly of a killer whale.

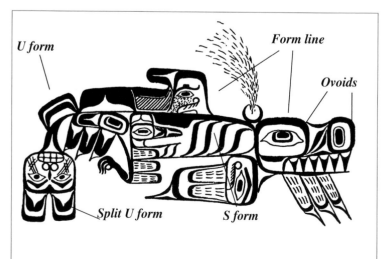

ment many of the traditional northern elements but with slight varia-
tions, such as detaching certain components from the main figure.
Kwagiutl art is recognized by its variety of colors, abundance of small
elements and the protruding beaks, fins and wings that are added to
totem poles.

West Coast (Nootka) art is more flexible than classic northern art,
with frequent breaks in the form lines or even the complete absence of
form lines. Shapes are often geometrical and fewer design elements,
such as ovoids, are used.

Coast Salish natives used no crest system, so their art traditionally
depicted animal and human figures rather than clan emblems. They are
noted for their excellent weaving and basketry as well as their carved
spindle whorls. The Cowichans on Vancouver Island still employ traditional methods when making their famous sweaters.

With a renewed interest in preserving the traditions of native art,
another concern has arisen – that of authenticity. By definition, anything created by a native Indian is authentic. However, some of the best
native artists are not content to replicate the work of their ancestors but
are experimenting with their art's classical components. As the
acclaimed Haida artist Robert Davidson says, if an art isn't changing,
it's dead. Davidson's professional career as a Haida artist began with
his carving miniature totem poles for customers at a Vancouver department store. His work is now displayed in art galleries, and his original
prints and sculptures are collectors items.

The late Bill Reid, of Haida and Scots-American ancestry, is credit-
ed with reviving West Coast native art and reintroducing it to the world.
His major works include *The Black Canoe*, which is the centrepiece of
the Canadian embassy in Washington. A second casting, *The Jade
Canoe*, stands in the departure hall of Vancouver's International
Airport. His *Killer Whale* bronze sits outside the entrance to the
Vancouver Aquarium, and his massive yellow cedar carving *The Raven
and The First Men* is housed at the University of British Columbia's
Museum of Anthropology.

When a Haida embarks on an artistic career, the first step is to
become an apprentice – one who copies the art of predecessors. The
next stage is that of journeyman – learning the symmetrical and classical forms of Haida art. The next stage is to become a master, which
entails experimenting with what has been learned. Finally, those with
exceptional talent become artists, their work reflecting both mastery
and emotion.

The most recent development in native art is the use of computer
graphics. Roy Henry Vickers, a talented Tsimshian artist, has recreated
traditional forms on a computer screen. He says that his computer-gen-
erated ovoids and U-shapes look no different than those created by his
ancestors a thousand years ago. The use of computer technology also
provides for long-term storage of totem pole designs on disks.

CHAPTER MAP

CH. THIRTEEN
• Fairbanks
Denali

CH. TWELVE
Anchorage •
Prince
William
Sound

CH. ELEVEN

CH. EIGHT
Skagway •

CH. NINE CH. SEVEN
Juneau •

CH. SIX

CH. TEN
Sitka •

CH. FIVE
Ketchikan •

CH. FOUR

CH. THREE

CH. TWO
Vancouver •
Victoria •

Seattle •
CH. ONE •

CH. FOURTEEN

KODIAK
ISLAND

PART II

The Voyage and the Ports

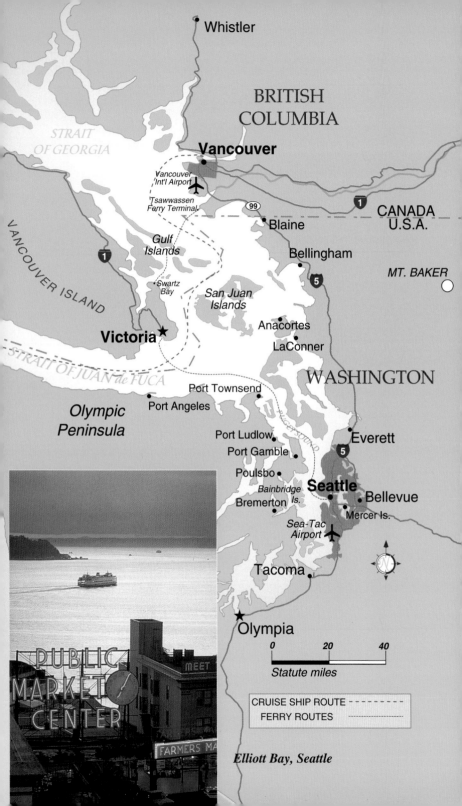

Whistler

BRITISH
COLUMBIA

STRAIT
OF GEORGIA

Vancouver

Vancouver
Int'l Airport ✈

Tsawwassen
Ferry Terminal

(99)

1

CANADA
U.S.A.

Blaine

Gulf
Islands

Bellingham

5

MT. BAKER ○

VANCOUVER ISLAND

1

Swartz
Bay

San Juan
Islands

Victoria ★

Anacortes

LaConner

WASHINGTON

STRAIT OF JUAN de FUCA

Port Townsend

Port Angeles

Olympic
Peninsula

PUGET SOUND

Port Ludlow

Port Gamble

Everett

5

Poulsbo

Bainbridge
Is.

Seattle

Bellevue

Bremerton

Mercer Is.

Sea-Tac
Airport ✈

N

Tacoma

0   20   40

Statute miles

★ Olympia

CRUISE SHIP ROUTE - - - - - -
FERRY ROUTES ··········

PUBLIC MARKET CENTER

MEET

FARMERS MA

Elliott Bay, Seattle

CHAPTER ONE

VICTORIA & SEATTLE

For several centuries the legend of the Strait of Juan de Fuca fascinated seafaring explorers. According to one version of the legend, this mysterious waterway was first sighted by the Greek mariner Juan de Fuca, who was a pilot on board Sir Francis Drake's *Golden Hind* when that daring British privateer ventured into these waters in 1579. In a story published some years later, the Strait of Juan de Fuca was said to be an inlet leading to the Atlantic Ocean.

Finally, after years of learned debate in universities and salons across Europe, the legend was put to rest in the summer of 1792. That's when British and Spanish naval ships sailed the length of Juan de Fuca Strait and found it connected not with a northwest passage, but with a coastal waterway of twisting channels bounded by snowcapped mountains to the east and forested islands to the west. A thousand miles in length, this protected but intricate stretch of water would eventually be called the Inside Passage.

The Strait of Juan de Fuca is the southernmost entrance to the Inside Passage and is now a busy marine highway. It is also part of the international border between the United States and Canada. On its south side lies Washington State's Olympic Peninsula and to the north is British Columbia's provincial capital of Victoria, on Vancouver Island.

Victoria's Inner Harbour

VICTORIA

FURS TO FLOWERS

On a clear day, Victoria's 75,000 residents can look across Juan de Fuca Strait to Washington State's Olympic Mountains. This vista is only one reason Victoria is a popular tourist destination. Others include the temperate climate, flourishing flower gardens and a British heritage preserved in the city's Tudor, Victorian and Edwardian architecture.

Victoria began as a fur trading post of the Hudson's Bay Company. Bastion Square is the site of the original fort, built in 1843, with Johnson, Government and Fort Streets the first commercial thoroughfares. A town sprang up south of the fort around James Bay, and the outlying area became farmland as settlers arrived.

Britain made Vancouver Island a crown colony in 1849. When the 1858 Fraser gold rush attracted boatloads of American prospectors to the region, a second colony was formed on the adjacent mainland. The two colonies soon merged to form British Columbia and, in 1868, Victoria became the capital.

Meanwhile, the sale of Alaska to the United States in 1867 placed the British colony in the middle of two tracts of American land – Washington State to the south and Alaska to the north. This prompted a lengthy debate and final decision on the part of British Columbians to join not with the United States but, in 1871, with the recently-formed Confederation of Canada. By the end of Queen Victoria's reign in 1901, the city that bears her name was coming into its own. The archi-

Victoria's Legislative Buildings, designed by British architect
Francis Rattenbury, are shown here in 1900 shortly after completion.

tectural achievements of Britain's Francis Rattenbury would soon define the city's Inner Harbour, the sight of which prompted Rudyard Kipling to say that a visit to Victoria was "worth a very long journey" – a sentiment still expressed to this day.

GETTING TO VICTORIA

All routes leading to Victoria are scenic. Linked to Vancouver and Seattle by sea and air, visitors can arrive at Victoria's Inner Harbour on board a passenger ferry, high-speed catamaran, floatplane or helicopter. The Victoria International Airport is a short drive north of the city, as are the car ferry terminals at Sidney and Swartz Bay. The cruise lines offer pre- and post-cruise trips to Victoria. Your travel agent will be able to advise you about booking these and other tours.

CITY SIGHTS

There's no better place to start a tour of downtown Victoria than strolling the Inner Harbour. Here the boats and docks are part of an imperial setting of lawns and lamp posts, overseen by the regal **Empress Hotel** 1. This grand hotel, which first opened its doors in 1908, was designed by a flamboyant British architect named Francis Rattenbury. Built by the Canadian Pacific Railway, the hotel has been restored to its original Edwardian opulence and afternoon tea at The Empress is a Victoria tradition.

Equally imperial in style and scale are the **Legislative Buildings** 2, designed by Rattenbury and completed in 1898. He was in his early twenties when he won a competition to design these buildings. Built of granite and other indigenous materials, this Beaux-Arts structure is a mix of Victorian, Roman and Italian Renaissance styles. At night its classical domes and arches are outlined by thousands of lights.

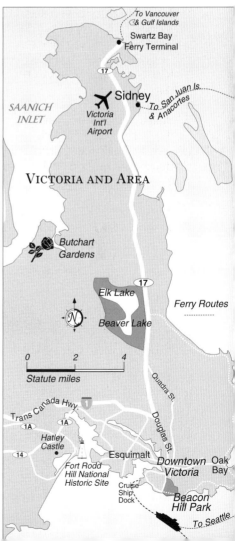

To Vancouver & Gulf Islands
Swartz Bay Ferry Terminal
17
SAANICH INLET
Sidney
To San Juan Is. & Anacortes
Victoria Int'l Airport

VICTORIA AND AREA

Butchart Gardens

17
Elk Lake
Ferry Routes
Beaver Lake

0   2   4
Statute miles

Trans Canada Hwy. 1
1A
1A
Hatley Castle
14
Fort Rodd Hill National Historic Site
Esquimalt
Cruise Ship Dock
Quadra St.
Douglas St.
Downtown Victoria   Oak Bay
Beacon Hill Park
To Seattle

The Empress, a grand rail hotel, was named for Britain's Queen Victoria, Empress of India.

(Right) Historic buildings line the pedestrian streets of Bastion Square.

Visitors from around the world enjoy the magnificent Butchart Gardens near Victoria.

Sailors of all ages enjoy the exhibits at the Maritime Museum.

Rattenbury trained with his uncle in England before moving to Canada where the wide-open spaces of the west suited his grand schemes. His life ended in scandal back in England when his young, second wife and her paramour (the chauffeur) were charged with bludgeoning him to death in 1935. Alma Rattenbury was acquitted, only to commit suicide by the side of a river, while George Stoner was sentenced to life imprisonment and later released.

Right behind The Empress, near the bus depot, is the **Crystal Garden** 🔢. It too was designed by Rattenbury, and this glass-roofed tropical paradise contains exotic flowers, birds and small monkeys. On the south harbourfront is yet another Rattenbury design – the former CPR steamship terminal. It now houses the **Royal London Wax Museum** 🔢 (based on the famous Madame Tussaud's) with over 200 life-size figures of royalty, presidents and other historic figures.

Across the water, on the north side of the harbour at the corner of Government and Wharf, is the **Visitor Info Centre** 🔢, where you'll find a helpful staff and selection of maps and brochures. City tours, such as the Scenic Drive to Oak Bay, are available by motor coach, double-decker bus and horsedrawn carriage.

Wharf Street leads north of the Inner Harbour, past the original Customs House, to historic **Bastion Square** 🔢, its narrow streets and restored brick buildings now housing restaurants, shops and art galleries. The original courthouse, at 28 Bastion Square, now houses the **Maritime Museum**. Inside this turreted building, visitors can ride an ornate elevator built in 1900 for an elderly judge. Exhibits include a dugout canoe named Tilikum which was sailed by Captain Voss from Victoria to England. Across the street is the Garrick's Head Pub, which opened for business in 1867.

VICTORIA

Esquimalt

Inner Harbour

Chinatown

Cruise Ship Terminal

To Anne Hathaway's Cottage

Beacon Hill Park

Craigdarroch Castle

Streets:
Pandora
Johnson
Yates
View
FORT
Broughton
Courtney
BLANSHARD
DOUGLAS ST.
GOVERNMENT
Wharf
Store
Oak Bay Rd.
Cook
Vancouver
Fairfield
Humboldt
Linden
Moss
Fairfield
Cook
Joan St.
Dallas (scenic drive)
Douglas
Government
Toronto
Menzies
Simcoe
Michagan
Superior
Oswego
Kingston
Quebec
Belleville
Montreal
St. Lawrence

1 2 3 4 5 6 7 8 9 10 11 12 13 14

Statute miles
0   1/4   1/2

N

Other downtown sights include the **Royal British Columbia Museum 6** which houses an outstanding exhibit on the area's natural and native history. Beside it is Thunderbird Park with an impressive display of totem poles, and behind it is **Helmcken House 7**, one of Victoria's oldest houses which was built in 1852 by a pioneer doctor.

A ten-minute stroll away, heading south on Government Street, will take you to **Carr House 8**. Now a museum, this Italianate-style house, built in the 1860s, was the birthplace of Emily Carr, one of Canada's most acclaimed artists and writers (see page 116). Two blocks east on Simcoe Street is Victoria's oldest and cherished municipal park – **Beacon Hill Park 9**, named for the navigational range markers which sat atop its hill in the 1840s. Today, visitors enjoy the classic English landscape garden while below in the strait a modern beacon marks a dangerous shoal's position outside the harbour entrance.

Another popular park is **Fort Rodd Hill & Fisgard Lighthouse National Historic Park,** a short drive to the far side of Esquimalt Harbour, where you can take a close look at the oldest working lighthouse on the British Columbia coast.

A mile east of the downtown core, in the upscale Rockland neighborhood, is **Craigdarroch Castle 10** – built in the late 1800s by the coal baron Robert Dunsmuir, a Scottish immigrant who became British Columbia's wealthiest and most influential businessman, and whose son James became premier of the province in 1900. The four-storey castle, complete with a tower, turrets and French Gothic roofline, is now a museum with the family's original furnishings and artwork on display. Nearby, housed in an 1889 mansion, is the **Art Gallery of Greater Victoria 11** where works of Emily Carr are exhibited.

CITY OF GARDENS

Victoria's rocky bluffs and sweeping sea views are tempered by gardens which bloom in early spring when other parts of the country are

The birthplace of Emily Carr is now a museum with some of her paintings and other items on display.

NOTABLE VICTORIANS

A Skidegate Pole by Emily Carr,
(Vancouver Art Gallery).

Victoria society, in its early days, reflected Victorian England's rigid rules of social behavior. There were, however, a few noteworthy Victorians who broke with convention when it came to living their own lives.

One was James Douglas, an agent of the Hudson's Bay Company, who oversaw the construction of Fort Victoria in 1843 and became governor of Vancouver Island in 1851. Douglas was born in British Guyana, the son of a Scotsman and a Creole woman. He came to British North America as a fur trader and married Amelia Connolly, a sixteen-year-old with auburn hair and grey eyes. She bore him 13 children and, when her husband was knighted, became Lady Douglas. Yet she was never fully accepted by the ladies of Victoria society because her mother was a native.

Governor Douglas obviously harbored no such prejudice. As governor he sympathised with the natives, believing they could prosper alongside the white settlers if provided protection for their villages and fishing/hunting grounds. However, after Douglas retired in 1864, native rights deteriorated under a steady influx of white settlers.

Many of these immigrants were from Britain, including Richard Carr, who established a grocery wholesale business in Victoria. He and his wife raised five daughters, encouraging the youngest's talent for drawing. Her name was Emily and she was still a teenager when her parents died within two years of each other. Buoyed by her tolerant upbringing, she defied Victorian social standards to pursue her artistic vision and become one of Canada's greatest painters.

In 1890 it was one thing for a young woman to study art as part of her 'finishing,' but to actually become an artist was most improper. Emily Carr's impropriety didn't stop with studies at the California School of Design in San Francisco or training in England and France. It continued with her remaining single, her smoking, her keeping a menagerie of pets which included a small monkey, and – perhaps most improper of all – her travelling the coast with native guides to visit their villages and sketch their totem poles and longhouses.

She was not content with painting just what she saw, but also what she felt, and her experimental works captured the spirit of a West Coast rainforest. Emily Carr was also a writer and her haunting stories are as vivid as her paintings, with anything ambiguous or unnecessary peeled away to expose the subject's core.

still in the grip of winter. Daffodils, rhododendron, honeysuckle and hyacinth are just a few of the flowers that thrive in Victoria's mild climate. A British fondness for gardening is reflected everywhere – streets lined with blossoming cherry trees, lawns bordered by rockeries and rose bushes, and enough public gardens to satisfy any flower aficionado. The gated grounds of **Government House** 🔢 (official residence of the Lieutenant-Governor, the Queen's representative in British Columbia) and **Hatley Castle** in Esquimalt (built by the coal heir James Dunsmuir), are both beautifully maintained and open to the public.

The gardens everyone wants to see, however, are the world-famous **Butchart Gardens**. A 20-minute drive north of Victoria, this 50-acre garden site took root in 1904 when Jennie Butchart decided to clean up the mess her husband left behind when his cement plant excavated a limestone quarry on their estate. Employing workers from her husband's cement company, Mrs. Butchart transformed an eyesore into the Sunken Garden. She spent hours tucking ivy into the rock wall's pockets and crevices while hanging over the sides of the quarry in a bosun's chair. For years the Butcharts welcomed all visitors to their gardens, serving afternoon tea in summer houses scattered about the property until the sheer number of visitors made this impossible. Today more than a million visitors arrive annually to view the grounds which include a Japanese Garden, Rose Garden, Italian Garden, Concert Lawn and Fireworks Viewing Area. At night the gardens are transformed when hundreds of hidden lights illuminate the flowers and fountains.

SHOPPING IN VICTORIA

Some of the best browsing can be done on Government Street where the late Victorian era is preserved in chocolate shops, bookstores, tobacconists and tea merchants. Here you can buy Scottish tweeds and tartans, English bone china, Waterford crystal and Irish linen. Munro's Bookstore and Rogers' Chocolates are worth popping into just for a look at their splendid interiors.

On Fort Street is 'Antique Row' and at **Market Square** 🔢, the Olde Town's former hotel and saloon district, the shops front an open-air square. **Fan Tan Alley**, 🔢 said to be the narrowest street in Canada, leads to colorful Chinatown.

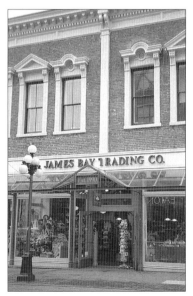

Shops on Government Street are housed in heritage buildings.

The restored Victorian facades of Market Square include the Milne Building and Strand Hotel (far right) on Johnson Street.

DINING IN VICTORIA

In addition to the many pubs and tea rooms in Victoria, some of the city's best meals can be enjoyed in the dining rooms of hotels such as **The Empress**, which serves award-winning cuisine in the Empress Room and a popular curry buffet in its famous Bengel Lounge where the British Colonial decor includes a Bengal tiger skin displayed over the marble fireplace. Tea with sandwiches, pastries and scones is served throughout the afternoon in the hotel's elegant Tea Lobby (reservations for one of the seatings is recommended).

Victoria's inviting pubs include **Swans Brewpub** (at Pandora and Store Streets) where draught ales and lagers are served on its flower-filled patio. The Snug, Victoria's oldest English pub, is at the **Oak Bay Beach Hotel** – an English country inn overlooking the sea.

Across the Inner Harbour in Esquimalt is the **Olde England Inn**, a Tudor-style mansion where the decor and staff attire are Elizabethan and the menu features traditional English fare. On the hotel grounds is a replica of **Anne Hathaway's Cottage** – birthplace of William Shakespeare's wife – complete with country garden.

SIDNEY BY THE SEA

The seaside town of Sidney is a pleasant detour for Victoria visitors heading to or from the B.C. Ferries terminal at Swartz Bay. Just south of the ferry terminal is Canoe Cove where you'll find the cozy Stonehouse Pub tucked in the hillside woods. Continuing south along the highway, you'll come to marina-filled Tsehum Harbour. At its southern end, off Harbour Road, is the rustic Latch Restaurant – built in

Active Pass is the main ferry route through the pastoral Gulf Islands to the Swartz Bay terminal near Victoria on Vancouver Island.

1920 as a summer retreat for a former Lieutenant-Governor of the province. More restaurants and shops await in downtown Sidney, especially on Beacon Avenue which runs through the centre of town down to the waterfront where a small museum, seaside walkway and more restaurants provide visitors with waterfront views of the San Juan Islands in Washington State.

Ferries ply the waters off Sidney where a string of islands – Canada's Gulf Islands and America's San Juan Islands – dot the horizon. Blessed with a Mediterranean-type climate and picturesque coves, both island groups attract plenty of visitors each summer. Recreational boaters, kayakers, campers, cyclists and nature lovers are all drawn to their shores.

Their histories include such colorful characters as Brother Twelve – a charismatic Englishman who established a cult on De Courcy Island in the 1930s. He had a knack for wooing women off visiting boats. Their husbands, providing they had money to contribute to the colony, were also invited ashore but relegated to the north end of the island. Brother Twelve's colony – called The Haven – eventually collapsed as people (and the police) caught on to his wily ways. He vanished with a jar of gold and was never seen again.

The hermits and eccentrics of bygone days have a tougher time of it now that the larger islands are easily accessible by inter-island ferries. Marina resorts and bed & breakfast inns provide pleasant accommodations from which to stroll the parks and beaches, browse the arts & crafts shops and enjoy the peaceful ambience of these island gems.

SEATTLE

CITY OF SPIRIT

When two ships of Britain's Royal Navy sailed into Puget Sound in the spring of 1792, the expedition's commander was so impressed with the "pleasing landscapes" and "serenity of climate" that his logbook entries read more like those of a travel writer than a sea captain. Yet, with uncanny foresight, Captain George Vancouver's comments were right on the mark.

He looked around at the forested shores and saw a potential lumber industry, noting "thousands of the finest spars the world produces." He gazed at the future site of Seattle and wrote that the verdant lawns and abundant fertility required "only to be enriched by the industry of man." But it was the esthetic beauty of the area which caused this skilled surveyor to momentarily forget about compass bearings and potential northwest passages. "To describe the beauties of this region," he wrote, "will, on some future occasion, be a very grateful task to the pen of a skilful panegyrist."

Captain Vancouver's prophetic words have been echoed time and again in recent years. Ranked in various surveys as the number one place in America to live, visit and do business, the city of Seattle has realized its potential. This achievement, however, was a long uphill struggle which began in 1851. In the fall of that year, when the lands around Puget Sound were still part of Oregon Territory, two men from

Seattle became a busy shipping port when gold fever sent men and women rushing north to the Klondike.

A horse-drawn carriage takes visitors on a tour of Pioneer Square.

Portland – John Low and Lee Terry – explored Puget Sound and chose Alki Point for a townsite.

Two months later the rest of their party arrived by schooner from Portland. This group of 12 adults and 12 children tried to forge a community but were unsuccessful. Low and Terry's sawmill venture failed and the group split, with the majority – led by Arthur Denny, Charles Boren and William Bell – relocating four miles away on the east side of Elliott Bay in what is now Seattle's downtown core.

This larger group was joined by Dr. Maynard and a Portland lumberman who came to build a steam sawmill. Land claims were quickly established and a name was chosen for their new townsite. They decided on Sealth (later altered to Seattle), after a chief of the local Duwamp natives.

Through the 1850s and '60s, increasing numbers of lumber schooners and supply vessels from San Francisco and Portland pulled into Puget Sound, but Seattle didn't grow beyond a sprinkling of houses and shops with a schoolhouse, church and hotel to serve its 200 residents. Then coal was discovered nearby, and Seattle began shipping coal as well as lumber.

The town became a service and supply centre for mining and logging camps, lumber mills and farms, and by 1870 Seattle was growing faster than other communities in the area. But the city's fate was still not certain. Its future hinged on the Northern Pacific Railroad, and land speculators eagerly anticipated that Seattle would be chosen as a western terminus. When Tacoma got the nod over Seattle, her disappointed citizens joined together to build their own railroad. This civic pride and energy became known as the 'Seattle Spirit.'

In 1880, railroad magnate Henry Villard bought the nearby Newcastle Mine, gained control of the Northern Pacific Railroad and, a few years later, a main line finally reached Seattle. This helped the brash young city sustain its growing prosperity, with three-quarters of the population employed in businesses which serviced the local lumber, mining and fishing industries.

Seattle Center

Space Needle

Monorail Terminal

1

2nd Ave N

John St

Denny Way

Broad St.

Clay St

Cedar St

Vine St

Wall St

Battery St

Bell St

Blanshard St.

Lenora St.

3rd Ave

2nd Ave

1st Ave

Western Way

Monorail

9th Ave

8th Ave

7th Ave

6th Ave

5th Ave

4th Ave

Virginia St

Stewart St

Olive Way

Terry Ave

Minor Ave

Howell St

Boren Ave

Terry Ave

Monorail Terminal

Visitor. Info.

i

Elliott Ave

Pier 70

Pier 69

Pier 67

Port of Seattle

Pier 66

Alaskan Way

Pike St. Market

2

Pine St

Pike St

Union St

University St

P.O.

1st Ave

Post Alley

6

Seneca St

Spring St

Madison St

Marion St

Columbia St

3rd Ave

4th Ave

5th Ave

6th Ave

9th Ave St

8th Ave St

Cherry St

James St

Pier 59

Pier 57

Pier 56

Pier 55

Pier 54

WA State Ferries

ELLIOTT BAY

SEATTLE

2nd Ave S

3rd Ave S

4th Ave S

5th Ave

3

Pioneer Square

Yesler Way

S Washington St

S Main St

5

Chinatown/ International District

S King St

1st Ave S

King Street Station

Kingdome

4

To Vancouver

0   5   10

Statute miles

I-5

Lake Washington

Bainbridge Is.

Seattle

Bellevue

Mercer Is.

90

405

Blake Is.

Museum of Flight

Exit 158

Sea-Tac Airport

A depression in the mid-80s caused a downturn and in 1889 a fire wiped out 60 city blocks. But the Seattle Spirit, fueled by immigrants from other parts of the country and Europe, propelled the city forward with dogged determination. Then, on July 17, 1897, the steamer Portland arrived from Alaska with gold prospectors on board. They had struck it rich in the Klondike and the great gold rush began.

Seattle, already shipping freight to Alaskan ports, quickly established itself as the outfitting center and port of departure for prospectors heading north. The city never looked back. Its economy diversified further with the establishment of Boeing Airplane Company in 1917 and, more recently, high-tech industries such as the Microsoft computer software company.

Seattle's roots, however, have not been lost to the 20th century. When Rolland Denny, the last survivor of the original 24 settlers, died in 1939 at age 88, Seattle had in his lifetime grown from frontier village to bustling metropolis. But the Seattle Spirit, born of hard work and self reliance, was firmly embedded in the city's pioneer soul.

WHERE TO STAY IN SEATTLE

In addition to the reliable chain hotels, Seattle's distinctive establishments include the stately Four Seasons Olympic Hotel, as well as the Alexis Hotel and the Hotel Vintage Park – both offering European-style luxury. The elegantly appointed Mayflower Park Hotel is located in the heart of the shopping district and the Inn at the Market is reminiscent of a French country inn. The Edgewater, at Pier 67, offers a mountain lodge decor with views of Elliott Bay and the Olympic Mountains. In 1992 it was used as a location for an episode of TV's Northern Exposure, called 'It Happened in Juneau.'

GETTING AROUND IN SEATTLE

The downtown Metro buses in the core area – between Battery and South Jackson Streets and between Sixth Avenue and Alaskan Way – are free from 4 a.m. to 9 p.m. A high-speed monorail whisks passengers between Westlake Center and the Seattle Center, while a more leisurely pace is taken by the tram and trolley cars servicing the waterfront piers and other downtown attractions.

The Visitor Information Bureau **i** is located at 7th and Union, in Level 1 Galleria of the Washington State Convention Center.

SEATTLE SHOPPING

During the Klondike Gold Rush, prospectors shopped in Seattle for tents, picks, shovels, beans and bacon. Today the outfitting stores supply freeze-dried food and Gore-Tex clothing. Outdoor recreation is popular here (the city's median age is 35), and in addition to the traditional hardware stores and ship chandlers, suppliers such as Eddie Bauer, Recreational Equipment Inc. and Northface now provide everything from skis to backpacks.

Seattle is a good place to do some pre-Alaska shopping for items such as a wide-brimmed hat, rain slicker or binoculars. If high fashion is more your taste, head for Fifth Avenue's shops and malls such as Westlake Center, Nordstrom and Rainier Square.

NORTHWEST CUISINE

In the mid-1980s, a new culinary trend began in the Pacific Northwest. With its moderate climate, rich soil and access to salt and fresh water, the region enjoys a year-round bounty of fruit, vegetables, meat, poultry and seafood from nearby farms and fishboats. These locally harvested products, enhanced with regional delicacies such as wild mushrooms, are highlighted in Northwest Cuisine.

Preparation may vary but the natural flavor of the ingredients is always the emphasis. To help wash down an oyster in the shell or a steaming bowl of clams, Seattle diners can choose from a growing list of local wines and brews.

In addition to Seattle's many old-fashioned pubs and specialty coffee bars, there are a number of award-winning restaurants serving Northwest cuisine, such as Fullers (in the Sheraton Seattle), The Painted Table (in the luxurious Alexis Hotel) and, on Fourth Avenue, The Dahlia Lounge (Northwest cuisine with an Asian influence). Also on Fourth is the Assaggio Ristorante, serving excellent Italian cuisine.

Seafood lovers might try Chandler's Crabhouse overlooking Lake Union, McCormick & Schmick's in downtown Seattle or Ray's Boathouse on Shilshole Bay where the sea and mountain views are as good as the food.

For American food served in a turn-of-the-century atmosphere there's F.X. McRory's Steak, Chop & Oyster House at Pioneer Square where, in addition to a wide selection of ales, lagers and stouts, the Whiskey Bar has the world's largest selection of bourbons. Another favorite for pub draughts and prime rib is Jake O'Shaughnessey's Saloon & Eatery beside the Seattle Center.

The Pike Place Market sells fresh seafood and farm produce – the key ingredients in Northwest Cuisine.

Seattle's skyline, with the Space Needle in the foreground, stands against the dramatic backdrop of Mount Rainier.

CITY SIGHTS

A good place to enjoy Seattle's beautiful mountain/sea setting is from atop the 600-foot **Space Needle** ■, built for the 1962 World's Fair. The observation deck's 360-degree view lets you gaze down at the city built on the hills between Puget Sound and Lake Washington. To the west lie the Olympic Mountains and eastward is the Cascade Range of snowcapped peaks which includes Mount Rainier and Mount Baker. The Space Needle is part of the 74-acre **Seattle Center** which encompasses a theater, opera house, children's museum and science center.

Six blocks south of the Space Needle is Seattle's waterfront – formerly called 'The Gold Rush Strip' when freighters and passenger liners from Alaska and other American ports docked here. It stretches the length of Alaskan Way, from Pier 70 – a restored wharf now filled with shops and restaurants – down to Pier 52. In between are restaurants, gift shops and tour boat operators offering harbour tours, cruises of the canal locks and trips to Blake Island State Park.

The **Seattle Aquarium** and **Omnidome Theatre** are located on historic **Pier 59**, and the recently renovated **Bell Street Pier (Pier 66)** is where **Odyssey, The Maritime Discovery Centre** is located. This interactive maritime centre contains four galleries and hands-on exhibits celebrating the city's marine environment, such as taking a simulated kayak ride through Puget Sound. A public rooftop deck, with telescopes, is a good spot to enjoy the harbor views.

Perched on a bluff overlooking the waterfront is the **Pike Place Market** ■. Its cobblestone streets are lined with stalls of fruit, vegetables, seafood, meats, cheeses, coffees, teas and spices. When you tire of strolling the busy aisles, there are three levels of shops and restaurants below the main arcade. The stairs of Pike Place Hillclimb connect the market with the waterfront below. Here pedestrians can hop aboard vintage trolleys which travel up and down Alaskan Way. They stop at various pier attractions, then carry on to Pioneer Square and the International District. Seattle trolley tours can be boarded at the waterfront or downtown booths for a one-hour narrated loop tour of the city's best attractions, with on/off privileges at each stop.

The restored brick buildings of **Pioneer Square** 3 stand where settlers' shacks stood before the Great Fire of 1889. Yesler Way, which runs through the middle of Pioneer Square down to the waterfront, was originally a skid road for logs. A guided underground tour follows sidewalks (one storey down) that were abandoned after the Great Fire. The Klondike Gold Rush National Historical Park, hidden away in a storefront at 117 South Main, commemorates Seattle's boomtown days as 'Gateway to the Gold.'

Next to Pioneer Square is the **Kingdome** 4 sports arena, home field for the Seattle Mariners baseball club and Seattle Seahawks football team. Due east of the Kingdome is the **International District** 5 where Asian restaurants, bazaars and exotic shops are bordered by the Kobe Terrace Park. Guided tours are available of this colorful area rich in Oriental culture.

The **Seattle Art Museum** 6, internationally known for its Native American and modern art of the Pacific Northwest, is at 100 University Street. On the block just uphill from the Museum is the Seattle Symphony's new concert hall – Benaroya Hall – which opened with a two-week gala celebration in September, 1998.

To the north, separated from downtown by the Lake Washington Ship Canal, is the Ballard area – settled by Scandinavian fishermen and loggers. The canal connects Lake Washington with Puget Sound and near its western entrance are the **Chittenden Locks**. Here sightseers can watch fishboats and other vessels being raised or lowered as they travel between fresh and salt water. Seattle's huge fishing fleet moors at nearby Fisherman's Terminal and each spring hundreds of seiners and gill netters head north to fish the waters of Alaska. The **Woodland Park Zoo**, on Phinney Avenue North, is one of the best zoos in the U.S. with its re-creation of natural habitats.

On the southern outskirts of the city, off Airport Way, is the **Museum of Flight**, a national historic landmark. Built around the Boeing Company's original factory on the edge of Boeing Field (King County Airport) the museum's Great Gallery contains vintage aircraft suspended in simulated flight from the ceiling, which is six storeys high. The Spirit of Washington dinner train will take you on a scenic trip around Lake Washington to the Chateau Ste. Michelle Winery situated on the landscaped grounds of Woodinville.

Farther afield, scenic country roads lead into the Cascade Mountains past rocky gorges, plunging falls and pretty alpine villages such as North Bend at the base of Mt. Si, Leavenworth with its charming Bavarian theme, and Roslyn – the fictional Cicely, Alaska of the TV series Northern Exposure.

To the west of the city, beautiful Puget Sound beckons. The Washington State ferry system (the nation's largest) provides access from downtown Seattle to Bainbridge Island and to Bremerton on the Olympic Peninsula.

A loop drive of the Peninsula can include stops at Poulsbo (settled by Norwegians), and the ports of Gamble, Ludlow and Townsend (all 19th century towns where schooners loaded lumber for shipment to California). Port Angeles, with its mile-long spit called Ediz Hook, is the gateway to Olympic National Park, where attractions include the Sol Duc Hot Springs. Ocean beaches beckon on the Peninsula's west coast, and the state capital of Olympia is situated on Puget Sound's southern shore.

North of Seattle, the Interstate 5 is the quickest land route to Vancouver, Canada – a 3-1/2 hour drive of 140 miles. Time permitting, you can turn off at Conway for a visit to LaConner – a century-old port town with interesting shops and restaurants. Another recommended detour is to turn at Burlington onto the scenic Chuckanut Drive, which hugs the coastline. Chuckanut Drive reconnects with the I-5 at Bellingham – southern terminus of the Alaska State Ferry and an interesting waterfront town with turn-of-the-century buildings. From here Mount Baker is a 62-mile detour east.

A Washington State Ferry plies the waters of Puget Sound with Mount Rainier in the background.

Chapter Two

VANCOUVER

I f there's a common sentiment expressed by people arriving in Vancouver to embark or disembark their Alaska cruise, it's likely this: "I wish I had arranged to spend more time in this beautiful city."

Greater Vancouver's 1.8 million residents will readily concede that their coastal city's backdrop of mountains and rainforest is what first impresses visitors. However, a closer look at this vibrant metropolis reveals an abundance of parks and gardens, marinas and promenades, restaurants and public markets, all of which complement the natural beauty surrounding them.

Vancouver sits at a crossroads – both geographically and culturally. Mountains meet sea, east meets west. The city, founded by British settlers in the late 1800s, began as a small lumbering village on the shores of Burrard Inlet and gradually grew into a major shipping port.

The 20th century brought continued immigration from other parts of North America, Britain and the rest of the world and, in recent years, Vancouver's growing trade with the Pacific Rim countries has brought steady immigration from Hong Kong and other Asian nations. This diversity of cultures has transformed Vancouver from provincial town to cosmopolitan city.

Vancouver celebrated its 100th birthday in 1986 by hosting an international transportation fair – the event that 'put Vancouver on the map' as it stepped proudly onto the world stage to take its place alongside

Stanley Park's Brockton Point stands near the entrance to Vancouver's scenic harbor.

other famous cities and ports of call. Britain's Prince Charles and the late Diana, Princess of Wales, officially opened Expo 86. Their mode of transportation to the opening ceremonies was, fittingly, by boat.

Planes, trains, cars and buses all converge in Vancouver but it remains first and foremost a port city. Freighters lie at anchor in English Bay waiting to unload their shipments. Barge-towing tugs chug in and out of port, as do fishboats and pleasure craft. And from May through September, amid this bustle of maritime commerce and recreation, gleaming passenger ships begin and end one of the world's most scenic cruises at one the world's most beautiful port cities – Vancouver.

A BRIEF HISTORY OF VANCOUVER

The first people to appreciate Vancouver's natural harbor were the Squamish tribe of Coast Salish natives. Their local villages were well established when, in the summer of 1792, Captain George Vancouver of the British Royal Navy sailed his ship's boats into the harbor to survey the surrounding shores. He was looking for the Northwest Passage, not a good restaurant, so his visit was cursory to say the least.

In seamanlike fashion, he ordered that the boats proceed "under an easy sail" as a welcoming party of natives paddled out to greet these strange-looking visitors. An exchange of goods (salmon for iron) took place on the run as the British survey boats sailed through the First Narrows and the Second Narrows toward the head of mountain-enclosed Burrard Inlet in search of an inland waterway. It was not to be found, so after a night spent camped on shore the British sailors left at dawn.

A crowd gathered as the **Empress of India** *– the first CPR liner to arrive in Vancouver – pulled into port on April 28th, 1891.*

Captain George Vancouver commanded one of the most demanding expeditions in naval history when he surveyed the Pacific Northwest's vast and intricate coastline.

In his journals Captain Vancouver frequently mentions the lofty barrier of mountains and snow which frustrated his efforts at finding an inland waterway. These coastal mountains, which extend from California to the Aleutian Islands, weren't his only source of frustration. Spain had also dispatched ships to these waters, much to the surprise of Captain Vancouver who thought he was the first European to venture into what we now call the Inside Passage. The British and Spanish vessels crossed paths off Point Grey and the names English Bay and Spanish Banks commemorate this friendly encounter.

But, apart from brief visits by naval ships, the waters off present-day Vancouver remained the domain of the Coast Salish natives who fished here for salmon and harvested shellfish. Merchant ships rarely ventured into the twisting channels of the Inside Passage, choosing to trade for furs with natives whose coastal villages bordered the open Pacific.

Eventually, however, the Hudson's Bay Company forged an overland route to the west coast where it established Fort Langley on the Fraser River in 1827. But it wasn't until gold was discovered in the Fraser Canyon, 30 years later, that settlers began moving into the area. The downstream settlement of New Westminster was declared the colony's Port of Entry to protect British lumber and mining interests, and prevent any land grabbing.

Meanwhile, three Englishmen decided to claim land on the sparsely inhabited shores of Burrard Inlet, beside a government reserve that is now Stanley Park. The locals back in New Westminster (financial hub of the region) thought these fellows were making a big mistake and dubbed them the 'Three Greenhorns.' But one man, 'Gassy Jack'

Deighton, also thought Burrard Inlet had potential. In 1867, with $6 in his pocket, he too settled there with his native wife and mother-in-law where they opened a small hotel and saloon to serve the workers of the nearby Hastings Sawmill.

A small settlement of boarding houses and stores sprang up and became known locally as Gastown although its official name was Granville. Then, in the 1880s, the privately-owned Canadian Pacific Railway pushed its tracks through the Rocky Mountains to the west coast. Its termination point was Burrard Inlet, and with the arrival of CPR's first locomotive on May 23, 1886, the newly incorporated city of Vancouver was born.

The young city's first setback came just weeks later when Gastown burned to the ground. It was quickly rebuilt and by the end of the century a booming sawmill industry was supporting a population of over 27,000. The city had an opera house, museum and horsedrawn coach tours of Stanley Park.

Vancouver Harbor had become a busy place. Merchant cargo ships – both the tall-masted and steam-driven variety – brought goods from overseas and loaded shipments of lumber, while CPR's Empress passenger ships offered luxury cruises to the Orient. The Alaska run began with American and Canadian shipping companies filling their extra berths. Then, in the 1950s, Vancouver's Union Steamships offered trips to Alaska aboard converted World War II Navy Corvettes.

Today Vancouver is one of North America's busiest ports, especially from May to October when the world's leading cruise lines make Vancouver their home port for the increasingly popular Alaska run.

North coast totem poles overlook the cricket pitch near Brockton Oval in Stanley Park.

An aerial view of Vancouver Harbor showing the West End, Stanley Park and English Bay, where freighters lie at anchor.

Over the centuries, Vancouver has seen everything from dugout canoes and square-rigged sailing ships to deepsea freighters and luxury liners visit its harbor. The tall ships have been replaced with tall buildings, but the city's timeless setting of sea and mountains remains as stunning as ever.

THE GREAT SURVEYOR

Captain George Vancouver, at the age of 33, was chosen by the British Admiralty to command a voyage of discovery to the North Pacific. This lengthy voyage took 4-1/2 years and covered 65,000 nautical miles, making it the longest continuous sailing expedition in history – both in time and distance.

The charts produced by Captain Vancouver and his skilled officers were unequalled in detail and accuracy, and are the basis for today's charts of coastal British Columbia and Alaska. He achieved all this without sacrificing the well-being of his men whose mortality rate aboard the two survey ships was lower than if they had remained in England.

Vancouver's own health began to fail him halfway through this challenging voyage and his temper frequently flared. Not particularly well liked by some of his crew, he did manage to inspire a team effort as they rowed in open boats up every mainland inlet of the Inside Passage. It was grueling work in which everyone pushed themselves to the limits of hunger and exhaustion.

Captain Vancouver died in 1798, a few years after his return to England, just as he was completing his journals of the voyage. His final days were spent outside London at Petersham, but his lifelong devotion to the sea began at his birthplace of King's Lynn on the Norfolk coast. A thriving port in the golden age of maritime trade, King's Lynn was a prosperous town and many who lived there were of Dutch ancestry, including Vancouver's father.

James Cook became the young Vancouver's mentor when he accepted the 14-year-old lad as midshipman aboard the *Resolution*. This was Cook's second voyage to the Pacific and under his tutelage Vancouver learned the work of sailors doing duty aloft and of officers steering the ship. Vancouver also served on Cook's third Pacific expedition and witnessed his commander's murder in Hawaii, caused by a tragic misunderstanding.

Cook, who opened up the vast Pacific and made sweeping surveys of the new lands he was sailing past, is remembered as the Great Navigator. Vancouver's rightful place in history is that of the Great Surveyor.

VANCOUVER'S ROYAL CONNECTION

When Britain's Royal Navy dispatched ships to explore and survey the New World, her officers were called "King George's Men" by the natives they encountered. Fortunately there were a number of King Georges who ruled Britain during this era of naval exploration.

Captain Vancouver was the first European explorer to survey in detail the waters of the Pacific Northwest, from Puget Sound in Washington to Cook Inlet in Alaska, and his charts and their place-names have endured to this day. Thus began the proliferation of British place names in and around the City of Vancouver, a trend which continued in the 1800s when Britain extensively surveyed all of her Empire's distant coastlines.

At the turn of the century, Vancouver was an Edwardian outpost of the British Empire. Many of the city's settlers built grand homes containing stained glass windows, potted palms and plush velvet furniture. Summer days were filled with lawn croquet and tennis, lemonade and tea parties on the verandah. Bath houses appeared along English Bay and those who dared wore bathing costumes guaranteed to protect their bodies from sun, sand and prying eyes.

Among Vancouver's first royal visitors were the future King George V and Queen Mary who came in 1901 as the Duke and Duchess of Cornwall and York. In May of 1939, King George VI and Queen Elizabeth (now called the Queen Mother) arrived by train.

Charles and Diana, the Prince and Princess of Wales, were the world's most famous couple when they cruised Vancouver's False Creek en route to the opening ceremonies of Expo 86.

One of Vancouver's most famous moments occurred in 1954, on the final day of the British Empire Games. Prince Philip was among those who witnessed Britain's Roger Bannister and Australia's John Landy break the 4-minute 'miracle' mile in a thrilling finish.

In the spring of 1982, Queen Elizabeth II arrived in port on board the Royal Yacht Britannia. Hundreds of Vancouverites sailed out to greet their visiting monarch and escort her into the harbor.

YOUR STAY IN VANCOUVER

Close to where your ship docks in downtown Vancouver, you'll find a wide range of accommodations, including several five-diamond hotels. Adjacent to the Canada Place Cruise Terminal is the luxury **Pan Pacific Hotel**, where British royalty has stayed, and right across the street is the **Waterfront Centre Hotel**, a Canadian Pacific Hotel. Vancouver's other CP Hotel is the **Hotel Vancouver**, a city landmark located a few blocks from the cruise terminal on Georgia Street. The Hotel Vancouver was built in 1939, but Vancouver's oldest heritage hotel, also on Georgia Street, is the **Hotel Georgia** which opened for business in 1929.

The five-diamond **Four Seasons Hotel** is situated a few blocks south of the harborfront at Howe and Georgia, and **The Sutton Place Hotel** (formerly Le Meridien) is located on Burrard Street just south of Robson. Both establishments are favored by entertainment celebrities when in town, as are the **Pacific Palisades** on Robson Street and the resort-like **Westin Bayshore** near Stanley Park on the waterfront. The **Hyatt Regency,** at Burrard and Georgia, hosted President Clinton when he was in town to meet with Russian leader Boris Yeltsin in April of 1993.

Waterfront condominiums overlook the marinas and seawalk that run along the north shore of False Creek in downtown Vancouver.

LOCAL SIGHTS

The first step to exploring Vancouver is a visit to the Travel InfoCentre in the Waterfront Centre. Here you will find information on local attractions, sightseeing tours and side trips. Modern coaches, British-style double-decker buses and turn-of-the century trolley cars are all available to take you on a scenic tour of Vancouver. For the energetic visitor, free walking tours are available. And for thrill seekers, helicopter and floatplane tours provide a bird's-eye view of the city.

While Vancouver is a relatively safe city, visitors should avoid the east side of the downtown core and not venture on foot past Carrall Street at night. Car break-ins are also a problem so be careful to park only in well-secured lots and never leave valuables in the trunk.

1 Vancouver Art Gallery

Located at Robson Square, this former court house was designed by British architect Francis Rattenbury, whose other turn-of-the-century designs include Victoria's Legislative Buildings and Empress Hotel.

Public transit includes ferry service across False Creek, between downtown and Granville Island.

When Vancouver's new Law Courts opened on Robson Street in 1979, Rattenbury's neo-classical court house became Vancouver's art gallery housing a permanent collection of works by Canadian artist Emily Carr (see profile on page 116). The building's former role of court house was revived in the film *Accused*, starring Jodie Foster.

2 Marine Building

Standing at the northwest corner of Burrard and West Hastings, this 1930s building is an award-winning example of Art Deco architecture. Be sure to take a stroll through the lobby, its murals a tribute to the days of sail and steam.

3 The Lookout!

Take a glass elevator to the top of Harbor Centre Tower for a 360-degree view of Vancouver and its surrounding scenery.

4 Gastown

The original site of present-day Vancouver, the town was named for Jack Deighton whose nickname was "Gassy Jack" because he talked a lot. Gastown's cobble-

(Above) Vancouver Art Gallery's main entrance fronts Robson Square, with the stately Hotel Vancouver next door. (Below) Queen Elizabeth Park provides sweeping views of the city skyline and North Shore mountains.

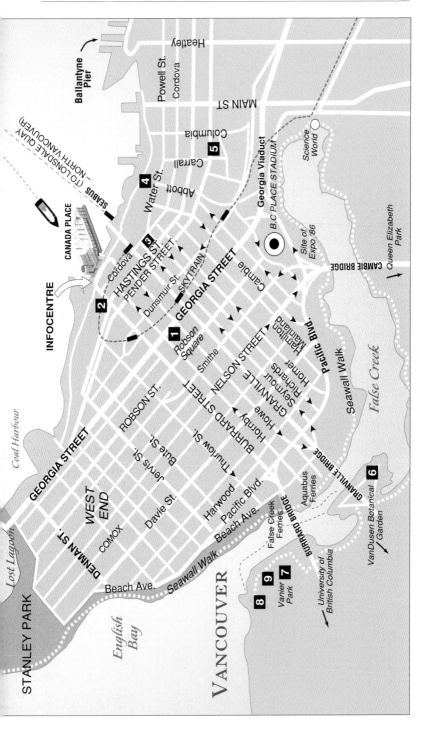

stone streets are today lined with shops and restaurants. A statue of Gassy Jack stands in Maple Tree Square (Water and Carrall) where he first established a hotel in 1867 and at the corner of Water and Cambie Streets is a chiming steam clock.

5 Chinatown

Some of the best chinese restaurants in North America are found here in its second-largest Chinatown. Other attractions are the pagoda telephone booths and the classical Dr. Sun Yat-Sen Garden containing architecture of the Ming Dynasty.

6 Granville Island

Hop aboard one of the little ferry boats at the foot of Thurlow or Hornby for a short ride across False Creek to Granville Island. Here you can wander through the public market and visit boutiques, restaurants and theatres.

7 Vanier Park

The seawall winds west of Granville Island past fishboat docks and marinas to the sweeping lawns of Vanier Park and an across-the-water view of Vancouver's West End.

8 Vancouver Maritime Museum

Located on the edge of Vanier Park, and accessible by the False Creek passenger ferries which depart from the Aquatic Centre on Beach Avenue, the Maritime Museum is a good place to learn about the city's nautical history and view the St. Roch – the first vessel to travel both ways through the Arctic Northwest Passage.

9 Vancouver Museum – H.R. MacMillan Planetarium

Also located in Vanier Park, these attractions are housed in the same building. The Museum contains a permanent exhibition on Vancouver's history as well as travelling exhibits. The Planetarium features astronomy shows and an observatory.

The Marine Building is Vancouver's finest example of Art Deco architecture.

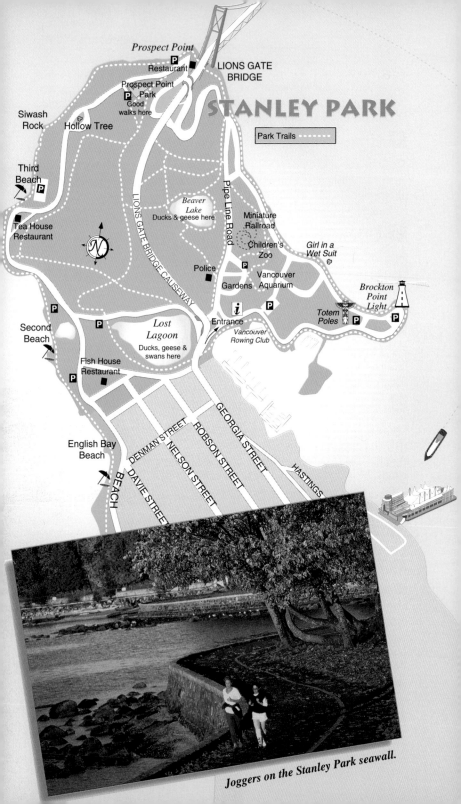

Prospect Point

Restaurant

LIONS GATE
BRIDGE

Prospect Point
Park
Good
walks here

STANLEY PARK

Siwash
Rock

Hollow Tree

Park Trails

Third
Beach

Beaver
Lake
Ducks & geese here

Miniature
Railroad

Tea House
Restaurant

Children's
Zoo

Girl in a
Wet Suit

Police

Vancouver
Aquarium

Brockton
Point
Light

Gardens

Second
Beach

Lost
Lagoon
Ducks, geese &
swans here

Entrance

Totem
Poles

Vancouver
Rowing Club

Fish House
Restaurant

English Bay
Beach

DENMAN STREET

NELSON STREET

ROBSON STREET

GEORGIA STREET

HASTINGS

BEACH

DAVIE STREET

Joggers on the Stanley Park seawall.

Stanley Park

No one visits Vancouver without seeing this 1000-acre park encircled by a five-and-a-half-mile pedestrian seawall. Squirrels, rabbits and raccoons live in the park, much of which is forest, while an aquarium houses other species such as killer whales and sea otters. A number of park tours, including one by horse-drawn tram and a free shuttle service, start in the lower parking lot beside the information booth. There is city bus service between the downtown core and the park, and bicycles can be rented just outside the park entrance.

In 1859, when Britain's navy was surveying the area, two officers – Colonel Moody and Captain Richards – recommended that this forested parkland be protected as a military reserve. A 12-pound muzzle loader was eventually installed near Brockton Point and was originally fired on Sundays at 6 p.m. The fishermen used this as a time check and early mariners for calibrating their chronometers. Today the aptly named Nine O'Clock Gun booms across the water each evening at nine o'clock.

Not far from Brockton Point stands an impressive display of north coast totem poles. Other park attractions include the Rose Garden and Prospect Point – a popular viewing site. Casual dining can be enjoyed at the Prospect Point Cafe or at one of several foodstands. A full day can easily be spent in Stanley Park, with its trails, beaches, tennis courts and pitch-and-putt golf course. And dinner can be enjoyed right in the park, at the Fish House or the elegant Ferguson Point Tea House overlooking English Bay.

Thunderbird sits atop this Kwagiutl totem pole, one of several on display near Brockton Point.

VanDusen Botanical Garden

Located south of the downtown core on 37th and Oak, these gardens are a favorite with visitors who enjoy the international display of plants and flowers, as well as Sprinklers Restaurant.

Queen Elizabeth Park

A beautiful park with sweeping views of downtown Vancouver, it contains a year-round display of tropical plants, birds and fish within the Bloedel Floral Conservatory – a large geodesic dome. The Seasons in the Park Restaurant offers fine dining, located within the Park at 33rd Avenue and Cambie Street.

University of British Columbia

This campus has a fortress-like location atop the cliffs of Point Grey and is highly acclaimed for its scientific research in such fields as genetics and biochemistry. On site is the **Museum of Anthropology**, famous for its Great Hall containing huge totem poles and massive sculptures by Haida artists, including the late Bill Reid.

Within walking distance of the museum is the Japanese-style Nitobe Memorial Garden. Farther along Marine Drive is the UBC Botanical Garden, with plants from around the world displayed in separate areas of the forest.

Capilano Suspension Bridge, the world's longest and highest suspension footbridge, draws over half a million visitors annually.

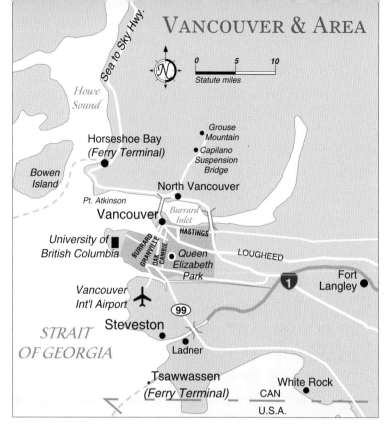

VANCOUVER & AREA

Sea to Sky Hwy.

Howe Sound

0   5   10
Statute miles

Horseshoe Bay
(Ferry Terminal)

Grouse Mountain

Capilano Suspension Bridge

Bowen Island

North Vancouver

Pt. Atkinson

Vancouver

Burrard Inlet

HASTINGS

University of British Columbia

BURRARD
GRANVILLE
OAK
CAMBIE

Queen Elizabeth Park

LOUGHEED

Fort Langley

Vancouver Int'l Airport

99

Steveston

STRAIT OF GEORGIA

Ladner

Tsawwassen
(Ferry Terminal)

White Rock

CAN
U.S.A.

OUT-OF-TOWN ATTRACTIONS

SOUTH OF THE CITY

The historic fishing port of **Steveston** is located on the banks of the mighty Fraser River. Freighters, tugs and fishboats are a passing sight for visitors to Steveston while enjoying the heritage buildings, water-front restaurants and specialty shops. Pedestrians and cyclists enjoy the miles of nearby dike paths and bird watchers flock year-round to the Reifel Bird Sanctuary, located on pastoral Westham Island near Ladner. A fleet of B.C. Ferries docks at Tsawwassen, just south of Ladner, and provides regular sailings to the Gulf Islands and to Sidney and Nanaimo on Vancouver Island.

EAST OF THE CITY

A scenic drive through the Fraser Valley farmlands will take you to historic Fort Langley, the Minter Gardens which contain a collection of Penjing Rock Bonsai, and Harrison Lake where you can stroll the village and relax in the hot springs.

NORTH OF THE CITY

Take the seabus across Vancouver Harbor to Lonsdale Quay in North Vancouver or cross Burrard Inlet via the Lions Gate Bridge – built

Steveston, once the heart of B.C.'s fishing industry, is home to the century-old Gulf of Georgia Cannery which was declared a national historic site in 1979 and is now a museum.

(Opposite page) The dramatic Sea to Sky Highway hugs the coastline along Howe Sound. (Left) Whistler Village is the social hub of this year-round alpine resort. (Below) The Grouse Mountain aerial tramway whisks visitors to a mountain plateau with panoramic views of city, sea and mountains.

in1938 by the Guinness brewing family of Dublin to provide access to their new North Shore subdivision called British Properties. This suspension bridge was named for The Lions – twin mountain peaks visible from the bridge. Its span is outlined at night by a string of lights which were a gift from the Guinness family to commemorate the city's 100th birthday in 1986.

While in North Vancouver, visit the **Capilano Suspension Bridge** which straddles the Capilano River at a height of 230 feet. The adjacent park contains forest trails and a dramatic waterfall.

To reach even greater heights, take the tram car at the base of **Grouse Mountain** for a 3700 foot ride up to a spectacular mountain plateau with sweeping views and alpine meadows.

If time permits, consider a trip by road, rail or air to the alpine village of **Whistler**, located 75 miles north of Vancouver. View fabulous scenery all the way along the Sea to Sky highway or rail route that leads to this year-round resort surrounded by snowy peaks, mountain lakes and valley trails. Outdoor activities include hiking, fishing and river rafting, while golf enthusiasts can choose from four championship courses. The European-style Whistler Village features pedestrian streets lined with sidewalk cafes, specialty shops and art galleries.

Another pleasant excursion is to ride the Royal Hudson Steam Train from North Vancouver along the coast to the logging port of Squamish. Come back the same way or board the M.V. Britannia for a cruise of fjord-like Howe Sound back to Vancouver. BC Rail also offers a round-trip dinner ride to Porteau Cove in Howe Sound.

SHOPPING IN VANCOUVER

Shopping complexes within easy walking distance of the Canada Place Cruise Terminal include the Sinclair Centre and The Landing, at the entrance to Gastown, both of which are restored heritage projects. The Pacific Centre, at the intersection of Georgia and Granville, is an underground mall connecting two major department stores – The Bay and Eaton's. The Bay still sells its original Hudson's Bay blankets and coats, and both stores are likely places to pick up some pure maple syrup and other Canadian souvenirs.

Robson is Vancouver's pre-eminent shopping street, especially the three blocks west of Burrard to Jervis. Lined with fashion boutiques, coffee houses and restaurants frequented by movie stars and other celebrities while in town, Robson Street is where everyone goes to stroll and people watch.

There are many fine art galleries and boutiques in Vancouver, including the Diane Farris Gallery which was recently listed in a Paris guide to the world's top 200 galleries. If you're looking for native northwest coast art, you might try the Marion Scott Gallery on Howe Street or the Inuit Gallery at the entrance to Gastown. Also in Gastown are Images for a Canadian Heritage and Hill's Indian Crafts which carries authentic Cowichan sweaters. Three Vets at 2200 Yukon (south of False Creek) is also a good bet, as are the Gallery of Tribal Art and Douglas Reynolds Gallery, both on South Granville.

DINING IN VANCOUVER

Just about any cuisine imaginable can be found in Vancouver, including Pacific Northwest fare which features the region's fresh produce and seafood. This style of cuisine can be enjoyed at Raincity Grill on Denman Street, Century Grill on Hamilton Street, and Raintree at The Landing on Water Street. For seafood, good choices include 'C' Restaurant at the foot of Howe on the False Creek waterfront and the Fish House in Stanley Park. For Italian fare, try Umberto's Il Giardino at Hornby and Pacific. Robson Street's popular dining spots include Cincin and Caffe de Medici. Bishop's on West 4th is considered one of Vancouver's finest dining spots.

A FEW FLEETING FACTS ABOUT VANCOUVER

The *S.S. Beaver* was a famous steamship employed by the Hudson's Bay Company during the fur trade. She also served as a survey ship, freighter, passenger vessel and tugboat. Today a replica of the ship takes passengers on sightseeing and dinner cruises. The original *Beaver* met its end in 1888 at the entrance to Vancouver Harbor when the

The paddle wheel Beaver, the first steamship on the North Pacific, ran aground off Prospect Point in 1888. A few years later the luxurious new CPR liner Empress of India swept out of port after stopping at Vancouver on her maiden voyage.

A modern cruise ship nudges up the dock at Canada Place Cruise
Terminal, which is situated in the heart of downtown Vancouver.

departing ship was gripped not by tidal rips and back eddies but by a
sense of panic in her crew when they discovered their liquor supply had
been left behind in port. They turned the ship sharply around and
grounded her.

The one place in Vancouver you're likely to see a Canadian
Mountie wearing the traditional red serge uniform is at the airport. You
may, however, see a policeman on horseback in Stanley Park where a
small mounted squad of officers patrols the park's network of trails.

Outside the former main branch of the Vancouver Public Library (at
Burrard and Robson), pedestrians will notice a water fountain with two
basins – one at waist level for thirsty people, the other at shin level for
thirsty dogs. The building itself is now occupied by a Virgin Megastore
which was opened in December 1996 when flamboyant British owner
Richard Branson rappelled down its five-storey side, spraying cham-
pagne on the crowd gathered below.

Vancouver, the third-largest film production centre in North
America after Los Angeles and New York, is a popular city with film
and television producers because of its laid-back style and wealth of
locations – everything from the streets of New York to the Mississippi
delta. When filming takes place in one of Vancouver's public parks, a

From the cricket pitch of Stanley Park, the view is of Coal Harbor and the Canada Place Cruise Terminal where passenger ships bound for Alaska dock throughout the summer.

supervisor is on location to make sure the film crew leave the park the way they found it. Weather is less easy to control and during one shoot in heavy rain an actor refused to come out of his trailer. He was a cat.

Vancouver weddings often take place outdoors – in parks, on boats, even in hot-air balloons. So it wasn't surprising to hear about the American couple who met on a cruise to Alaska and, falling in love with each other and with Vancouver, decided to fly back there to get married on Granville Island.

Shore to Ship

Vancouver is home port to the Alaska cruise, and passengers who embark here are off to a smooth start.

Canada Place Cruise Ship Terminal is located at the north end of Howe Street in the very heart of downtown Vancouver. It's a city landmark and instantly recognized for its majestic white sails which crown a complex containing the Pan Pacific Hotel, the Prow Restaurant, a Food Fair, promenade shops, and IMAX 3D Theatre. Long-term parking is provided here, and taxis, limousines, public transportation and car rentals are all easily available. The Vancouver International Airport is thirty minutes away, and Seattle a three-and-a-half hour drive.

Ballantyne Pier, Vancouver's other cruise terminal, is a beautifully refurbished and modernized heritage building.

The terminal itself is a gleaming model of spacious efficiency. Baggage handlers quickly relieve passengers of their luggage while port staff are on hand to answer any questions about ship boarding and the various sights to see in Vancouver prior to departure. Strict control over ship access is enforced as passengers are whisked through check-in and security, then onto the waiting ship. Passengers are usually advised to board no later than an hour prior to departure and can some-times board early if the ship is ready.

Vancouver's secondary cruise facility – **Ballantyne Pier** – is located about one mile east of Canada Place at the foot of Heatley Avenue. This terminal received many plaudits when completed in 1923 and it recently underwent a major renovation and expansion to transform it into an ultramodern cruise facility while retaining its original character.

Passengers departing from either terminal will be treated to a unique view of the city's waterfront. On the industrial North Shore are docked freighters loading lumber, wheat, coal and piles of yellow sulphur. To the south stand the office towers and hotels of downtown Vancouver.

These gleaming highrises, fronted by docks and marinas, quickly give way to the lawns and trees of Stanley Park where you may catch a glimpse of the Cricket Grounds. Perched on a foreshore rock is the Girl

A captain eases his ship away from Canada Place Cruise Terminal and sets sail for Alaska.

in a Wetsuit – Vancouver's answer to Copenhagen's mermaid. As your ship passes under the suspended span of Lions Gate Bridge and heads into English Bay, sailboats can often be seen tacking back and forth among the anchored freighters. Beyond lies Georgia Strait and the protected waters of the Inside Passage.

Passengers disembarking in Vancouver will find their arrival equally smooth. Color-coded luggage retrieval, individual baggage carts and a red door/green door system of customs clearance, all ensure a swift transfer of passengers from ship back to shore.

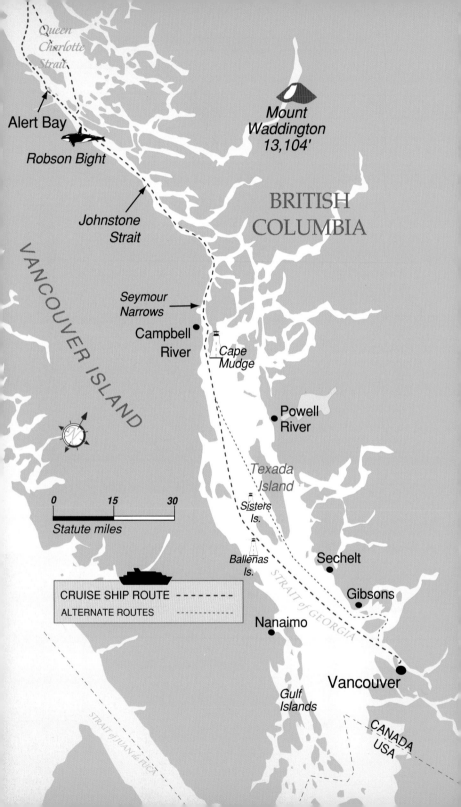

CHAPTER THREE

CANADA'S INSIDE PASSAGE
VANCOUVER TO ALERT BAY

A single, mountainous island protects the southern waters of Canada's Inside Passage. Named for the British sea captain who first circumnavigated it, **Vancouver Island** extends almost 300 miles from the Strait of Juan de Fuca up to Queen Charlotte Sound. Its rugged west coast buffers the Inside Passage from rain, wind and waves but there's one thing it can't stop from reaching these protected waters – the tide.

Controlled by the gravitational pull of the moon and to a lesser degree the sun, a rising tide rushes with cyclical predictability around both ends of Vancouver Island and pours into the straits and channels of the Inside Passage. When this onslaught of water is compressed through narrow passes and channels, bottlenecks occur. But, unlike car traffic which comes to a standstill in such circumstances, water does the opposite – it turns into a churning rapids complete with whirlpools, back eddies and rip tides.

The numerous channels that weave through the islands clogging the Inside Passage between Vancouver Island and the mainland are all affected by tidal currents. Mariners pay special attention to the area's tide tables (published annually by the Canadian Hydrographic Service) in order to reach a pass when the water is slack and presents no danger. Even large cruise ships try to time their transit of **Seymour Narrows** – one of the most impressive tidal passes of the Inside Passage – to coincide with slack water.

A northbound cruise ship approaches Texada Island on a quiet evening in the Strait of Georgia.

Upon leaving Vancouver Harbor to commence a northbound cruise of the Inside Passage, cruise ships will sometimes take an unexpected detour into the scenic waterways of **Howe Sound**. This is not just to provide passengers with a lovely porthole view during dinner, but to delay the ship's arrival at Seymour Narrows. The side trip ensures a safe passage through the Narrows – especially if a large tide is running.

Point Atkinson, one of British Columbia's first lighthouses when built in 1874, marks the eastern entrance to Howe Sound. It is also a marine weather station and tidal reference point for this part of the Strait of Georgia. The lighthouse sits atop smooth granite rock on the edge of Lighthouse Park, where wooded trails and valleys border a shoreline of sea caves and tidal pools.

Opposite Point Atkinson lies **Bowen Island**, a popular resort for Vancouverites since 1924 when the Union Steamships began ferrying people there for company picnics and moonlight dance cruises. The steamships, which departed Vancouver at Whyte Cove (now Whytecliff Park), stopped running in 1950. Local residents continue to enjoy Howe Sound, either on board a BC Ferry (out of **Horseshoe Bay**) or from the deck of their own recreational boat. More than one surprised boater, anchored in a quiet cove, has looked up from a smoking barbecue to see the unexpected sight of a cruise ship gliding past the entrance to the anchorage.

Until recently, Howe Sound was the world's largest log booming ground and recreational boats often tied to these log booms, their skippers hammering a couple of 'dogs' (metal eye hooks) into the outer log for attaching the mooring lines. The only drawback to docking at a log

A sailboat lies at anchor in Howe Sound – a popular weekend retreat for Vancouver boaters.

The wine is poured, the sun is warm and there's plenty of time to relax on deck and enjoy the passing scenery before dinner.

boom was the possibility of a tug arriving in the middle of the night to tow the 'dock' away, complete with attached boats. These log booms featured prominently in the popular TV show *The Beachcombers* which ran for 370 episodes and gained an international audience. The series was based in the town of **Gibsons**, at the western entrance to Howe Sound, where an abandoned liquor store was converted into Molly's Reach – a fictitious coffee shop which has since become a seafood restaurant. The town's *Beachcomber* days are over but several movie directors have also discovered Gibsons.

Gibsons is located at the bottom of the **Sunshine Coast,** which stretches up the mainland to the Swedish-founded fishing port of Lund. In between lies the Sechelt Peninsula, first inhabited by a large population of Salish natives. Traces of their early civilization remain in pictographs on rock faces of Agamemnon Channel. Painted with a mixture of berries, oils and an unidentified preserving agent, these pictographs often mark fishing holes which, thousands of years later, still offer good cod and red snapper jigging.

One of the prettiest anchorages along the Sechelt Peninsula is **Smuggler Cove**. It's now a marine park but during Prohibition in the 1920s it was a storage area for bootleg whiskey that was smuggled by boat into the U.S.A. American yachtsmen who visited Smuggler Cove in those days had a favorite song which went like this:

Four and twenty Yankees feeling rather dry,
Sailed into Canada to have a drink of rye,
When the rye was open they all began to sing,
God bless America, but God Save the King!

The Sunshine Coast is today renowned for its scenic cruising which includes **Princess Louisa Inlet** – one of Canada's most spectacular fjords. Three steep-sided reaches twist inland past hanging waterfalls before culminating at Princess Louisa Inlet where the Chatterbox Falls, fed by glaciers and lakes, plunge 1,800 feet down granite cliffs into the still water.

Erle Stanley Gardner, the American writer who created Perry Mason, wrote in his *Log of a Landlubber* that he didn't need to see the rest of the world after seeing Princess Louisa Inlet. "One views the scenery with bared head and choking feeling of the throat," he wrote. "It is more than beautiful. It is sacred."

The natives called the inlet Suivoolot, meaning warm and sunny. When James (Mac) Macdonald, a Nevada prospector, laid eyes on 'The Princess' in 1919 he instantly succumbed to her charms, obtained land by the falls and built a log cabin. After years of welcoming maritime travellers to his very own Yosemite Valley and fjords of Norway, Mac turned this prized property over to the newly formed Princess Louisa International Society to preserve the inlet "as God created it, unspoiled by the hand of man" so that "all may enjoy its peace and beauty." The

Smuggler Cove is one of hundreds of small-boat anchorages hidden behind islands and headlands along B.C.'s Inside Passage.

Society has chapters in Renton, Washington, and Victoria, British Columbia, and functions in cooperation with BC Parks in maintaining the floats, wharves and picnic shelter.

While the water in Princess Louisa Inlet is a chalky turquoise typical of glacial runoff, the waters at nearby **Saltery Bay** are clear, warm and excellent for diving. Here a sunken bronze mermaid rests twenty metres beneath the sea and shares her submarine gardens with wolf eels, sea lions and octopuses.

Ferry service connects Saltery Cove with **Powell River**, a city of about 20,000 which is easily visible by the smoke stacks of its large paper mill. The mill's log storage basin is protected by a floating break-water of old ships' hulls which include the pre-World War I American cruisers *Charleston* and *Huron*, several Liberty supply ships from World War II, and the Canadian patrol vessel *Malaspina*, which chased down rum runners during prohibition. Although some of these hulks are listing, the ones built of ferro-cement become increasingly watertight as the cement cures.

Texada Island lies opposite and it was here, on its northeast side, that a large whiskey still produced the bootleg liquor which reached thirsty Americans via Smuggler Cove. Before that, in the 1870s, whaling was a profitable enterprise with processing operations set up in Blubber Bay at the island's northern tip. Over the years, Texada has also been mined for gold, copper, iron ore and limestone.

With Vancouver Island in the distance, a northbound sailboat runs with an evening breeze up the Strait of Georgia.

The next island over, called **Lasqueti**, is home to domestic and wild sheep which wander the rugged hillsides and cliff-edged shorelines. In rocky coves oysters grow in abundance, the commercially-farmed ones shipped to gourmet restaurants in faraway cities. The pace of life on Lasqueti is tranquil and the island residents carefully guard their isolation. No car ferry calls at Lasqueti, so motor vehicles and other large items must be brought in by barge. The people who live here prefer it this way, with the community wanting to preserve the island's natural and peaceful setting for future generations.

A small passenger ferry connects Lasqueti with French Creek on Vancouver Island. From here the Island Highway stretches in both directions along the eastern shores of Vancouver Island. To the south is the City of **Nanaimo**, founded in the 1850s by the Hudson's Bay Company when coal deposits were found in the area. The wooden military bastion is now a museum overlooking the harbor where Nanaimo's Annual World Championship Nanaimo-to-Vancouver Bathtub Race is held each July.

Year-round bungy jumping takes place from the world's first specially designed bungy bridges. They span a 140-foot gorge of the Nanaimo River where the water is 40 feet deep and – as they say – you really don't have to worry about hitting bottom. When a nude bungy jump was held here (for a charitable cause), the event attracted more spectators than usual, including television cameras.

Newcastle Island, located a short passenger ferry ride across Nanaimo Harbor, has been the site of a coal mine, cannery, boatyard and sandstone quarry. The sandstone found here was exceptionally strong and used in construction of the San Francisco Mint – one of the few buildings to withstand that city's 1906 earthquake. In the early thirties, Canadian Pacific Steamships Limited opened a resort on Newcastle Island. The Pavilion has been restored and serves as a Visitor Centre, with the entire island now a public park with picnic tables and overnight camping sites. Deer, rabbits and raccoons inhabit the island, which is criss-crossed with mapped trails.

In the waters just north of Nanaimo is a naval testing range, jointly operated by the Canadian and American navies, its relatively flat seabed of soft mud ideal for retrieving torpedos. A torpedo tracking base is located on the adjacent **Winchelsea Islands**, and during testing any boats caught wandering through the restricted zone are escorted to safer waters.

North of here, beautiful sand beaches stretch along the east side of Vancouver Island past Parksville and Qualicum Beach. Another lovely beach is found at Tribune Bay on **Hornby Island** which was called 'leg o'mutton' by early mariners because of its shape. In the 1800s sperm, humpback and bowhead whales were brought here for processing at Whaling Station Bay.

Another naval and airforce base is located at Comox Harbor, its eastern entrance marked by **Cape Lazo** – named the 'snare' in 1791 by Spanish explorer Jose Maria Narvaez. He was likely referring to the Cape's deceptive appearance, jutting like an island into the Strait of Georgia, or to its extensive sand bars that create dangerous shoal water.

The stretch of water from Cape Lazo to Cape Mudge offers few protected anchorages for small boats, and most yachtsmen favor the east side of the Strait of Georgia. Both Savary and Hernando Islands have lovely beaches which are in fact drift deposits left behind by retreating glaciers 10,000 years ago. Barren **Mitlenatch Island** is a breeding and nesting site for thousands of birds, especially glaucous-winged gulls. The island, which is a nature park, receives relatively little rain (the prickly pear cactus grows here) and, because of the long swim, few predatory mammals threaten the young nesting birds.

The nearby **Twin Islands** have been owned since 1961 by a German aristocrat and nephew of Prince Philip. The Prince and Queen Elizabeth, accompanied on board the Royal Yacht Britannia by their daughter Princess Anne, anchored off these islands (joined at low tide) in 1971 and spent a day ashore where a huge log lodge and manicured grounds are maintained by caretakers. Across the water on the mainland is **Desolation Sound Marine Park** – a mecca for yachtsmen with its beautiful stream-fed anchorages, mountain lakes and cascading falls. There is little tidal current in the Desolation Sound area, so the water is warm for swimming in summer.

Along B.C.'s Inside Passage, red-and-white lighthouses dot the winding route made famous by the Klondike Gold Rush when steamships carried hundreds of prospectors north to Skagway.

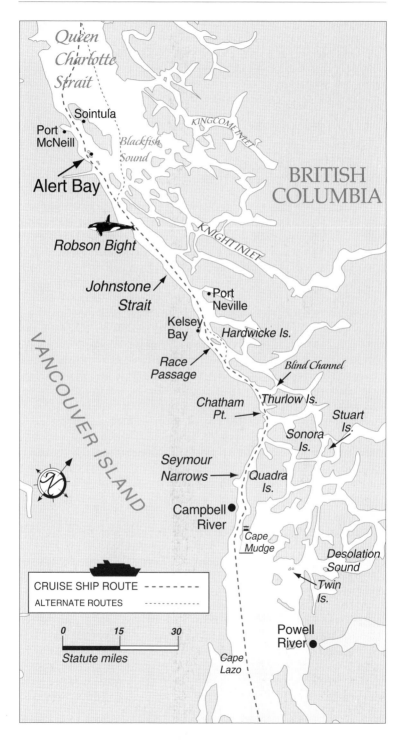

Queen Charlotte Strait

Sointula

Port McNeill

KINGCOME INLET

Blackfish Sound

Alert Bay

BRITISH COLUMBIA

Robson Bight

KNIGHT INLET

Johnstone Strait

Port Neville

Kelsey Bay

Hardwicke Is.

Race Passage

Blind Channel

Chatham Pt.

Thurlow Is.

Stuart Is.

Sonora Is.

Seymour Narrows

Quadra Is.

Campbell River

Cape Mudge

Desolation Sound

Twin Is.

VANCOUVER ISLAND

Powell River

Cape Lazo

CRUISE SHIP ROUTE - - - - -

ALTERNATE ROUTES ·········

0   15   30

Statute miles

The same cannot be said of the waters in Discovery Passage (part of the cruise ship route), where tidal currents are extremely swift. When the tide floods around each end of Vancouver Island, it meets somewhere between Cape Lazo and **Cape Mudge** at the southern entrance to Discovery Passage. Turbulence generated by these opposing tides can worsen into steep, confused seas when a strong southeasterly wind blows against currents flowing out of Discovery Passage.

In 1927 a ship loaded with Christmas provisions was bound for Alaska when it got caught in a snowstorm and foundered in the waters off Cape Mudge. The residents of Quadra Island wasted no time exercising salvage rights on the beached ship and Christmas that year was especially festive.

When Captain Vancouver anchored off Cape Mudge in the summer of 1792, a Salish chief greeted him on shore and escorted the British captain and his officers up a steep path to the village perched atop white sand cliffs. This was a strategic location overlooking Georgia Strait and it marked the border between the Salish and Kwagiutl natives. Captain Vancouver wrote that he and his men enjoyed a "refreshing walk" accompanied by a number of native hosts who picked "berries from the trees as we passed, and with much civility presented them to us on green leaves." About fifty years after Captain Vancouver's visit, the Kwagiutl – who had obtained firearms from fur traders – raided the Salish village at Cape Mudge. Both sides suffered heavy losses during protracted warfare throughout the Strait of Georgia and Puget Sound. Eventually the surviving Salish at Cape Mudge and Campbell River fled south to Comox, abandoning this territory to the Kwagiutl.

Cape Mudge is now the site of the Tsa-Kwa-Luten Lodge – designed to resemble a Kwagiulth 'Big House' with massive interior posts and cross beams supporting a cathedral ceiling. This modern lodge and the nearby Kwagiulth Museum, which has an outstanding 'potlatch' collection, are both operated by the Cape Mudge band. Gazing out from Cape Mudge are petroglyphs carved into granite boulders. In prehistoric times this was likely a shaman site.

A more recent sign of man's industry is the lighthouse, erected on the Cape in 1898 when vessels were streaming up Discovery Passage on their way to the Klondike gold fields. Salmon also stream up and down Discovery Passage and sportfishing lodges can be spotted on either side of the channel.

At the mill town of **Campbell River**, residents are often up at dawn in the summer to do a bit of fishing before heading to work. Sportfishing is a tradition here, dating back to 1924 when the Tyee Club was established. It was inspired by Sir Richard Musgrave who, in 1896, was Campbell River's first sportfisherman. Fishing from a dugout canoe with native guides, he afterwards wrote an article for Field magazine in which he praised their simple but skillful method of catching chinook salmon weighing up to 70 pounds.

The rules for inclusion in the prestigious Tyee Club are that the fish must weigh more than 30 pounds and be caught in the Tyee Pool, from a rowing boat, using an artificial lure with only a single hook. Simply rowing a boat in these current-ridden waters is a challenge, let alone catching one of these famous Tyee salmon. Not all sportfishermen come to Campbell River to fish the Tyee Pool. Many are after one of the trophy-sized chinook that gather in swirling back eddies near Seymour Narrows.

The salmon caught in Discovery Passage are returning from the open ocean to their spawning rivers. Scientists speculate that outflow from the Fraser, a major river just south of Vancouver, reaches all the way up Discovery Passage to the northern end of Johnstone Strait where it ebbs into the Pacific. This outflow, although minimal and highly-diluted by the time it reaches the open ocean, is still substantial enough for returning salmon to 'smell' its source. That is why any-where from 10-to-80% of riverbound sockeye salmon will make a diversion down Johnstone Strait instead of entering the Inside Passage via Juan de Fuca Strait.

Salmon like the cold, swift-flowing waters that race down the east side of Vancouver Island, and experienced fishing guides learn how to read the tides and currents in their area to figure out where the best fishing is each day. Mariners also read the tide tables but their goal is to avoid contrary currents, especially at the narrowest part of Discovery Passage, called **Seymour Narrows**.

Challenging Seymour Narrows, where currents can reach 16 miles per hour, is the major pass for all Alaska-bound cruise ships.

The top of dreaded Ripple Rock, in the middle of Seymour Narrows, was finally blown off on April 5, 1958.

Ripple Rock, a two-headed pinnacle rock in the middle of the Narrows, used to lie just nine feet below the water's surface at low tide. It caused the sinking of more than 100 vessels before its top was blown off in 1958. Explosives were inserted into the core of Ripple Rock via an underwater tunnel that connected with Maud Island. When the world's largest non-atomic explosion was over, the top of Ripple Rock lay a safe 45 feet below chart datum.

Even with that hazard removed, Seymour Narrows can generate more than 13 knots of mid-channel current on a large tide. When this jet-like stream rubs against the nearly motionless peripheral waters, it produces a line of whirlpools down both sides of the pass. Most passengers will be spared this impressive sight because captains usually time their ship's transit of the Narrows to coincide with calm waters.

It's worth stepping out on deck to watch as your ship glides under the power line spanning Seymour Narrows. The vertical clearance used to be 161 feet – just high enough for cruise liners to pass beneath it at high water. Then, in 1995, Royal Caribbean Cruises positioned its new megaship *Legend of the Seas* on an Inside Passage itinerary and the hydro line had to raised by about 20 feet. The perspective when looking skyward from a ship's deck makes the wires appear unnervingly close to a ship's superstructure.

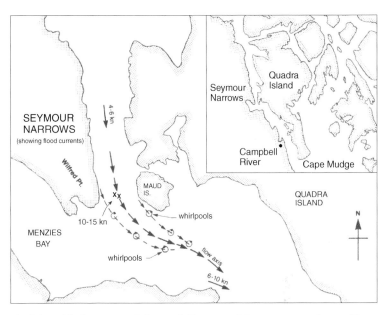

A rising tide is squeezed through Seymour Narrows, creating swift currents and churning whirlpools. Twin X's mark the location of Ripple Rock.

Chatham Point marks the intersection of Discovery Passage with **Johnstone Strait** – the most direct route through the Inside Passage and the one used by commercial traffic. Smaller boats often take the 'back route,' winding their way through the Discovery Islands.

This was the route taken by Lieutenant James Johnstone in 1792 when leading one of Captain Vancouver's survey parties in search of a northwest passage. These survey expeditions were carried out in open boats while the ships remained anchored in one spot. Officers would head each boat party, and crewmen would draw on the oars from dawn until dusk and sometimes well into the night. Stowed in the boats were two weeks' provisions, survey instruments, muskets for shooting game, and trinkets for trade with the natives.

These expeditions were not pleasant jaunts. The climate then was wetter and cooler than it is today, and the men were constantly drenched by rain. They often ran low on food when an expedition took longer than anticipated so, to supplement their provisions, they hunted, fished and bartered with the natives. At night they camped on shore while the men on watch cooked the next day's food over open fires. If the forest above the highwater mark was impenetrable, they were forced to sleep in the boats. This was something the men detested and some preferred to take their chances on the foreshore. On one occasion, when swamped by a rising tide, an oarsman was so tired he didn't wake up and was floating away when roused by his companions.

Johnstone, a talented young officer, was pushing his survey party to its limit as they made their way north. They tried in vain to row through one set of rapids and had to haul the boat through with ropes. Some natives were watching all this activity from shore and lent a hand.

Johnstone's first clue to the existence of Vancouver Island came with the tide. While he and his men were sleeping on shore one night, they were unexpectedly swamped by a tide that was rising instead of falling. This meant the tide was coming in through a northern entrance and this revelation diverted Johnstone's attention from tracing the continental shoreline to locating a seaward passage at the top of Vancouver Island. He followed Sunderland Channel into the strait and rowed all the way to **Pine Island** for an unobstructed view of the open waters of the Pacific Ocean. Johnstone and his men were exhausted and hungry by the time they backtracked 130 miles to the ships at anchor in Desolation Sound. But they had found a navigable channel to the Pacific Ocean.

Johnstone Strait is now a marine highway travelled by ships, tugs and fishboats. Much of the forested land on either side of the Strait is Crown Land (owned by the provincial government) and tree farm licenses are granted to private forestry companies. Considerable controversy surrounds a common logging practice called clearcutting and the

A hiker on the Blind Channel forest trails gazes up at a cedar snag left standing by hand loggers at the turn of the 19th century.

British Columbia government has drafted a forest practices code outlawing clearcuts in sensitive areas such as wildlife habitats and salmon streams.

Some forestry companies have already tried to be more responsive to public concerns. A glowing example of this is at **Blind Channel**, a few miles off Johnstone Strait via Mayne Passage. Like many settlements in this remote area, Blind Channel's roots are the logging industry. In 1910 a sawmill was built here and the surrounding forest was handlogged by nine lumbermen, who used teams of oxen to drag the felled trees to the mill.

The community became a center for nearby logging camps and gold mines, with a hotel and dock built to accommodate the Union Steamship boats which called regularly with freight and passengers. By 1918 the population at Blind Channel had soared to 120 with a cannery and shingle mill in operation. The mill's boiler usually had enough steam left at the end of the day to power a generator which lit up everyone's home with a recent invention called the light bulb. A gas engine provided auxiliary power on Saturday nights when the dance hall was lit. Loggers from nearby camps would descend on Blind Channel and forget their worries as they kicked up their heels and "skidded the ladies across the floor."

In the 1930s bootlegging attracted additional entrepreneurs to Blind Channel, but a decade later the population peaked. The repeal of prohibition, dwindling salmon stocks and mechanization of logging and mining all conspired to shut the place down. Logging crews, using improved machinery, shrunk in size and were flown in and out of camps by floatplanes, which contributed to the demise of the Union Steamship Company.

Blind Channel's revival began in the summer of 1969 when the Richter family, cruising the coast in their small boat, pulled up to a lonely dock and noticed a 'For Sale' sign on the store. Within months the family sold their Vancouver home and, with entrepreneurial vision and hard work, began transforming Blind Channel into a resort marina complete with manicured grounds and fine dining. Boats, large and small, pull in here all summer long.

Logging has also returned to Blind Channel, but the forestry company which owns the nearby tree farm license has refrained from logging the second-growth forest next to the resort. Instead they maintain a system of hiking trails, mapped and signposted, so the public can walk through a forest once logged and see its various stages of regrowth.

Interspersed with logging camps along the steep shores of Johnstone Strait are pockets of homesteaders – people pursuing a subsistence lifestyle of farming, fishing and cottage industries. But Johnstone Strait remains, for the most part, a saltwater river wending its timeless way past timbered mountains and evergreen islands.

Killer whales are frequently sighted in the salmon-rich waters of Johnstone Strait.

The Strait's salmon-rich waters attract natural predators such as seals and eagles, as well as a resident pod of killer whales that is frequently sighted in the vicinity of **Robson Bight**. Here they visit some special beaches where they sink to the sea bottom and rub against rounded pebbles. Whale watching is a popular pastime at the nearby boardwalk village of **Telegraph Cove**, where some residents even listen to them through hydrophones installed in Johnstone Strait. Each pod of killer whales has its own dialect of calls and squeaking noises.

In addition to informative whale watching tours out of Telegraph Cove, scuba diving at nearby sites has attracted the likes of Jacques Cousteau and underwater cinematographers Al Giddings and Stan Waterman seeking subsea footage for movies such as *The Deep, Jaws* and the James Bond flicks.

A few miles north of Telegraph Cove is the mouth of the Nimpkish River. A Kwagiutl village thrived here when Captain Vancouver paid a visit to the home of Chief Cheslakee. The hospitality was reciprocated on board the ship *Discovery* but things turned momentarily sour when Captain Vancouver found his native guest trying to steal one of his logbooks – an item of idle curiosity to the chief but of irreplaceable value to the captain.

In the late 1800s, the Nimpkish River villagers were persuaded to move across the channel to **Alert Bay** on Cormorant Island where work was available in the newly-established salmon saltery. In recent years a resurgence of native pride and a growing international interest in their culture has made Alert Bay an important centre for Kwagiutl art and

A dugout canoe bobs on its moorings in front of the U-mista Cultural Centre at Alert Bay.

customs. Enjoying the highest profile in Alert Bay is a 170-foot-high totem pole – currently the world's tallest. It was raised in 1972 and tells the story of the Kwagiutl peoples. Other impressive totem poles, including one carved by the late Mungo Martin (a renowned Kwagiutl artist) can be viewed at the Nimpkish Burial Grounds. The highlight of a visit to Alert Bay is the U'mista Cultural Centre, built in the tradition-al plank-and-beam style. Inside is a collection of potlatch treasures con-fiscated by the Canadian government in 1922 and returned in 1979.

A car ferry connects Alert Bay with another fishing port on nearby Malcolm Island. **Sointula** – a Finnish word meaning 'harmony' – was founded at the turn of the century by farmers from Finland who wanted to create a utopia of co-operative, rural living in a scenic, seaside set-ting. They must have been on to a good thing because a bidding war recently ensued over a 10-acre waterfront lot for sale on the island. It was eventually bought by a German airline pilot for 25% more than its listed price.

The inter-island ferry also calls at **Port McNeill** on Vancouver Island. This prosperous logging town was named for a Boston-born captain hired by the Hudson's Bay Company during the fur trade. Captain McNeill married a native woman with whom he had six chil-dren, and during his 12 years of trading along the coast, he gained the respect of both the native peoples and his employers. He was eventually given command of the *S.S. Beaver*, first steam-driven paddlewheeler on the North Pacific.

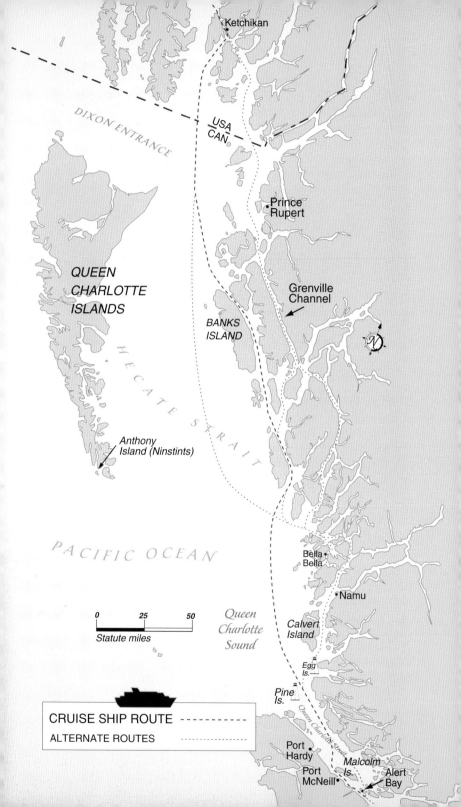

Ketchikan

DIXON ENTRANCE

USA
CAN

Prince
Rupert

*QUEEN
CHARLOTTE
ISLANDS*

Grenville
Channel

*BANKS
ISLAND*

H E C A T E   S T R A I T

Anthony
Island (Ninstints)

N

PACIFIC OCEAN

Bella
Bella

Namu

| 0 | 25 | 50 |

Statute miles

*Queen
Charlotte
Sound*

*Calvert
Island*

Egg
Is.

Pine
Is.

Queen Charlotte Strait

CRUISE SHIP ROUTE — — — —

ALTERNATE ROUTES ·············

Port
Hardy

Port
McNeill

*Malcolm
Is.*

Alert
Bay

CHAPTER FOUR

CANADA'S INSIDE PASSAGE
PORT HARDY TO PRINCE RUPERT

Port Hardy marks the end of the road and the beginning of the marine highway that winds north through the coastal waters of British Columbia and Alaska. Located near the northern tip of Vancouver Island, this major fishing port of 5,500 residents is also the terminal for B.C. Ferries' Day Cruise up the Inside Passage to Prince Rupert.

The port is named in honor of Sir Thomas Hardy who was right-hand man to Lord Horatio Nelson, Britain's greatest naval hero. At the legendary Battle of Trafalgar in 1805, Hardy was pacing the decks of the *Victory* with Nelson when he was hit by enemy fire. Taken belowdecks, Nelson died in Hardy's arms.

No naval battles were staged in the waters off Port Hardy but Britain's Hudson's Bay Company did establish **Fort Rupert** at nearby **Beaver Harbor** in 1849. Engraved on the sandstone foreshore in front of the old fort site are some ancient petroglyphs. Others are found at Port Hardy, on the beaches beside Kinsmen Park's seawall. Archaeologists estimate that **Bear Cove** – location of the B.C. Ferries terminal – was first occupied 8,000 years ago.

Coal was discovered at Beaver Harbor in the 1830s but permanent settlement of Port Hardy didn't begin until the turn of the century when it slowly grew along with the local industries of fishing, logging and mining. Visitors to Port Hardy can enjoy a stroll past Fisherman's

Barge-towing tugs are a regular sight along the Inside Passage.

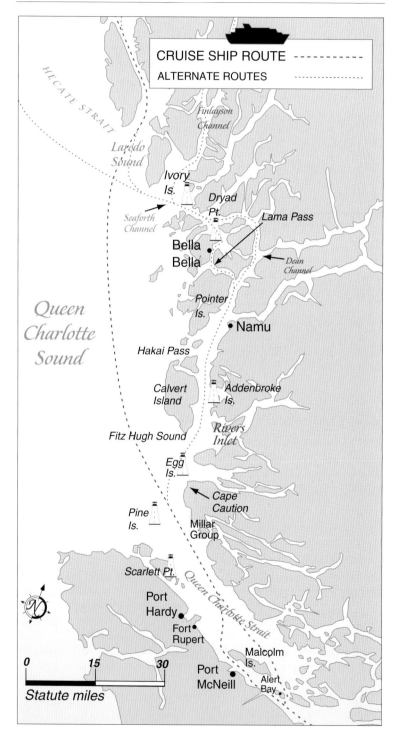

CRUISE SHIP ROUTE - - - - - - - - - - -

ALTERNATE ROUTES · · · · · · · · · · · · ·

HECATE STRAIT

Finlayson
Channel

Laredo
Sound

Ivory
Is.

Dryad
Pt.

Lama Pass

Seaforth
Channel

Bella
Bella

Dean
Channel

Pointer
Is.

Namu

Queen
Charlotte
Sound

Hakai Pass

Calvert
Island

Addenbroke
Is.

Rivers
Inlet

Fitz Hugh Sound

Egg
Is.

Cape
Caution

Pine
Is.

Millar
Group

Scarlett Pt.

Queen Charlotte Strait

Port
Hardy

Fort
Rupert

Malcolm
Is.

N

0   15   30

Port
McNeill

Alert
Bay

Statute miles

Wharf and along Market Street with its interesting shops. Also worth viewing are the town's art gallery and local museum.

When B.C. Ferries' Queen of the North pulls out of Port Hardy, she heads into **Queen Charlotte Strai**t. Here gentle swells indicate that the open waters of Queen Charlotte Sound are not far away. The only thing that lies between are clusters of islets and rocks. These hazards to navigation are well-charted and marked with buoys, beacons and lighthouses. Such was not the case 200 years ago.

Then, Captain Vancouver sailed up Queen Charlotte Strait with no chart to guide his course. The air was thick with fog and in light winds his square-rigged ships were at the mercy of the currents. The water was too deep for soundings as they groped their way through the mist and, late one afternoon, the *Discovery* grounded on a submerged rock just east of the **Millar Group**. As the tide dropped, the ship heaved onto her starboard side. She faced imminent wreckage as the water crept within three inches of her chainplates. Fortunately the sea was calm and a few hours later she was afloat again on a rising tide.

Modern cruise ships ply these same waters in safety, thanks to a legacy of seafaring exploration which began in the Mediterranean in the 13th century. These early mariners sailed with primitive charts drawn on goatskin, which showed a coastal outline and the position of ports. In the 1500s, Flemish geographer Gerardus Mercator provided the means of projecting a sphere onto a plane, and by the mid-1600s chartmaking as we now know it had begun.

A century later European explorers were constantly pushing the frontiers of ocean and coastal navigation. Best known is the British sea captain James Cook, who made daring voyages into the vast Pacific Ocean's unknown waters. Aids to coastal navigation at this time lagged behind those of ocean navigation. Deviation of the magnetic compass was by then understood and the sextant was an accurate measuring instrument at sea. The most recent breakthrough was the chronometer – a clock which allowed ocean navigators to determine longitude. But this state-of-the-art equipment was of limited use when a ship entered uncharted coastal waters. This was when pilotage skills became critical.

The term 'pilotage' derives from the Dutch word *peillood* which means 'sounding lead' – a device used to measure the depth of water. Attached to a hemp line was a 7-lb lead weight, its lower end cap-shaped to hold a pressed lump of tallow which, when dragged across the bottom, picked up whatever was down there – sand, mud, shell or, if the tallow came up clean, rock.

A sounding line was usually 25 fathoms (150 feet) in length and marked at regular intervals with pieces of leather, cord or cloth woven through the line. Their different textures allowed the leadsman to feel the "marks" in the dark and call out the depth. For example, 'Mark Twain' – the pen name used by Mississippi riverboat pilot Samuel Clemens – means 'two fathoms' (or 12 feet of depth).

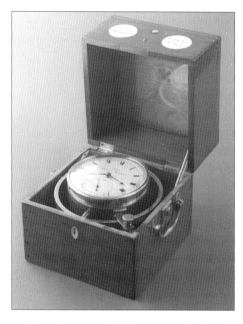

This 18th century chronometer (a ship's clock) was used by Captain Vancouver when navigating the coastlines of British Columbia and Alaska in the 1790s.

Experience and skill were needed to take soundings with this hand line. The leadsman, hanging from the forechains by a bight of line, would swing the lead over and over, then heave it far ahead of the ship so that it was straight below when the bow glided over it. For deeper waters, a 100-fathom line with a heavier lead was used.

The search by Captain Vancouver and other European explorers for a navigable northwest passage was futile, but their surveys laid the groundwork for further detailed charting in the 19th century. As seaborne trade in the Pacific Northwest increased, so did the construction of beacons and lighthouses. You will notice such buoys and light stations as your ship plies the waters of Queen Charlotte Strait.

The lighthouse at **Scarlett Point** on Balaclava Island was established in 1905. It marks the entrance to Christie Passage, an important pass off Queen Charlotte Strait. A number of vessels have suffered shipwreck off Scarlett Point, including a Scandinavian ship that ran aground in 1916. When the lighthouse keeper rowed out to retrieve the crew, the ship's captain is quoted as saying, "I know all the rocks around here. And this," he said, gesturing to the one that had just ripped a hole in his keel, "is one of them."

Pine Island, site of a lighthouse since 1907, sits alone at the entrance to Queen Charlotte Strait. The island is a nesting place for the Rhinoceros Auklet. These nocturnal seabirds tend to make ungraceful landings when flying back from the sea after dark. Veering in for a landing, they often run into a tree and fall with a thud to the ground, which is where they burrow anyway.

As your ship passes **Cape Caution**, a gentle wave motion is sometimes noticeable on the short leg across **Queen Charlotte Sound**. This open body of water is, beneath the surface, an underwater maze of shallow banks and deep troughs that twist their way seaward to the edge of the continental shelf, where the depth plunges thousands of fathoms to the bottom of the Pacific. Sea floor crustal movements forged these submarine canyons. Retreating glaciers, leaving deposits when sea levels were much lower, are responsible for the shallow banks now dragged by commercial fishermen.

On the western side of the Sound, near the edge of the shelf, the seas can be dramatic in winter. During an October storm in 1968, an oil rig off Cape St. James recorded a freak wave close to 100 feet high when one wave climbed onto the back of another. In his classic adventure tale *The Call of the Wild*, American author Jack London gives Queen Charlotte Sound a special mention when the ship carrying "Buck" crosses it in stormy weather.

Egg Island lies a few miles north of Cape Caution, on the eastern edge of Queen Charlotte Sound. The lighthouse keepers on this isolated island have an unobstructed view of the Sound and the seas it produces – from the gentle swells of summer to the frenzied breakers of a winter storm. Stan and Judy Westhaver have run the light on Egg Island since 1977 and are well known to local mariners. Fishermen often call them on their radio as they pass the island. Once a month a helicopter lands with supplies.

Stan and Judy Westhaver – the resident lightkeepers at Egg Island – pose for a photo while an Alaska State Ferry sails past in Queen Charlotte Sound.

Previous lighthouse keepers on Egg Island have had their share of excitement. The original building was twice washed away by storm waves, but the current buildings are positioned in a more secure spot. This doesn't mean the Westhavers haven't seen their share of action. After one storm Stan was asked what 77-knot winds look like at Egg Island, and he said, "Not as bad as 100-knot winds."

The Westhavers see everything from cruise ships to kayaks pass their island. Long before a lighthouse was first built here in 1898, marine traffic around Egg Island consisted of dugout canoes paddled by Kwagiutl natives. A large village was situated at the mouth of **Rivers Inlet** at what is now called Fury Island. Thousands of years ago, the abundance of salmon supported a thriving native population, and this area is now world famous for sportfishing

Fury Island lies at the entrance to **Fitz Hugh Sound** – a long wide channel that hugs the mainland coast and is shielded by islands from the open ocean. Near its southern end, on the east side, is **Addenbroke Island**. In the 1920s this lighthouse was manned by a lone woman who stayed on as lightkeeper after her husband's sudden death. For three and half years Mrs. Smith lived a solitary existence with only her dogs, chickens and goats for company. The odd fishboat stopped for a visit and she would sometimes row the five miles across Fitz Hugh Sound to call on friends in Safety Cove.

Mrs. Smith eventually remarried, and in 1928 she and her husband moved to Lucy Island. Her replacement, Ernie Maynard, didn't last long at Addenbroke. One night that August a crazed hermit from Calvert Island pulled up to the island's dock. When Ernie came down to investigate, he was shot dead. The suspected murderer disappeared before an arrest was made and to this day the Lighthouse Murder Case remains unsolved.

The northern half of **Calvert Island** is part of the Hakai Recreation Area which, at close to 123,000 hectares, is British Columbia's largest

coastal marine park. Miles of ocean beaches stretch along the west side of Calvert Island. **Hakai Pass**, at its top end, is well known to sportfishermen who frequent the area's many fishing camps each summer.

Parallel with Hakai Pass, on the mainland side of Fitz Hugh Sound, is the **Koeye River** – a scenic waterway and another hot fishing spot. The salmon in this river also attract grizzly bears. When fisheries officers fly in to Koeye Lake to monitor salmon stocks, they often see – from the air – a few of these big bruins. A boat waits downstream for the men, who hike a grizzly trail out from the lake to reach the waiting vessel, and for self defense they each carry a rifle or shotgun. Counting fish can sometimes be dangerous work.

A lot of fish were counted and canned at nearby **Namu** during its heyday in the early 1900s. The old cannery, hotel and boardwalk streets still stand on pilings at Namu, but the workers – many of them native or Chinese – are long gone.

Namu's first fish cannery was built in 1893, and by 1917 close to a hundred canneries operated up and down the British Columbia coast. Fifty years later, with the advent of fast transport and improved refrigeration, the industry became centralized and outlying canneries turned into ghost towns. Namu is one of the few original canneries still in partial operation, with a small staff running its freezing plant. Visitors can stroll the plank streets past weatherbeaten buildings or hike a boardwalk trail to scenic Namu Lake.

Fitz Hugh Sound, at its north end, narrows into Fisher Channel, which in turn leads into **Dean Channel** – a steep-sided fjord twisting its way into the mountains. Elcho Harbor lies off Dean Channel and it was

These sportfishermen are netting a ling cod in Fitz Hugh Sound near Hakai Pass. (Opposite page) The white sand beaches on Calvert Island are among the best of the B.C. coast.

A purse seiner sets its net in the fertile waters of Fitz Hugh Sound near the old cannery town of Namu.

here, in the summer of 1793, that the Scottish explorer/fur trader Alexander Mackenzie broke through the brush and became the first white man to forge an overland route through the Canadian Rockies to the Pacific. Mackenzie inscribed his arrival on a rock that bears the date of July 22, 1793. Just 47 days earlier, Captain Vancouver and his men were in the very same spot conducting their coastal survey.

Ships following the main Inside Passage route don't proceed into Dean Channel but often turn instead where **Lama Pass** joins Fisher Channel. A lighthouse used to sit at this marine intersection, on Pointer Island, which is connected to shore by a ledge that dries at low tide. The first lightkeepers stationed here in 1899 were a family named Codville. In fact, James Codville helped build the lighthouse, insisting that a large cedar tree containing an eagle's nest be saved. That eagle earned its keep by catching salmon which supplemented the family's meagre provisions.

When James died in 1917 at the age of 83, his son Ben took over the station. But James's widow grew concerned that her 34-year-old son, who had spent his entire life at this isolated light station, was never going to meet any women, let alone the "right woman." So she gave a photo of her son to the captain of a visiting mission boat. He showed it around back in the city of Vancouver but could find no young lady interested in travelling to Pointer Island for a blind date with a light-house keeper and his mother.

Finally he found a willing candidate – a lonesome woman who had been jilted by her fiancee. She took a steamship up to Namu where the cannery manager rowed her over to Pointer Island. Annie and Ben were married by the mission boat captain, and they remained on Pointer Island until Ben's retirement.

From Pointer Island the narrow channel snakes around Denny Island up to **Bella Bella**, a native community stretching along the east side of Campbell Island. With a population of 1,700, Bella Bella is the main centre of the Heiltsuk people (members of the larger Kwagiutl group). In the summer of 1993 the town hosted a week-long festival and its population doubled when people from thirty different native groups converged on Bella Bella. Many arrived in traditional dugout canoes they had paddled from as far away as Washington State.

The Tsimshian artist Roy Henry Vickers, whose grandfather was born in Bella Bella, attended the festival and created a special print to commemorate both the gathering of native people and his personal homecoming. Vickers, born of a Tshimshian/Heiltsuk father and a British mother, bridges his two cultures with a unique blending of native imagery, vivid colors and modern graphic techniques. His distinctive prints have been presented as gifts to various dignitaries, including President Clinton and Queen Elizabeth.

Cruise passengers can take a close look at the Kwagiutl fishing village of Bella Bella as their ship slowly glides past Campbell Island.

The fishing and logging town of Bella Bella used to be located across the channel on Denny Island. When a Hudson's Bay Company trading post was built on Campbell Island, the natives moved to the present-day site which they called Waglisla – a name still used on postal addresses.

Just north of Bella Bella is **Dryad Point Lighthouse**. Ship passengers are treated to a close look as the ship makes a tight turn around this point. The lighthouse, like many others along the Inside Passage, was established during the Gold Rush when a flood of steamships began using this route to the Klondike.

The lighthouse on **Ivory Island**, at the other end of Seaforth Channel, was built a year earlier – in 1898. Farther along the meandering maze of interconnecting waterways is **Boat Bluff Lighthouse**. This scenic lighthouse overlooks Sarah Passage and sits on an island inhabited by wolves. One former keeper, fearing for the safety of his small children, asked for a transfer from this lighthouse.

The natives were always wary and respectful of wolves. In her *Klee Wyck* stories the artist Emily Carr talks of an elder who, upon seeing her about to enter a forest, "ran and pulled me back, shaking his head and scolding me…The Indians forbade their children to go into the forest, not even into its edge. I was to them a child, ignorant about the wild things which they knew so well."

Dryad Point Lighthouse, just north of Bella Bella, was established in 1899 to aid steamships travelling the Inside Passage. Its red-and-white light is visible for 18 miles.

A northbound tug heads up Princess Royal Channel.

Wild things are found throughout the Inside Passage of British Columbia. Whales, dolphins, porpoises, seals and sea lions are commonly sighted while eagles soar overhead on the thermal winds. Occasionally a black bear will be sighted on shore or a lone deer swimming bravely across a channel.

On **Princess Royal Island** there lives a rare type of black bear called a kermode. A genetic mutation has given this black bear a fur coat that is not black, brown or cinnamon – but pure white. These rare bears are not easy to find in the old-growth forest of an island the size of Princess Royal, but biologists with the Valhalla Wilderness Society have been conducting annual research here since 1990 to gradually determine the bears' population and habitat. The Society has proposed that a kermode sanctuary be established on Princess Royal Island to save the white 'spirit' bears that live here and their position is supported by America's Great Bear Foundation.

The narrow reaches of **Princess Royal Channel** are lined on either side with cliff-hanging waterfalls that vary from single strands to tumbling cascades. Halfway along this watery corridor a small island splits the channel. Ships often steer to the south of **Work Island**, affording passengers a full view of the abandoned cannery at **Butedale** on Princess Royal Island. To the right of the weatherbeaten cannery is a spectacular waterfall.

Of all the channels of sheer cliff and clinging cedar that comprise the Inside Passage, none is more impressive than **Grenville Channel** – squeezed between the mainland and Pitt Island. Not only do the precip-

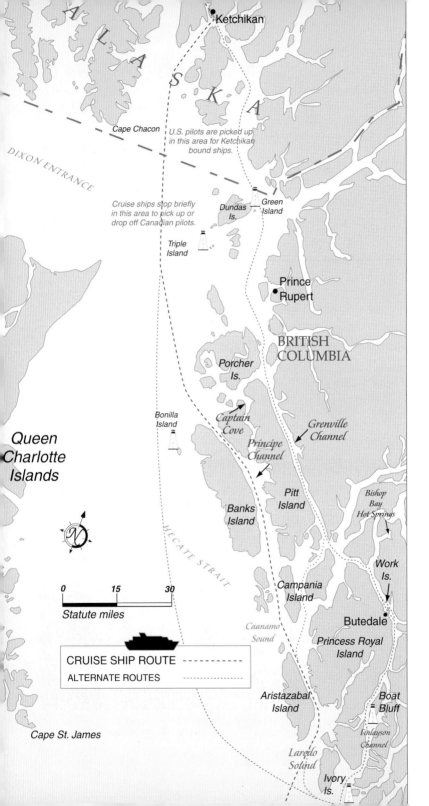

Ketchikan

A L A S K A

Cape Chacon

DIXON ENTRANCE

U.S. pilots are picked up
in this area for Ketchikan
bound ships.

Cruise ships stop briefly
in this area to pick up or
drop off Canadian pilots.

Dundas
Is.

Green
Island

Triple
Island

Prince
Rupert

BRITISH
COLUMBIA

Porcher
Is.

Bonilla
Island

Queen
Charlotte
Islands

Captain
Cove

Grenville
Channel

Principe
Channel

Pitt
Island

Bishop
Bay
Hot Springs

Banks
Island

HECATE STRAIT

N

Campania
Island

Work
Is.

0   15   30

Statute miles

Caanamo
Sound

Butedale

Princess Royal
Island

CRUISE SHIP ROUTE - - - - - - -
ALTERNATE ROUTES · · · · · · · · ·

Aristazabal
Island

Boat
Bluff

Cape St. James

Finlayson
Channel

Laredo
Sound

Ivory
Is.

itous sides of this channel rise from watery depths of 1,600 feet to forested heights of 3,500 feet, they form such a narrow corridor that large ships entering from the south look like they're going to get stuck in the first bend. This is of course an optical illusion, but the channel is, at its narrowest point, only a fifth of a mile wide.

The small cruise ships pull into a variety of pristine anchorages along the Inside Passage, one being the natural harbor of **Captain Cove** on the northwest end of Pitt Island. Passengers who visit this beautiful setting of low, forested mountains might catch a glimpse of a sailboat anchored behind the wooded islets or see black bears near the salmon stream at the head of the cove.

Cruise ships often bypass Grenville and Princess Royal Channels if they are clogged with fishboats. Salmon fishing is highly regulated and when a brief 'opening' is announced, dozens of fishboats will converge on that area to set their nets. With little room to maneuver in these tight channels, large ships face the unpleasant prospect of running over a fisherman's net if he's slow to pull it out of the way. A wayward net poses no hazard to a large ship – its large propellers simply chew it to shreds – but losing a net is a major financial loss for fishermen. Fog will also prompt the ship's captain to take an easier route and avoid the more intricate and restricted channels.

The main route follows Principe and Laredo Channels past **Campania Island**, which is a striking sight with its high barren mountains. The dome-shaped summit of Mount Pender is completely bare and is the island's most conspicuous landmark.

A small cruise ship pulls into Captain Cove where passengers enjoy a remote wilderness setting.

The view from the lido deck of a cruise ship as it steams up Laredo Sound.

The main route also takes in part of **Hecate Strait**, a wide body of water separating the mainland islands from the mystical **Queen Charlotte Islands** – homeland of the Haida. These islands are the peaks of a submerged volcanic ridge of the continental shelf. When the last Ice Age glaciers advanced, parts of this 175-mile long archipelago were left untouched, which is why the islands contain species of plants and animals found nowhere else in the world. Others that thrive here are rare, such as a type of moss found only in the Himalayas and Scotland.

Helping to preserve the unique biology of these 'Canadian Galapagos' is their isolated location. For centuries the only seafarers who plied the shallow, choppy waters of Hecate Strait were the Haida. Travelling in canoes carved out of cedar logs, these skilled mariners established villages throughout what they called Gwaii Haanas, meaning Islands of Wonder. The southern islands are a wilderness park reserve and are reached only by boat, kayak or floatplane. Visitors can wander in solitude through moss-carpeted forests of spruce and cedar, the toppled ones now 'nurse' logs to seedlings which sprout from their trunks.

Near the southern tip of the archipelago is **Anthony Island**, a small island exposed to the Pacific. On it stands the abandoned village of **Ninstints** which was declared a World Heritage Site in 1981. The village is named for a wealthy chief who was head of the Kunghit Haida when they had settlements throughout the southern islands. Some of the totem poles are still standing at Ninstints, where they overlook a lagoon protected by an islet. In summer Haida caretakers live in a nearby cabin and keep these cedar monuments – now bleached by the elements – free of moss to prevent further rotting.

B.C. Ferries connects the northernmost island of the Queen Charlottes – Graham Island – with the mainland. A car ferry sails between Skidegate and **Prince Rupert**, which is the northern terminus for passengers riding the *Queen of the North* through the Inside Passage. The Alaska state ferry also docks in Prince Rupert.

Prince Rupert is located at the mouth of the Skeena River on Kaien Island – a native name meaning Foam on Water – and the townsite was once a gathering place for the Tsimshian and Haida. It eventually became a gathering place for white men when they realized the location's potential as a deep-sea port. Railway magnate Charles Hays, general manager of the Grand Trunk Pacific Railway, envisioned a shipping port here that would rival Vancouver and Seattle with its boast of being a day or two closer in shipping time to the Orient.

A competition was held in 1906 to choose a namesake for the new port. The winner, chosen from history, was Prince Rupert – a cousin of Britain's King Charles II and first governor of the Hudson's Bay Company. The first sod was turned in 1908, followed by a hydrograph-

The abandoned Haida village of Ninstints, in the Queen Charlotte Islands, is a World Heritage Site.

An Alaska-bound cruise ship steams up Grenville Channel in the fading light of a September sunset.

ic survey of the harbor and its approaches so that lighthouses and navigational beacons could be installed to guide steamships arriving at night or in fog. All that remained to establish Prince Rupert as a major port was construction of a rail line by the Grand Trunk Pacific Railway.

Charles Hays, the man who masterminded the founding of Prince Rupert, set off for England to raise investment capital for completion of his railway's western terminus. He decided to do some networking on the return trip and chose the ill-fated maiden voyage of the *Titanic*. His life (and vision for Prince Rupert) was lost along with 1,500 other lives when the "unsinkable" British liner sideswiped an iceberg and sank in the North Atlantic.

A railway terminus was completed a few years later but fishing became the town's main industry.With the outbreak of World War II, Prince Rupert received an economic boost as thousands of American troops passed through on their way to the Aleutians and the Pacific. The port also handled freight and equipment for construction of the Alaska Highway.

Today Prince Rupert is a major port handling overseas shipments of coal, pulp and grain, in addition to traditional fishing, canning and processing. It's also the western terminus of the Yellowhead Highway and tourism is starting to blossom here as well. Local attractions include Mariners' Park, the Museum of Northern B.C. and gondola rides to the top of Mount Hays. The lovely, grotto-like Sunken Gardens are located behind the Government Courthouse on a site originally excavated for the courthouse's foundations. The gardens' adjacent tunnels were used to store munitions during World War II.

Smiles Seafood Cafe, on the waterfront at Cow Bay, has been a town landmark since 1934. During World War II, it stayed open 24 hours a day to serve the local shift workers and the Canadian and American troops stationed in Prince Rupert. Its tasty meals ranged in price from 35 cents to a dollar, and the menu included Canned Crabmeat à la Louis and Fried Filleted Chicken à la Maryland. Smiles' famous halibut and chips are still a favorite with both locals and visitors.

Prince Rupert's pioneer past is reflected in buildings such as this one, located near the tunnel entrance to the Sunken Gardens.

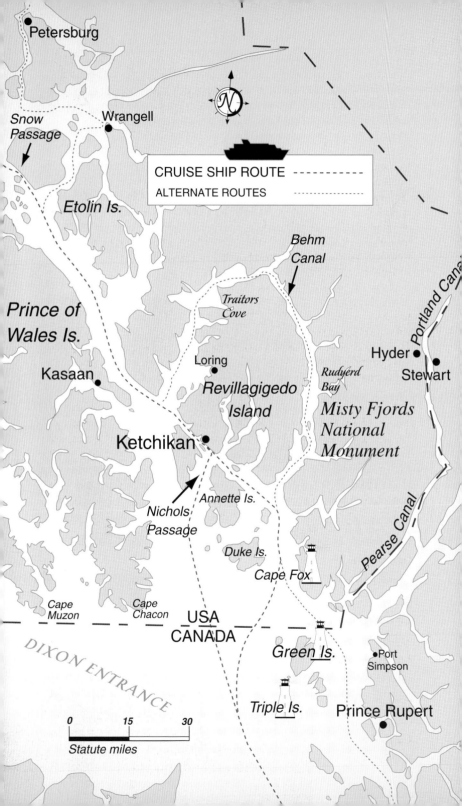

Chapter Five

KETCHIKAN

Mariners have dominated the evolution of the Inside Passage. First they plied its waters in dugout canoes, then in square-rigged sailing ships. They conducted arduous surveys and drew detailed charts of its routes and hazards for future mariners. They delivered people and materials to far-flung ports, pioneers who forged a livelihood from this raw and beautiful land.

Roads now connect some of these towns and cities to the rest of North America, as do planes. But ships still provide a major link and mariners continue to dominate coastal Alaska, where the land is inextricably tied to the sea.

Many of us live far removed from a maritime world and quickly lose our bearings out on the water. Distances become hard to gauge and the many channels and islands passing by our porthole are hard to differentiate. Now and then we might ask ourselves, "Where are we?"

Fortunately the trained mariners on the ship's bridge know exactly where we are. Not only is the officer on watch an experienced navigator, he has at his side a local pilot who is familiar with these waters and highly trained at piloting ships through the intricate waterways of the Inside Passage.

At **Dixon Entrance** there is a changing of the guard, for this open body of water is also the border between Canada and Alaska. The two Canadian pilots embark or disembark on the south side of Dixon Entrance and the American pilots do likewise on its north side.

Green Island Lighthouse lies on the Canadian side of Dixon Entrance – the international boundary between Canada and Alaska.

*The Misty Fjords National Monument contains granite ridges
and alpine lakes.*

The border, lying as it does on water, is not as easy to pinpoint as
one on land. It lies at latitude 54 degrees 40 minutes, and runs from
Cape Muzon to the entrance of Pearse Canal, then follows the Portland
Canal to its head. Called the A-B Line, this border was set in 1903 but
its has, over the years, been a source of controversy. Fishboats caught
on the wrong side of the Line are often seized and charged with illegal
fishing.

Meanwhile, marine traffic carries on as usual, as does life at the
head of Portland Canal where the Alaskan town of **Hyder** (population
73) on the American side of the Line is located two miles west of the
Canadian town of **Stewart**. Connected to the rest of mainland British
Columbia by a spur of the Cassiar Highway and to the Alaska Marine
Highway by once-a-week ferry service from Ketchikan, these two communities share their facilities. The airstrip, school, hospital and police
station are in Stewart while the seaplane base, fire hall and post office
are in Hyder. Both places have a few inns, restaurants and shops as well
as sightseeing tours. The nearby hills are no longer mined for their
gold, silver and copper, but their scenic beauty endures.

Hyder sits on the edge of the **Misty Fjords National Monument**, a
2.3-million-acre wilderness preserve – accessible only by boat or plane
– which lies within the 17-million-acre **Tongass National Forest**. This
huge tract of forested land encompasses 90% of Southeast Alaska and
was created in 1907 by President Theodore Roosevelt. An outdoorsman
and preservationist, Roosevelt wanted to save the forests and mountains
of America from profiteers. The demand for lumber was strong as rail-

roads were built and new towns were constructed across the American West. Minnesota and Wisconsin had already been stripped of their timber stands when Roosevelt camped with the famous naturalist John Muir at Yosemite in 1903. This experience convinced him of the need for wilderness protection. He established the first National Wildlife Refuge on Florida's Pelican Island to stop the killing of egrets, herons and other birds whose feathers were popular fashion accessories of the time.

About one-third of Tongass National Forest is designated wilderness. The rest is managed as a working forest, with logging and mining in operation alongside wilderness recreation and fishery management. Timber harvesting is limited to 1.7 acres and little replanting is required due to the area's temperate climate and abundance of rainfall.

Muir visited this area in 1899 as a member the Harriman Expedition – a private steamship voyage hosted by railroad magnate Edward H. Harriman to provide some of America's top scientists, writers, artists and photographers an opportunity to observe and record the nature, geology and history of Alaska. This philanthropic gesture was sometimes lost on the brusque Muir who disapproved of Victorian values being imposed on nature.

In those days, scientists didn't think twice about shooting animals for specimens. Muir, whose sympathies lay with the specimens, was often sickened at the sight of their "murder." He wreaked his revenge by sending an unsuspecting bear-hunting party on a trek he portrayed as unstrenuous when he knew from personal experience just how challenging it would be for the greenhorns. The enthusiastic hunters were reduced to hungry and exhausted men by the time they returned empty handed a few days later.

There was, however, nothing Muir could do to vent his bitterness when the scientific expedition stopped at **Cape Fox** on the southern tip of today's Misty Fjords National Monument. There, on the shores of Foggy Bay, they discovered an abandoned Tlingit village. The expedition members excitedly poked about the recently vacated cabins for artifacts, but it was the row of weathered totem poles overlooking the beach that most fascinated them. Sweating crewmen felled, one by one, a half dozen of the carved poles and hauled them out to the steamship for transport to various museums.

Nearby **Annette Island** was the site of another native village, but this one was far from abandoned. The settlement was called **New Metlakatla** and run by a Scottish clergyman named William Duncan. Duncan had come to Canada as an Anglican missionary in 1857 and quickly gained a devoted following of Tsimshian natives at Fort Simpson. A few years later Duncan led his converts away from the debauched atmosphere of Fort Simpson to establish a new village on Venn Passage near present-day Prince Rupert.

At his model village of Metlakatla, Duncan supervised the building of a church and schoolhouse as well as a sawmill, blacksmith and cannery. The neat rows of two-storey houses were bordered by picket fences and the self-sufficient community flourished for two decades until Duncan clashed with Anglican authorities over church ritual – specifically his refusal to use wine for the sacrament.

After successfully appealing to the American government for land, Duncan moved his flock to Annette Island in 1887 where they built a new village. No white men were allowed on the island for fear they would corrupt the natives with their greed for gold and liquor. So when the Harriman Expedition stopped for a visit in 1899, their presence was a rare event.

Duncan invited them all to a church service at which he delivered an impassioned sermon in the Tsimshian language. Most of his guests were impressed with Duncan's benevolent powers of persuasion with which he converted so-called savages into church-going ladies and gentlemen.

However, Muir and fellow naturalist John Burroughs were more interested in the birds, flowers and trees of Annette Island than in the social experiment of Reverend Duncan. Perhaps Duncan reminded Muir too much of his own dictatorial father – also a Scottish clergyman. Over time Duncan's followers grew tired of his rigid control and rebelled, demanding their political and economic rights.

Reverend Duncan died in 1918 but his well-planned community

lives on with a population today of 1,000 and facilities such as a recreation centre, Olympic-size swimming pool, state ferry service to Ketchikan, and several churches and schools. Annette Island has retained its status as a federal Indian reservation, allowing the natives of Metlakatla to use fish traps (which are banned elsewhere). The cottage in which Father Duncan lived is now the Duncan Museum and a replica of the original church (destroyed by fire in 1948) is open to the public.

Replicas of the Cape Fox totem poles now stand at Saxman Village outside Ketchikan.

While uncorrupted Christianity and capitalism thrived at New Metlakatla, a more free-for-all style of settlement was taking root at nearby **Ketchikan**. It began with a saltery in 1883, followed by a cannery a few years later. As more canneries were built, a boardwalk town sprung up along the waterfront straddling Ketchikan Creek – a major spawning river for salmon. In 1903 the new sawmill began making boxes for the cases of salmon being shipped out of local canneries and by the 1930s – the industry's heyday – more than a dozen canneries were packing two million cases of salmon annually.

Ketchikan was a rowdy town embodying all the vices so deplored by Reverend Duncan of New Metlakatla. Many of Ketchikan's fishermen, miners and loggers spent much of their free time drinking, gambling and visiting the madams of Creek Street, whose houses were built on pilings and connected by boardwalks. Business didn't slow during prohibition when bootleg whiskey was smuggled into Ketchikan. It was delivered by skiff at high tide and lifted through trap doors in the madams' floors.

During the steamship days, Ketchikan was dubbed 'Alaska's First City' because it was the first Alaskan port of call to receive mail and supplies from the south. Ketchikan is still the first stop for Alaska State Ferries arriving from Bellingham and Prince Rupert. The town stretches along the west shore of Revillagigedo Island at the base of Deer Mountain and is reached only by sea or air. An airport lies

(Above) Ketchikan's streets bustle with cruise passengers. (Below) Salmon still swim in Ketchikan Creek.

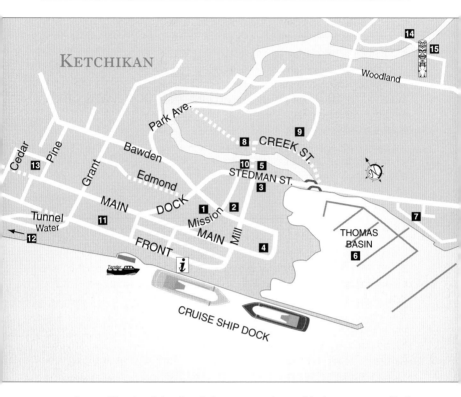

opposite on Gravina Island and the narrow channel in between – called Tongass Narrows – is busy with boats and floatplanes.

When fighter planes were built during World War I, Ketchikan's lumber industry provided the Sitka spruce – a strong and lightweight wood. In the 1950s Ketchikan's wood products industry overtook its declining salmon industry, which nearly collapsed in the '70s due to overfishing. Only two canneries are currently in operation but a few million pounds of fresh seafood are now airfreighted annually. The Deer Mountain Hatchery, built on Ketchikan Creek in 1954, currently releases 300,000 salmon a year.

Mining is another local industry. Gold was discovered in the area in 1897 and copper shortly after on nearby Prince of Wales Island. Ketchikan's latest mining prospect is at Quartz Hill where a huge deposit – possibly the world's largest – of molybdenum (a metallic chemical element used to strengthen and harden steel) has been discovered. However, this deposit is located within the Misty Fjords National Monument and many Alaskans are opposed to its development.

Another thriving industry in Ketchikan is tourism. In addition to its turn-of-the-century boardwalk streets and buildings, the town has become a showpiece for Tlingit culture with totem poles and other native art on display at local museums, parks and nearby villages. The name Ketchikan is based on a Tlingit word which, loosely translated, means 'thundering wings of an eagle', and the Tongass National Forest is named after a Tlingit clan.

Ketchikan's numerous church spires serve as perches for eagles attracted to the salmon in Ketchikan Creek, at the mouth of which residents often gather on a summer evening for a bit of fishing off the Stedman Street Bridge. This is also a popular swimming hole for kids who like to leap into the water from Creek Street's wooden balconies.

With 14,000 residents, Ketchikan has banks, gift shops and a local radio station that plays jazz and classical music. A popular cruise destination, this lively town embraces visitors today with the same exuberance it applied to salmon fishing at the turn of the century. When your ship pulls into port, Ketchikan is open for business.

SIGHTS TO SEE IN KETCHIKAN

The first thing you may notice about Ketchikan is that it rains a lot. This fact is readily admitted by a Rain Gauge proudly displayed on the **Cruise Ship Dock**. This sign shows the Ketchikan Rainbird – which looks like an oystercatcher holding an umbrella – standing beside a gauge that measures how many inches of rain the town receives annually – an impressive 162 inches.

Fortunately there's a general store right on the dock, called Tongass Trading Company, where you can buy an umbrella, rain slicker and widebrimmed hat if you haven't done so already. Also on the Cruise Ship Dock is the **Travel Information Office** ℹ️ where you can pick up a newsprint guide, brochures and walking map of Ketchikan.

A WALKING TOUR OF DOWNTOWN

Many of Ketchikan's attractions are best seen on foot and a stroll along its streets, even in the rain, is a pleasant way to acquaint yourself with the town.

As shown on the official map, start at the bottom of Mission Street where it intersects with Front Street (Tom Sawyer's gift store is on the corner). Follow Mission Street past the Trading Post (a post office is inside) and into the next block. You'll pass **St. John's Episcopal Church** 1 – built in 1903 – and the **Seamen's Center**, built a year later as a hospital.

Kittycorner to the church is **Whale Park** 2 where flower gardens and benches create an inviting setting for Ketchikan's historic Knox Brothers Clock and a replica of the Chief Kyan Totem Pole, carved by Stanley Marsden in 1964. It was first erected beside Ketchikan Creek where the Tlingit Chief Kyan held rights to a summer fish camp.

From Whale Park you can see the **U.S. Forest Service building** 3 which contains displays and information on the Tongass National Forest. On the far side of Mill Street, along the waterfront, is the **Southeast Visitors Information Center** 4. Built in the cannery style,

Ketchikan's rowdy past is preserved in the boardwalk buildings of Creek Street.

Thomas Basin and the cruise ship dock can be viewed from historic Thomas Street – a wood-plank street set on pilings where a cannery once operated.

this modern center contains impressive exhibits on the area's natural environment, wildlife and native heritage.

Standing opposite the Forest Service building is the **Chief Johnson Totem Pole** ⑤, carved by Tlingit artist Israel Shotridge and raised in 1989. It's an exact replica of the original pole raised in 1901 by Chief Johnson, which is now housed in the Totem Heritage Center.

Follow Stedman Street to the bridge spanning the mouth of **Ketchikan Creek**. Look down and you might see salmon milling about in the water while they adjust to fresh water before beginning their uphill swim to their spawning grounds.

Carry on along Stedman, past picturesque **Thomas Basin** ⑥ with its small boat marinas. In the early part of this century, before a break-water was built, the basin's long tidal flats were used as a baseball park. The game was called when a rising tide started flooding the outfield.

On the far side of Thomas Basin is a wood-plank street built over the water. Called **Thomas Street** ⑦, it was once part of the New England Fish Co. cannery and its historic buildings are now used by local businesses such as Fjord Photography.

Retrace your steps along Thomas and Stedman Streets, past The New York Hotel & Cafe, to Ketchikan's famous **Creek Street** ⑧. This former red-light district is now a respectable part of town and a major

Monrean House stands beside the wooden steps of Main Street. The totem pole is now at Whale Park.

tourist attraction. A boardwalk set on pilings, it will take you along the shores of Ketchikan Creek, past interesting shops and a museum called Dolly's House. Dolly was the town's most successful madam and her house has been preserved, complete with furnishings and other memorabilia.

About halfway along Creek Street is a tramway car that whisks passengers (for a small charge) up the hill to **Westmark's Cape Fox Lodge 9**. Here you have a sweeping view of downtown Ketchikan and Tongass Narrows.

Back down on Creek Street, pause at the footbridge where again you may see salmon heading upstream. On the other side of the bridge is the **Tongass Historical Museum and Public Library 10**. Here you can view exhibits depicting Ketchikan's earlier days.

Dock Street leads from the Museum back down to Front Street. On the way you will pass the foot of Edmond Street, which is a long set of wooden stairs going up the hillside. A stroll along Front Street takes you past the historic **Gilmore Hotel 11** (on the National Historic Register) to the tunnel under Knob Hill.

The tunnel was built in 1954 so that historic homes on Knob Hill could be preserved. Had a road been built, part of the hill would have been blasted away and the houses demolished. Many stories are told to visitors regarding this tunnel's construction, the best one being that federal funds were available at the time for building a bomb shelter, so Ketchikan built one with two entrances and road running through it.

If you carry on along Front Street, you'll reach **Harborview Park 12** overlooking Ketchikan's main boat basin. Benches here provide both a resting spot and a view of the busy harbor's fishboat and floatplane activity.

The heritage homes of Knob Hill straddle the Water Street Tunnel.

AN EXTENDED WALKING TOUR

Ketchikan is built on the slopes of Deer Mountain, so to see more of the local sights on foot involves a bit of climbing. Recommended is a hike up Front Street's steps to Cedar Street where you can overlook the waterfront.

Take the Main Street stairs back down to Pine Street. At the corner stands the **Monrean House** **13** – built in 1904 for one of the town's leading businessmen. Preserving the Queen Anne style so popular at the turn of the century, this house is on the National Register of Historic Places. Continue along Main Street, turn left at Grant and at the next block turn right on Edmond. Now you're at the top of the long wooden staircase leading down to Dock Street.

At the bottom of the stairs, turn left on Dock Street, then left again on Bawden. Stay with Bawden until you reach Park Avenue, which veers to the right. Follow Park along Ketchikan Creek to the **Deer Mountain Hatchery** **14** which backs onto a peaceful park containing ornamental ponds once used by the town's first hatchery.

A footbridge leads between the hatchery and the **Totem Heritage Centre** **15** which houses a major collection of authentic totem poles. Outside on the grounds is a self-guided nature path.

Retrace your route along Ketchikan Creek, turning off at Venetia Avenue to the Cape Fox Lodge (mentioned earlier), then take the tram car down to Creek Street. It and nearby attractions are outlined in the Downtown Walking Tour.

SAXMAN VILLAGE

One of Ketchikan's most popular shore excursions is **Saxman Village**, located two miles south of town. Coaches transport passengers to the village for a two-hour visit immersed in Tlingit culture. Your hosts are descendents of those who lived at Cape Fox and Fort Tongass until the late 1880s, when they were persuaded by Presbyterian missionaries to relocate here. The village was founded in 1894 and named for school teacher Samuel Saxman.

In the 1930s, the people of Saxman returned to their original village sites to retrieve the totem poles they had left behind. New poles have been carved since then and they stand in a semi-circle overlooking the village and Tongass Narrows. Guests arriving at Saxman are treated to the live enactment of a Tlingit legend, followed by an impressive slideshow presentation at the village's multi-media center.

Guests are also ushered into the Clan House, which is built of red cedar and displays the Beaver crest on its carved corner poles. In keeping with a traditional potlatch, the **Cape Fox Dancers** perform a series of dances, then invite members of the audience to join them. Upon leaving, each guest is given a small packet of trading beads – again in keeping with potlatch customs.

Outside the Beaver Clan House, a guide explains the stories behind some of the totem poles displayed in the park. A few minutes are allowed for visiting the gift shop before the tour concludes in the Carving Center, where the art of totem carving is explained. Anyone interested in native culture will find a visit to Saxman both enlightening and entertaining.

Wearing traditional regalia, a young Tlingit performs a potlatch dance in the Beaver clan house.

*(Above) The ceremonial clan house at Totem Bight State Park.
(Below) A Tlingit totem pole stands tall outside the Cape Fox
clan house.*

OUT-OF-TOWN EXCURSIONS

There is no shortage of shore excursions to take while in Ketchikan, and if you plan ahead there should be time for both a walking tour of downtown (including the shopping area) and an out-of-town excursion.

Tlingit heritage is strong in the Ketchikan area and eight miles north of town is a former village site now called **Totem Bight State Park**. A short trail through the forest opens into an old campsite containing a collection of authentic totem poles and a ceremonial clan house.

Just being in a coastal rainforest is a treat for many people, which is why there are also nature hike tours available. A knowledgeable guide helps you identify plant and tree species, adding to your enjoyment of the forest's natural beauty. (See A Walk in a Rainforest on page 89.)

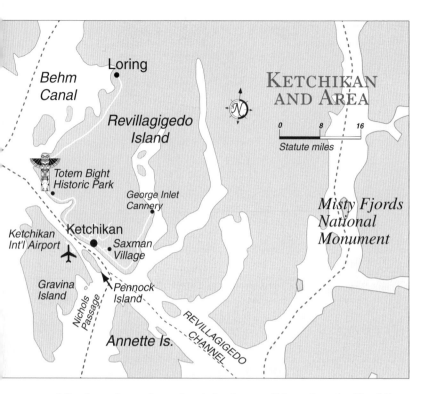

Viewing a forest from the air is also possible on board a Ketchikan air taxi (floatplane). Not only will you get an eagle's eye view of the steeply treed slopes, you'll see mountain lakes, hanging waterfalls and winding fjords that were carved long ago by retreating glaciers. You may even spot some wildlife – mountain goats, bear and moose on shore; killer whales, seals and sea lions in the surrounding channels.

Ketchikan is right next door to the **Misty Fjords National Monument** – a wilderness reserve created in 1978 and, at 2.3 million acres, almost four times the size of Rhode Island. Weather checks are made every hour but planes still fly in overcast weather; the fjords are said to be their most beautiful when mist rises off the water and wisps of cloud cling to the mountaintops.

A flightseeing tour lasts about an hour and offers aerial views of the **Behm Canal**, which is about a hundred miles long and wraps right round Revillagigedo Island. Pillar-shaped New Eddystone Rock – a volcanic plug – juts 234 feet skyward from the middle of the Canal's eastern arm. Eagles like to perch here.

Also in the Behm Canal (but outside the National Monument) is the U.S. Navy's submarine testing facility, which is located in these remote waters to escape marine traffic noise. The submarines being tested are so quiet that navy scientists need an equally silent location to plant their

T H E   B E A V E R

One of the most common sights in Alaska – and especially in Ketchikan – is the floatplane. Used as an important link between coastal villages, remote logging camps and main ports, the floatplane has served Alaska since the 1930s. However, it was the introduction of the Beaver aircraft just after the Second World War that made short-haul air connections in Southeast Alaska inexpensive and, most importantly, safe.

BEAVER MK 1

Engine: 450 hp
Pratt & Whiney
Wing Span: 48 ft.
Length: 30 ft.
Weight: 3000 lb
Performance –
Maximum Speed: 160 mph
Cruising Speed: 130 mph
Rate of Climb: 1020 ft/min
Service Ceiling: 18,000 feet

Developed by De Havilland Canada, the Beaver was designed to handle payloads over 1,000 pounds, and to take off and land in tight places, whether on land, ice, snow or water. The plane went on to become one of the most successful and long-lived designs in aviation history, with over 1,600 built. Of the 1,000 still operating most are working along the B.C. and Alaska coast.

Beaver floatplanes line up like taxi cabs along Ketchikan's waterfront. The Beaver has been the bush-plane of choice for 50 years.

(Above) Hanging waterfalls ribbon the rock walls of Misty Fjords' watery canyons.

(Below) A floatplane lands on an alpine lake in Granite Basin.

rows of hydrophones and record the rhythms of the subs as they race past. Data collected from these underwater tests is analysed and used to make the submarines even quieter.

The silence of these watery canyons is demonstrated when your plane lands on an alpine lake or one of the inlet's upper reaches and the pilot shuts off his engine. You can climb onto one of the plane's pontoons and listen to the subtle sounds of a mountain wilderness.

Highlights of the Monument are: **Rudyerd Bay** – a spectacular, steep-sided fjord; **Punchbowl Cove** – a dramatic cove of sheer cliffs; **Big Goat Lake** – an alpine lake containing a waterfall that plunges almost 1000 feet; **Nooya Lake** – left behind by a melting valley glacier; and **Granite Basin** – where bare rock ridges separate a row of deep-blue alpine lakes.

Other guided tours available during your stop in Ketchikan are sport-fishing by charter boat, kayaking along the waterfront and canoeing on a mountain lake. Beginners are usually welcome and wet weather gear may or may not be provided. Wear warm clothing in layers – the outer layer should be waterproof. More leisurely tours of Ketchikan's waterfront are provided in excursion yachts. Your on-board guide will explain the local sights and activities.

Jet boats and air taxis can whisk visitors to outlying resorts and canneries, such as Loring in the western arm of the Behm Canal. Loring was a cannery site from 1885 to 1930, and pieces of the wrecked side-paddle steamer Ancon can be seen here at low tide. The steamer used to deliver mail, freight and passengers to **Loring** until one day in 1889 when an overly enthusiastic cannery worker cast off the departing ship's dock lines before an officer was ready at the controls. The steamer drifted onto a reef where it holed and sank with no loss of life – except maybe the cannery worker's!

When Captain Vancouver's two ships were anchored in 1793 at Port Stewart, on the other side of the Behm Canal, they were visited both by Tlingits from the Stikine River and by Haidas from Kasaan. The British sailors, who had been attacked by some Tlingits in **Traitors Cove**, watched with apprehension when it looked as though a fight was going to break out between the two native groups. Peace prevailed, however, after an exchange of words between their leaders. On board one of the British ships was a Tlingit who told Captain Vancouver he wanted to sail with him to England, then promptly changed his mind when he saw a crew member being whipped.

A Misty Fjords flight seeing excursion whisks passengers over forested mountains and pristine fjords.

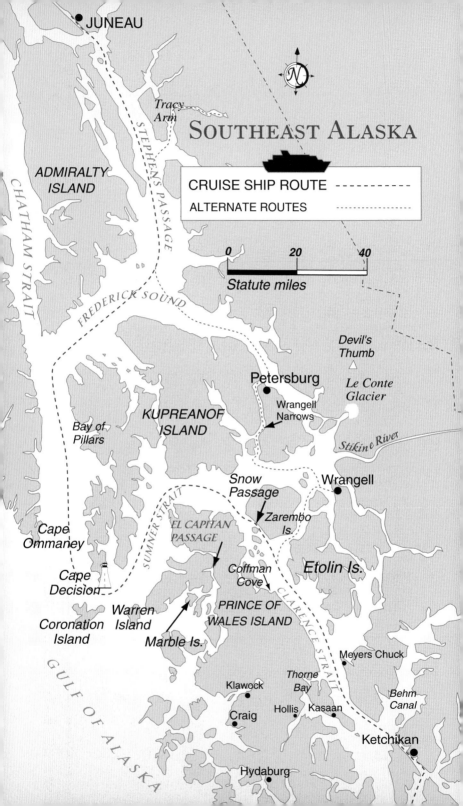

CHAPTER SIX

PIONEER PORTS

L and is scarce in Alaska – private land, that is. Of the state's massive land area covering 365 million acres, less than one per cent is currently in private hands.

For almost a century Alaska's single landowner was the U.S. Government. Statehood was granted in 1959, but the complex and controversial process of land allocation is ongoing. Millions of acres lie within national parks and wilderness refuges and, in 1971, the Alaska Native Claims Settlement Act – involving 44 million acres – was passed.

In Southeast Alaska the land is either national park or part of the Tongass National Forest. Developed property in towns such as Ketchikan is scarce and expensive, with house prices considerably higher than the national average. People who decide to homestead in Alaska cannot simply squat on their chosen piece of land – certain procedures must be followed.

Under the state's Homesite Program, each Alaskan is eligible to five acres of free land. Those enrolled in the program must pay for a survey and build a permanent, single-family dwelling within five years. Under the Homestead Program, a person can acquire from 40 to 160 acres (depending on its land-use classification) but must survey, occupy and

The moon rises over Clarence Strait at the entrance to Thorne Bay on Prince of Wales Island.

improve the land in certain ways within set time periods in order to receive title. If they purchase the land, the restrictions are fewer, but one year's residency is required to participate in either program.

Despite these restrictions, the lure of the north still beckons. In 1984, the ABC television program 20/20 featured the remote Alaskan village of **Coffman Cove**. Afterwards the residents of this tiny logging community, located on the northeast side of **Prince of Wales Island**, were deluged with mail from viewers who wanted to move there. The show's portrayal of Coffman Cove's wholesome lifestyle – fresh air, clean water and freedom from urban crime – appealed to many Americans living in the Lower 48.

Yet Alaskans who live in outlying ports similar to Coffman Cove don't harbor any illusions about their lifestyle. Living in isolation is not for everyone. The work is often seasonal and incomes are sporadic. The winters can be long, dark and wet. Supplies must be shipped or flown into port, there are few conveniences and, for many, a trip south each winter is mandatory to their mental health. Yet most say they wouldn't live anywhere else.

Alaska breeds a hardiness in people. Early pioneers came to fish the waters, mine and log the land. Margaret Bell Wiks, well known for her children's books about Alaska's early days, was of pioneering stock. Her Scottish grandparents – James and Margaret Millar – arrived in Alaska in 1879 and established salteries on Prince of Wales Island. Their daughter Florence married a fellow named James Bell who raced his sloop against a steamer – from Puget Sound to Alaska – and won.

The Bells' daughter Margaret was born in December 1898. She was delivered by her Scottish grandmother while the doctor rested in bed. He had suffered a heart attack when the sailboat bringing him to **Thorne Bay** was caught in a storm. Margaret weighed only three pounds at birth and spent the first few weeks of her life in a shoebox on the door of an opened oven. Despite her tentative start, Margaret lived for 91 years.

Wrangell Narrows is a scenic waterway connecting the smaller ports of Wrangell and Petersburg.

Alaska's state ferries – called the Alaska Marine Highway – provide a transportation link between remote villages and coastal towns.

Millar Street in Ketchikan is named for the family, as is the town of **Craig** on Prince of Wales Island. Craig was one of Margaret's uncles and he ran a cannery there in the early 1900s. With a present population of 1,200, Craig is home port to a substantial fishing fleet and has become the service centre for Prince of Wales – the largest island in Southeast Alaska. The island is indented with inlets and coves, many of which were fishing camps for the Haida and Tlingit before the arrival of white settlers.

Klawock, about 10 miles north of Craig, was originally a Tlingit summer village. It is also the site of Alaska's first cannery, built in 1878. The local totem park contains 21 carved poles – both replicas and originals – from the abandoned village of Tuxekan, situated farther up island.

There is also a collection of restored totems at **Hydaburg** which was established in 1911 when several Haida villages in the vicinity joined together. The Haida – fearless seafarers – live in the Queen Charlotte Islands. About 300 years ago they extended the northern boundary of their territory to encompass the southern half of Prince of Wales Island. Their numbers, like those of other native groups, dwindled when European-imported diseases such as smallpox wiped out entire families and clans along the coast. Many villages were abandoned as survivors coalesced at central locations.

A state ferry runs between Ketchikan and Prince of Wales Island. It pulls into Hollis, a former mining and logging town, and each summer more and more visitors come to the island for its superb sportfishing and wildlife viewing. The National Forest Service is still identifying and cataloguing historic and prehistoric sites on the island including a system of limestone caves.

On the northwest side of Prince of Wales Island lie a number of smaller islands, including **Marble Island**. At the turn of the 19th century, when ornamental and building stone was popular on the west coast, the island's quarry near Tokeen produced almost $2 million worth of marble. The Juneau State Capitol's four exterior columns are made of Tokeen marble.

Extensive logging has taken place on Prince of Wales Island and logging roads connect most settlements with the Hollis ferry terminal. But the communities of **Point Baker** and **Port Protection**, at the north end of the island, don't want to be connected. When the forest service proposed extending the road system to include them, a ruckus ensued, with environmental organizations getting involved.

The 150 or so residents of these two fishing ports are quite happy in their isolation. They get about in skiffs and out-of-town visitors arrive by boat or floatplane. There's a free-and-easy atmosphere here – no rules or regulations, just a great deal of friendliness.

In Port Protection, boardwalks lead past homes and the local school. A general store overlooks the fuel dock, its liquor section located out back in a wood hut. Customers are led through the fishpacking building and along a short trail to get to it. The men and women who live here troll for salmon in **Sumner Strait** and are satisfied with a moderate day's catch – just enough to pay for their simple lifestyle.

Most cruise ships pass through Sumner Strait on their way to or from Ketchikan. Whales and dolphins also use this major channel. Its southern end is open to the Gulf of Alaska and marked by **Cape Decision** – a rocky bluff atop which sits an unmanned lighthouse.

Located at the southern tip of Kuiu Island, Cape Decision was named in 1793 by Captain Vancouver when his survey thus far decisively proved that no northwest passage existed in the area. He named nearby **Coronation Island** in honor of Britain's King George III because his ships sailed past it on the anniversary of their monarch's coronation.

When cruise ships round Cape Decision, mountainous Coronation Island and nearby **Warren Island** lie to seaward. Both are wilderness reserves. Seabirds nest on rocky cliffs and bears feed in the streams. Tall stands of spruce inland give way to wind-bent trees along the islands' lee shores, exposed to the open sea.

A September storm forced Captain Vancouver's two ships to seek shelter in Port Protection before heading out to sea. That summer their survey boats had covered hundreds of miles of shoreline, including the channels that lead to the mouth of the great **Stikine River**. This river delta is one of the most productive estuaries in Southeast Alaska. Its tidal flats attract half a million migrating seabirds each year and the silt it deposits in adjacent Dry Strait prevents vessels of any size from navigating that channel.

Before the arrival of European explorers and fur traders, Tlingit natives had established a major village at the mouth of the Stikine under a series of leaders named Chief Shakes. As the fur trade heated up, the 400-mile-long Stikine River turned into a conveyor belt for furs, with Chief Shakes and his people reaping the profits as middlemen.

The Russian-American Company had been steadily working its way eastward from the Aleutian Islands in pursuit of sea otters and seals while the Hudson's Bay Company of Britain had been working its way westward across the continent in pursuit of beaver pelts. In 1821, the HBC merged with the competing Northwest Company's operations west of the Rockies, but its monopoly ended on the shores of the Pacific where it faced competition not only from the Russians but also from American merchant ships.

These freewheeling Yankee traders were known as 'Boston men' because almost all of them were from that port. Transient traders with no permanent bases in the Pacific Northwest, the Boston men paid higher prices for beaver pelts than the HBC. They obtained these pelts – which rose five times in market value in the 1820s – from natives living at the mouths of the Stikine, Nass and Skeena Rivers, who regularly travelled upriver to trade with natives of the interior.

The HBC realized some corporate restructuring was needed to counter the American traders, so it began building trading posts on the banks of strategic rivers to intercept the seaward flow of beaver pelts. Fort Vancouver was built in 1825 on the Columbia River, Fort Langley in 1827 on the Fraser River, Fort Simpson in 1831 near the mouth of the Nass, and Fort McLoughlin in 1833 on the edge of Queen Charlotte Sound.

Meanwhile the Russian-American Company tried to ban foreign vessels from its coastal territory, but this Csarist decree was ineffective because the Russian outpost of Sitka relied on Boston ships for supplies. These provisions were paid for with seal skins which the Yankee traders then sold in Asia for threefold the price.

There was little Russia could do about the American presence but they could do something about the British wave of fort building. A year before the HBC coaster arrived at the Stikine River

The fishing community of Port Protection has no roads but plenty of trees for building boardwalks.

to build yet another upstream fort, the Russians began building their own at the river's mouth. Called Saint Dionysius Redoubt, its commander prevented the British from ascending the Stikine River when they arrived in 1834.

The British, who were regaining their monopoly on beaver pelts, accepted this minor setback. They bided their time with the Russians and redoubled their efforts against the Yankee traders. The HBC's newly formed naval department hired American skippers (veterans of the coastal trade) to shadow the Boston ships and outbid the Yankee traders. As their profits dwindled, the Boston men gradually withdrew from the fur trade and turned their sights on whaling.

Their withdrawal also meant a loss of supply ships for the Russians at Sitka. They had no alternative but to turn to the British who had offered, on a number of occasions, to supply the Russian outpost with surplus food from their forts' surrounding farms. So, in return for a reliable food source, the Russians granted the British exclusive access to coastal waters bordering the mainland. The HBC moved into Saint Dionysius Redoubt and changed its name to Fort Stikine. A brisk trade continued between local Tlingit clans and the British, who offered cloth and woolen Hudson's Bay blankets in exchange for furs.

The fur trade eventually dwindled and the British fort had been abandoned when a prospector named Buck Choquette discovered gold on the Stikine River in 1861. Men rushed upriver by steamer to Buck's Bar to pan for gold. A second strike was made farther upriver at Cassiar in 1874. Fort Stikine was now called **Wrangell** – its name changed when the United States bought Russian America in 1867. Baron Von Wrangell, a former chief manager of the Russian-American Company, had ordered the fort's initial construction.

The American schooner **Lady Washington,** *a replica shown here at Vancouver's Maritime Museum, was commanded by 'Boston men' during the fur trade.*

When the famous naturalist John Muir of California arrived at Wrangell by steamer in July 1879, about 1,800 miners and prospectors had already passed through that spring en route to the Cassiar gold mines. This was Muir's first visit to Alaska and his initial impression of Wrangell was that "no mining hamlet in the placer gulches of California, nor any backwoods village I ever saw, approached it in picturesque, devil-may-care abandon." Muir did concede that despite the town's haphazard collection of houses built on swampy ground, Wrangell was a tranquil place. There were no noisy brawls in the streets and the weather was mild.

Muir himself was a bit of a curiosity. The townspeople wondered what he was up to wandering about the forest, examining plants and trees with no apparent objective. One resident observed Muir "on his knees, looking at a stump as if he expected to find gold in it."

A Presbyterian mission was established in Wrangell, where Muir met Dr. Sheldon Jackson (a missionary who would become widely known in Southeast Alaska) and Reverend Samuel Hall Young, who became Muir's lifelong friend. In his book *Travels in Alaska*, Muir describes Young as an adventurous evangelist. Of course, anyone who associated with Muir had no choice but to embrace adventure.

On the first climb Young made with Muir, the young missionary dislocated both arms when he slipped near the top of Glenora Peak and found himself hanging from a crumbling precipice on the edge of a thousand-foot drop. Muir saved his new climbing companion and it was the beginning of a close friendship.

During his stay at Wrangell, Muir also met the current Chief Shakes of the Stikine tribe who invited Muir and the missionaries to a potlatch. The floor of the great chief's house was "strewn with fresh hemlock boughs" while "bunches of showy wild flowers adorned the walls" and huckleberry branches filled the hearth. "Altogether it was a wonderful show," wrote Muir.

He enjoyed the dancing – the rhythmic stamping of feet and clapping of hands – and described the chief dancer's headdress as being filled with feathers. With each jerk of his head, he "scattered great quantities of downy feathers like a snowstorm as blessings on everybody." Theatrical imitations of several animals were performed so convincingly that when "the door of the big house was suddenly thrown open and in bounced a bear," they were all quite startled until they realized it was a man wearing a bear skin.

Gifts were handed out at the end of the ceremonies and Muir was given a headdress once worn by shamans – medicine men (and sometimes women) who had supernatural powers and could cure illnesses. Muir was also, on this occasion, adopted by the tribe and given the Tlingit name of Ancoutahan ('adopted chief') which would protect him in his travels. Other tribes wouldn't risk harming him for fear of retaliation from the powerful Stikines.

Wrangell, a former fur trading post and gold mining town, sits at the top of Wrangell Island near the mouth of the Stikine River.

WRANGELL (POP. 2,500)

During his stay in Wrangell, John Muir visited the site of the former Stikine village – called Kotslitna – which had been abandoned some 70 years earlier when Chief Shakes moved the community closer to the Russian fort. The small island on which they settled became known as **Shakes Island** and a replica of their tribal house is now a major tourist attraction. It was built in the traditional manner, without nails but by using adzes to shape and join the posts, beams and planks. Muir was so impressed with the Tlingit workmanship he stated that "with the same tools, not one in a thousand of our skilled mechanics could do as good work."

The original interior houseposts of the clan house, which were brought from the first village, are now housed in the Wrangell Museum. Replica poles grace the inside and outside of the tribal house and the clan's bear crest frames the entrance.

Other carved poles about town include a replica of the Three Frogs Totem, designed to shame the neighboring Kiksadi clan (whose crest was the frog) into repaying a debt. Bear Up The Mountain pole tells the story of a grizzly bear (his prints shown climbing up the pole) who led the Shakes clan to safety when threatened by a great flood. Totem poles of the Kiksadi clan are displayed in a small park on Front Street where false-fronted wooden buildings preserve the town's pioneer heritage.

On Church Street is the oldest protestant church in Alaska, the First Presbyterian Church. It was founded in 1879 and, twice damaged by fire, has been extensively renovated. A large, red neon cross was erected in 1939 and serves as a navigational light for local mariners.

Outside the **public library**, located on 2nd Street, are two totem poles as well as some petroglyphs carved on rocks in the grass. Several petroglyphs can also be viewed in the **Wrangell Museum** next door and even more petroglyphs are found (after some searching) on the beach a half mile north of the **ferry terminal**. At low tide, about 40 rock engravings of prehistoric images – animals and human faces – are exposed. People are allowed to take rubbings of them and museum staff are happy to explain how this is best done.

Northwest of Wrangell, opposite the south end of Sergief Island, is Garnet Ledge. Its red transparent mineral was mined in 1915 by Alaska Garnet & Manufacturing Company – apparently the world's first all-women corporation. The ledge is now the property of the children of Wrangell (adults need a permit to remove garnets) and youngsters here spend part of their summer holidays selling these local gems to visitors.

Baron Von Wrangell's name was also given to **Wrangell Narrows** – an important waterway in Southeast Alaska which is used by fish-boats, tugs, small cruise ships and the Alaska State Ferry. This long, narrow channel (20 miles in length and, at places, only 300 feet in width) is squeezed between two islands and well marked with over 60 navigational aids. Wrangell Narrows has been dubbed Christmas Tree Lane for its nightly blinking of red and green lights. The narrows are very scenic, winding past log cabins and fishing lodges nestled at the foot of treed slopes.

PETERSBURG (POP. 3,600)

At the north end of Wrangell Narrows, on Mitkof Island, is the pretty fishing port of **Petersburg**. Founded by Norwegian immigrants at the turn of the century, the town's site was chosen for its natural harbor and dramatic backdrop of glacier-draped mountains which reminded Peter Buschmann of the fjords back home. He moved here in 1897 and began fishing for salmon and halibut. Pack ice was supplied by the nearby Le Conte Glacier.

'Peter's Burg' grew quickly as fellow Norwegians joined Busch-mann and, from the ample timber supply, started building a neatly planned Scandinavian community. Buschmann was manager of the Icy Straits Packing Company, which constructed a sawmill, wharf, ware-houses, bunkhouses, store and cannery. Fish packing was a year-round operation with salmon caught each summer, halibut and herring in the spring, crab over the winter and shrimp throughout the year.

Unlike some of the goldmining towns of this era, there was no boom and bust cycle in Petersburg. The people here were industrious, com-munity minded and proud of their Scandinavian heritage. They decorat-ed their neat wooden homes with traditional rosemaling (fanciful floral designs painted in bright colors) and built a Sons of Norway Hall in 1912 for Saturday night socials. Many a Petersburg fisherman met his future wife at one of these dances.

Norwegian Independence Day is celebrated annually with a Little Norway Festival held on the weekend nearest May 17th. The people of

Petersburg dress in traditional costume, prepare lavish smorgasbords and dance to Norwegian folk music. As part of the festivities, a replica Viking ship called *Valhalla* (built in 1976 for the nation's bicentennial) is launched by local fishermen dressed as fierce Norsemen.

PETERSBURG ATTRACTIONS

Town maps and brochures are available at the Chamber of Commerce **Information Center**, located in the Harbor Master Office overlooking North Harbor.

The Valhalla is on display beside the **Sons of Norway Hall** at the entrance to Hammer Slough. Inside the hall is a crafts shop where visitors can browse for Norwegian knicknacks. Built on pilings, Hammer Slough's plank streets and brightly colored buildings are a favorite subject for local artists and their paintings are displayed in the town's shop windows.

Historic **Sing Yee Alley** is named for a local businessman who was mysteriously murdered in the 1930s. Scandal rocked the town when its local marshalls were implicated in the crime. The town marshall was soon murdered and the federal marshall left Petersburg only to turn up dead in Seattle.

The **Clausen Museum**, with displays of the different types of fishing gear used, provides insight into Alaska's fishing industry as well as Petersburg's past. Steamers used to deliver freight from the south, and whalers on their way north would pull into Petersburg to stock up with coal. In the Dirty Thirties, farmers from the Dakota Dustbowl came to try their hand at fishing, quickly learning how to lasso icebergs in Frederick Sound and tow them into port for crushed ice.

The fishing port of Petersburg on Mitkof Island has retained its Norwegian ancestry with such attractions as the historic Sons of Norway Hall and a replica Viking ship called **Valhalla.**

Glacier-clad mountains loom above Frederick Sound, forming a dramatic backdrop for the port of Petersburg.

At **Eagle's Roost Park**, just past the cannery plant along Nordic Drive, the women of Petersburg used to gather (before fishboats carried radios) and watch anxiously for their husbands and sons returning from the fishing grounds. Today this is a good vantage for watching both the marine traffic in Wrangell Narrows and the eagles that roost in the spruce trees here.

Another good spot to view Wrangell Narrows is at **Papke's Landing** – located along Mitkof Highway which runs parallel with the Narrows. An old-timer named Herman Papke lived here in a cabin and would phone the Petersburg switchboard when he saw a steamer coming up the narrows so that the townspeople could be ready on the dock to greet it. Other sights along **Mitkof Highway** are the Falls Creek Fish Ladder and Blind Slough, where trumpeter swans spend the winter.

On the other side of the Narrows is sparsely-populated **Kupreanof Island**. Those who live in the town of Kupreanof, about 50 in number, value their independent lifestyle which is based largely on self employment and subsistence activities such as fishing and shellfish harvesting.

Glaciers of the Stikine Icefield drain into Frederick Sound and nearby **Le Conte Glacier** is the southernmost active tidewater glacier in Alaska. Visible from Petersburg, it has retreated two to three miles since it was first charted in 1887. The glacier stabilized in the early 1980s and in recent years appears to be advancing again.

When John Muir visited Le Conte in 1879, he said it was one of the most imposing glaciers he had seen. Besides producing ice for Petersburg's fish packing plants, Le Conte played a starring role (alongside Richard Burton) in the 1960 film *Ice Palace*. Looming above Le Conte Glacier is **Devil's Thumb** peak – a majestic sight with a pyramid-like peak jutting through the ice and snow.

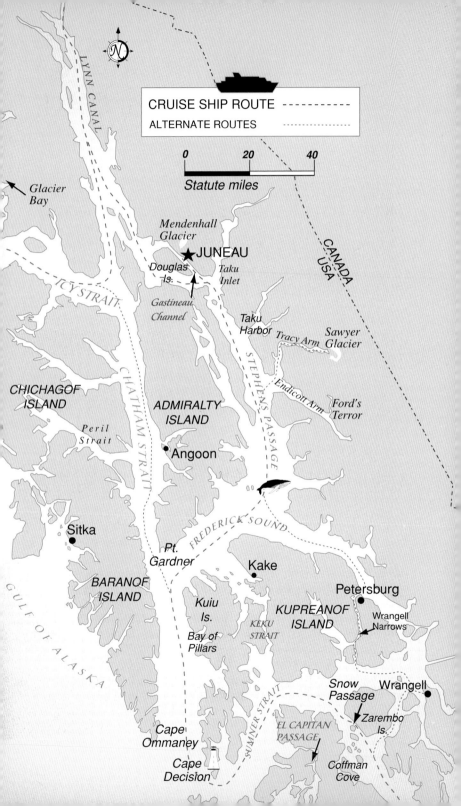

CHAPTER SEVEN

JUNEAU

T he mainland mountains of southeastern Alaska are dominated by two massive ice fields. Down rugged slopes and steep valleys flow glaciers, some of which reach tidewater. These water-lapped walls of ice hide at the heads of various fjords between Wrangell and Juneau, but there are clues to their whereabouts. Crystalline ice chunks – some as big as bungalows – can be seen floating down certain fjords and channels of the Inside Passage.

The U.S./Canada border runs through the middle of these icefields and is marked by mountains which poke their craggy peaks through thick layers of ice and snow. On the Alaska side of this lonely border, the combined area of these two icefields is more than 2,500 square miles.

The southerly Stikine Icefield stretches for 120 miles and drains its glacial meltwater into the fjords and inlets of Frederick Sound and Stephens Passage. These two bodies of water join at the top of Kupreanof Island where they form a major marine intersection with 138-mile-long Chatham Strait – the most extensive of southeast Alaska's channels. Because of Chatham Strait's long fetch and exposure to the Gulf of Alaska, the seas off Point Gardner (southern tip of Admiralty Island) can be steep and choppy in a winter storm. This is of

A flight over the sprawling Juneau Icefield is a journey back in time to the last Great Ice Age.

little concern to the large cruise ships that glide past this point throughout the summer, but it was of great concern to the native guides who were paddling these waters in October of 1879.

The man who had chartered their canoe was John Muir, the famous and fearless naturalist who was determined to see as many glaciers as possible on his first visit to Alaska. His new friend, the Presbyterian missionary Samuel Hall Young, came along to spread the gospel while the irrepressible Muir preached his own 'glacial gospel' to anyone who cared to listen.

The canoe's crew were, in Muir's words: "Toyatte, a grand old Stickeen nobleman, who was made captain, not only because he owned the canoe, but for his skill in woodcraft and seamanship; Kadachan, the son of a Chilcat chief; John, a Stickeen, who acted as interpreter; and Sitka Charley."

Their departure from Wrangell was not a happy scene. There were, as Muir said, a few domestic difficulties. Toyatte's wife wept bitterly for fear he would be killed by his enemies and Kadachan's mother accused Mr. Young of talking her son into going on a dangerous voyage among unfriendly tribes. "If my son comes not back," she said, "on you will be his blood, and you shall pay." Needless to say, no one wished them a bon voyage.

The crew's main concern was crossing Frederick Sound so late in the season and they spoke of it repeatedly as they headed north up **Keku Strait**, which cuts between Kuiu and Kupreanof Islands. At the top end of Keku Strait, which is a winding, intricate channel strewn with reefs and used only by small craft, is the Tlingit village of **Kake**. In his book *Travels in Alaska*, Muir describes the Kakes of his day as "shrewd, industrious and rather good looking" but tragedy had befallen them a decade earlier when a Kake was shot by a Sitka sentry. In revenge, the Kakes murdered two traders from Sitka. The U.S. Government retaliated by shelling and destroying three of their villages. Differences were eventually resolved and in 1891 the government established a school at the present site of Kake. The band's traditional subsistence lifestyle has, over time, given way to logging, commercial fishing and working at the local cannery.

Mr. Young, the missionary travelling with Muir, was well received by the Kakes who had heard all about Reverend Duncan's success at Metlakatla. They too wanted the benefits of white man's knowledge "about God, and ships and guns and the growing of things to eat."

Meanwhile, the crossing of Frederick Sound awaited and Toyatte had been having sleepless nights in anticipation of this "broad water." Their canoe was "tossed like a bubble on the swells coming in from the ocean," but the wind was calm and they rounded Point Gardner without incident to proceed up Chatham Strait along the west side of **Admiralty Island.**

A humpback whale feeds in Stephens Passage.

In 1978 Admiralty Island was granted monument status. Two years later, close to 95 percent of the island's 1,500 square miles became a designated wilderness area called Kotznoowoo – the island's Tlingit name meaning 'Fortress of the Bears.' The Tlingit village of Angoon and some mining interests at the north end of the island lie outside the monument, but the rest of this forested land belongs to the numerous brown bears and Sitka blacktail deer who live here.

The Forest Service manages a bear viewing sanctuary at Pack Creek in the **Seymour Canal**, on the east side of Admiralty Island, and visitor permits control the number of people who come here in late summer to view the salmon-feeding bears from either a spit or a tower farther up the creek. Seymour Canal also supports a high concentration of bald eagles and offshore, in the waters of Stephens Passage, whales and seals are plentiful.

On the return leg of their late-season trip to Glacier Bay, Muir's party came back along Stephens Passage and nearly ran into a humpback whale in the dark, at first mistaking its smooth round back for a rock. Humpback whales are a frequent sight in Stephens Passage. They come here each summer to feed and they remain until early autumn. At night, when the air is still, the thunderclap sound of their tails smacking the water can be heard in distant bays.

A daylight trip along Stephens Passage is one filled with natural wonders. Shimmering icefields grace the mainland mountains, floating ice sculptures drift down the wide channel and humpback whales blow puffs of mist into the air as they feed near the water's surface.

Halfway along Stephens Passage lies a dramatic inlet containing two fjords – Endicott Arm and **Tracy Arm**. They each branch into the mainland mountains for a distance of 25 miles before reaching the retreating glaciers that carved them. Muir explored both these arms the following summer, in 1880, when they were not yet named or even shown on Captain Vancouver's chart – a copy of which Muir was using. Vancouver's chart did show **Holkham Bay** at the entrance to the two fjords. Muir refers to this bay as Sum Dum – the Tlingit name for the glacier-covered mountain overlooking it.

A gold mining camp was located beside the large stream into which the Sum Dum Glacier drains. Muir came upon these prospectors the previous fall and noted at the time how evasive they were. He suspected they had discovered placer gold in the glacier's moraine and didn't want the news to spread. Muir was interested not in gold but in the beauty of nature, while Mr. Young was looking not for riches but for souls to save. As for Muir's new crew on this second trip – Captain Tyeen, Hunter Joe and Smart Billy – they just wanted to save their canoe from being crushed by the ice that clogged Endicott Arm.

They carefully picked their way through the thick ice to the head of the fjord, spotting along the way flocks of wild goats high on the mountain ledges. After 14-1/2 hours of paddling, Muir and his native guides reached the terminus of North Dawes Glacier. A few chunks of ice fell off the front, raising a cloud of spray, and Tyeen said to Muir, "The ice mountain is well disposed toward you. He is firing his big guns to welcome you."

They camped for the night on a rock shelf and next morning they investigated a canyon of water that was later named **Ford's Terror** for a man who, in 1889, rowed through its narrow entrance at slack tide. The water was as still as a pond when he rowed in. Then the tide started running and he was trapped inside for six hours, while his boat was pushed about by swift currents and battered by chunks of ice sweeping towards the bottleneck entrance.

Muir also explored Tracy Arm, tracing the twisting fjord to its head. Again it took a full day to reach the tidewater glacier and that night Muir pitched his tent on a boulder-covered shore while his guides remained in the canoe to prevent it from being crushed by drifting ice. Muir was awakened "by the beating of the spent ends of berg-waves against the side of my tent."

When a large chunk of ice falls into the water, it sends waves fanning outward until they hit the steep-sided shores of the inlet and rebound. When these rebounding waves collide with the initial waves, they create erratic seas which set the ice pack into motion. Small vessels must be careful not to get too close to a glacier that is actively discharging ice in case they get caught in a churning ice pack. Harbor seals raise their pups on these icepacks, which are relatively safe from predators. Whenever a wave surges through an icepack, seals lounging on the floes will slowly rise with the swell as if nonchalantly enjoying the ride.

Tracy Arm is less than a mile wide throughout most of its length, its cliffed walls rising 2,000 feet into the sky. Clinging to the schist and granite rock are moss, scrub and spruce trees. Hanging falls plunge down these steep sides into water a thousand feet deep and milky green in color, due to suspended sediments in the glacial runoff.

A retreating tidewater glacier will leave behind an end moraine of silt and stones beneath the water. The shallow bars at the mouths of Tracy Arm and Endicott Arm are the end moraines of their glaciers, and mariners entering either fjord use navigational markers to line themselves up with a gap in the bar, through which they can safely pilot their vessels.

The situation is quite different in **Taku Inlet** (at the top of Stephens Passage) where Taku Glacier, fed by the massive **Juneau Icefield**, is advancing seaward. This tidewater glacier is not losing any ice, however, because its snout has pushed up a ridge of sediment – called a push moraine – which prevents the ice from calving (dropping off into the water). If Taku Glacier continues tunneling its way across Taku Inlet at its current pace of a few hundred feet per year, in three or four decades Taku Inlet will be closed off from Stephens Passage, becoming a glacier-dammed lake.

An arm of Taku Glacier called Hole in the Wall, also flows into Taku Inlet. This tributary was formed in 1940 when part of the glacier jumped the valley wall and found its own way down to the sea.

The Taku River extends from the head of Taku Inlet and this river valley has been considered a potential highway route linking the city of Juneau with the interior road systems of British Columbia. But uncertainty about Taku Glacier's behavior makes construction of a road here a risky proposition.

Glacier-fed waterfalls stream down the sheer, rock walls of Tracy Arm.

Taku Inlet was the last mainland inlet examined and charted by Captain Vancouver's officers in the course of their three-year survey. In the words of the expedition's botanist, Archibald Menzies, the survey party found Taku Inlet "surrounded by a range of high steep rugged mountains covered with perpetual snow almost down to the water's edge." The ice-choked inlet held no promise of an inland waterway and the men, unable to land their boats, headed back to Stephens Passage in wind-driven sleet.

The Little Ice Age was just ending when Captain Vancouver's ships sailed these waters in 1794, and the weather was more inclement than today. The **Gastineau Channel** – upon the shores of which Juneau would eventually be founded – was also clogged with ice back then. The channel is today unnavigable at its north end because of shallow waters created by the Mendenhall River delta.

Gastineau Channel lies along a fault (a fracture in the earth's crust) and when ice covered this entire area it ground away the weakened bedrock of the Gastineau fault. These sediments, both coarse and fine grained, ended up as surface material covering much of the Juneau-Douglas area.

In 1880, on the south shore of Gastineau Channel, gold particles were discovered on the beach. The following year Pierre "French Pete" Eurrusard sold his lode claim to John Treadwell. A mine was built and the Treadwell mining complex eventually became the largest in the world, extracting more than $70 million worth of gold out of the metamorphosed rock.

Juneau, nestled at the base of mountains along Gastineau Channel, began as a collection of shacks built by gold prospectors.

Meanwhile, on the other side of the Gastineau Channel, two down-and-out prospectors named Richard Harris and Joe Juneau were looking for gold in Silverbow Basin. They had been hired by a German mining engineer named George Pilz of Sitka, who was offering a reward of 100 Hudson's Bay blankets to anyone who could show them where a substantial deposit of gold-bearing ore existed. In October 1880, a Tlingit named Kowee led Juneau and Harris up Gold Creek to Quartz Gulch – so named by Harris when he saw the quartz veins of this metamorphic rock. They contained more brilliant streaks of gold than he had ever before seen in one gulch.

Claims were quickly staked and within a year the number of prospectors camped in shacks on Gastineau Channel near Gold Creek was large enough to form a small town. Mining companies took over after the prospectors, who had found nuggets as big as beans, cleaned out the placer gold. Between 1881 and World War II, the Juneau Gold Belt yielded 6.7 million ounces of gold and 3.1 million ounces of silver. The last of three major mines closed in 1944 but a Canadian company called Echo Bay Alaska has since sought approval to reopen the Alaska-Juneau mine.

The Juneau Gold Belt extends south of Juneau to Holkham and Windham Bays. The prospectors whom John Muir encountered at the base of the Sum Dum Glacier were indeed panning the stream gravels for gold that had been washed downstream from the mountain's ore-bodies. The Sumdum Mine eventually produced close to half a million dollars in gold and silver before closing in 1903.

A Juneau street mural opposite Marine Park reflects the area's Tlingit history.

*The view of Gastineau Channel from Mt. Roberts takes in the
Juneau waterfront and Douglas Island lying opposite.*

At the turn of the century, Alaska's capital was moved from declining Sitka to the bustling new city of **Juneau**. Whaling and fur trading –
once a thriving industry at Sitka – were on the way out; gold rushes
were in. In addition to its lucrative gold mining operations, Juneau was
on the steamer route to the gold-rich Klondike in Canada's Yukon territory.

In 1906 the governor's office was transferred from Sitka to Juneau
and six years later the governor's mansion was built. Construction of
the capitol building was completed in 1930 and Alaska was granted
statehood in 1959. Juneau has remained the capital despite complaints
that the city is not accessible by road and that a location near the major
population centers of Anchorage and Fairbanks would make more
sense. Government jobs – at the city, state and federal levels – provide
50 percent of Juneau's employment, so whenever a 'move-the-capital'
campaign surfaces, the resisting residents of Juneau make their stand on
the issue perfectly clear.

Juneau, with a population of 30,000, is the largest city in Southeast
Alaska, and home port to one of the state's largest fishing fleets with
over a thousand boats docking here year round. The mining industry is
also showing signs of revival, but tourism is the leading private-sector
industry in Juneau. Each summer half a million cruise passengers visit
Juneau, a major port of call for ships sailing the Inside Passage. They
pull into Gastineau Channel, which is Juneau's major waterway and a
source of entertainment for Juneau residents who can watch live cover-
age of its activities on a local cable TV station. The cable company first
ran footage of Gastineau Channel as a filler during a technical glitch,

The pioneer past has been retained in several heritage buildings located on Franklin Street, Juneau's main shopping strip.

but the soothing footage of maritime traffic became so popular with local residents, the cable network decided not to bump it for commercial programming.

Despite Juneau's urbanization, wilderness remains right at the town's doorstep. Eagles, perched on power poles, are a common sight and black bears frequently show up in the downtown area where they risk being hit by motorists or destroyed by authorities. Bears who lose their fear of humans are often dangerous and improperly-disposed-of garbage is what attracts them to areas of human habitation.

There was a happy ending for one bear who came to town. An orphaned cub, she fended for herself in the woods near Bartlett Memorial Hospital. Then one day she admitted herself to the hospital by climbing onto a trash receptacle outside the Emergency Department. "Bartlett" was quickly transferred to Bear Country USA in South Dakota, leaving behind one of Juneau's best bear tales.

JUNEAU ATTRACTIONS

In terms of area, Juneau is a sprawling city, but the downtown area is fairly compact. Right on the cruise ship dock is a small building where you'll find **Juneau's Visitor Information** *i*. A visitor information

Franklin Street fills with shoppers when cruise ships arrive in port. (Below) St. Nicholas Orthodox Church was built in 1894.

kiosk is also situated in waterfront **Marine Park** **1**. Nearby are sculptures commemorating Juneau's pioneer miners, the USS *Juneau* and Patsy Ann – an English Bull terrier and local celebrity who lived at the long-shoremen's hall in the 1930s and '40s, and spent her days greeting steamship passengers. Also on the waterfront is the Naa Kahidi Theater, a clan-house style theater where performers dramatize tradi-tional native legends. It is located in the **Cultural Arts Park** **2** adjacent to the Alaska Native Artists Market. Not to be missed is the **Mount Roberts Tramway** **3** which whisks visitors 2,000 feet above the harbor to an observatory offering panoramic views of Juneau and area. Forest trails lead from the restaurant/theater com-plex to colorful alpine meadows.

*The Mount Roberts tramway provides spectacular views and the
opportunity to hike through an alpine meadow.*

Back on the cruise dock, it's a short walk to Franklin and Front
Streets. Shopping streets, they are lined with historic buildings such as
the restored Alaskan Hotel & Bar which first opened in 1913 and,
across the street at 174 S. Franklin, the turreted Alaska Steam Laundry
Building, built in 1901. At 202 Front Street you'll find the elegant
Valentine Building, built in 1914 by a local jeweller and long-time
mayor.

The **Red Dog Saloon 4** is one of the first landmark buildings to
your left if you're walking up South Franklin Street from the cruise
ship dock. This building is not historic
but is a popular attraction because of the
selection of Alaska draft beer and good-
humored pioneer atmosphere inside.

A post office is located on Seward, not
far from the main **Juneau Visitor
Information Centre i** which is housed
in the **Davis Log Cabin 5**, a replica of
Juneau's first public school. One block

*Sawdust-covered floors and a friendly
bartender greet visitors to the Red Dog
Saloon, many of whom step inside just
to see what it looks like.*

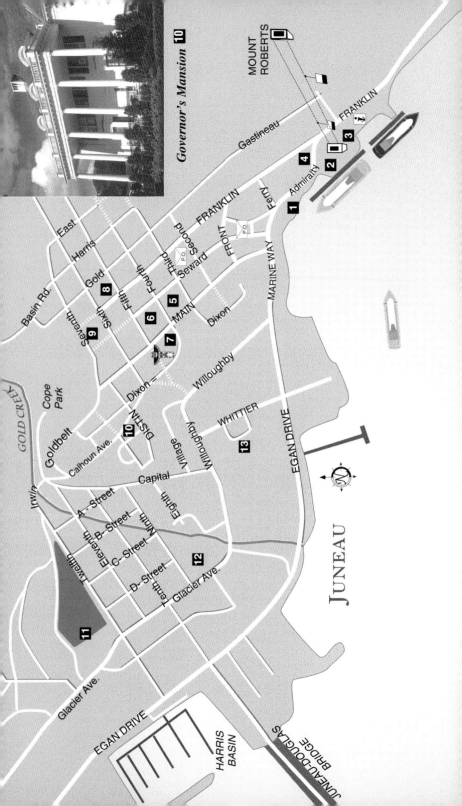

Governor's Mansion **10**

MOUNT ROBERTS

JUNEAU

up from here, on Fourth, is the **Alaska State Capitol** 6. It was built as the Federal & Territorial Building in 1930 and while it does not have the traditional domed roof of a capitol, it does have an impressive facade of Tokeen marble columns. The ground floor lobby, decorated in blue and gilt, houses an information desk for visitors interested in taking a guided tour. Across from the Capitol, on Main and Fourth, is the **Juneau-Douglas City Museum** 7 with displays that capture the city's gold mining era.

On Fifth and Gold, about three blocks from the State Capitol, is the **St. Nicholas Orthodox Church** 8, built in 1894 – nearly 30 years after Russia sold Alaska to the United States. Although the majority of Russian priests left Alaska at the time of the sale in 1867, they soon regrouped and began returning under the terms of the Treaty of Cession which guaranteed freedom of religion and allowed the Orthodox Church to retain its property and continue its mission in Alaska.

Gold Street leads up to Seventh Avenue where the **Wickersham House** 9 is also open to the public. James Wickersham was a pioneer judge who came to Alaska in 1900. He travelled throughout much of interior Alaska – by sternwheeler in summer and dogsled in winter – and delivered justice to goldmining settlements along the Yukon River.

A respected judge, Wickersham was also a consummate politician who strove tirelessly for Alaska's territorial status, which was granted in 1912. He introduced the first statehood bill four years later and won congressional approval for the establishment of Mount McKinley (now Denali) National Park in 1917. Judge Wickersham spent his final years in Juneau and the house in which he lived is furnished with such items as his 1904 gramophone and his Chickering concert piano, previously owned by the Russian government in Sitka.

Outside the Wickersham House, stairs lead back down to Fifth Avenue, as does Main Street – one block over. A right-hand turn onto Fifth will take you across a pedestrian bypass on your way to the **Governor's Mansion** 10 at the corner of Calhoun and Distin. Built in a colonial style and fronted with white pillars, it's the biggest house in the neighborhood and has a totem pole standing out front. The mansion is the official residence of Alaska's governor and is open for viewing only by advance special request. The one exception is at Christmastime when Juneau residents line up to receive a handshake and cookies from the governor and his wife.

If you follow Calhoun Street up the hillside and across Gold Creek, you'll come to the **Evergreen Cemetery** 11, where the prospectors Joe Juneau and Richard Harris are buried near the east end of the grave-yard. At the other end, off Glacier Avenue, is a monument to their Tlingit guide Kowee. Also buried here are some of those who died in 1918 when the *Princess Sophia* sank off Vanderbilt Reef in Lynn Canal. Near here is the Alaska State Ferry ticket office and the fishboat

The lovely home of James Wickersham, a pioneer judge, is now a museum.

harbors. A few blocks down Glacier Avenue, at the corner of Ninth, is the **Federal Building** 🄄. Outside is a bronze sculpture depicting pelicans. It was, according to local tour guides, intended for the Federal Building in Florida but a mix-up in shipping orders sent the eagle sculpture to Florida and the pelicans to Alaska. Florida decided to keep the eagle sculpture, the rationale being that eagles have been sighted there. But, as Juneau residents are fond of saying, these are the only pelicans you're going to see in Alaska.

As for eagle exhibits, you'll find a wonderful one in the **Alaska State Museum** 🄅. To reach this major attraction, carry on down Glacier Avenue, across Gold Creek and proceed along Willoughby to Whittier. Located to the right off Whittier, the State Museum features travelling collections from around the world in addition to its permanent exhibits on wildlife (the highlight of which is an eagle-nesting tree), native culture (the famous Lincoln totem pole is here) and Alaska's Russian heritage.

OUT-OF-TOWN ATTRACTIONS

Gold panning and salmon bakes along **Gold Creek** are popular with visitors to Juneau, as is the coach trip to **Mendenhall Glacier** – the state's most-visited glacier. A pretty stop along the way is the **Auke Lake Chapel**. Built of spruce logs, it overlooks the lake with Mendenhall Glacier in the distance.

A visit to Mendenhall Glacier is, for many people, their first lesson in how glaciers are formed and behave. The Visitor Center is equipped with books, pamphlets, videotapes and a model display to help explain glacial dynamics. A theater features a videotape on the Mendenhall Glacier and Juneau Icefield, and staff are there to answer any questions.

Outside, nature trails lead to various viewing points. Because Mendenhall Glacier has been retreating about 25 to 30 feet per year since 1750, a half mile of lake water now lies between the Visitor Center and the front of the glacier. The water of Mendenhall Lake reaches 200 feet in depth while the height of the glacier's terminus (snout) is 100 feet above lake level. One and a half miles wide at its snout, Mendenhall Glacier is 12 miles in length and its measured rate of flow is two feet per day. Based on these calculations, the ice at its terminus is about 150 years old.

Another way to view the Mendenhall Glacier is by helicopter. Not only do you get a close look at its icescape of pinnacles and crevasses, you get to walk on its brittle surface. The helicopter will find a safe spot to land and a guide will take you right to the edge of a deep crevasse.

Visitors to Juneau can try their hand at gold panning.

Other helicopter tours cover not only the Mendenhall Glacier but some of the other hanging and valley glaciers of the vast Juneau Icefield. Floatplane tours also whisk passengers over the icefield. Below the plane's wings you'll see craggy peaks all but buried in ice and snow, and valleys filled with pinnacles of blue ice.

One popular flightseeing excursion takes you over the Juneau Icefield to Taku Inlet where you land on a river in front of the historic **Taku Lodge**. Built of logs in 1923, this rustic lodge is well known for its delicious salmon bakes and spectacular vistas, all enjoyed in a peaceful, forested setting.

Other excursions available in Juneau are sportfishing in the area's bountiful waters, golfing on a course with views of the Mendenhall Glacier, and rafting down the Mendenhall River. The **Gastineau Salmon Hatchery** is usually included with coach tours to Mendenhall Glacier. Visitors to the hatchery will learn how salmon spawn and can view different species of fish swimming in the saltwater aquariums.

The **Last Chance Mining Museum**, situated just outside town at the Jualpa Mine Camp National Historic District, reopened in 1996 after being closed for decades.

Helicopter excursions to Mendenhall Glacier provide an up-close look at a glacier.

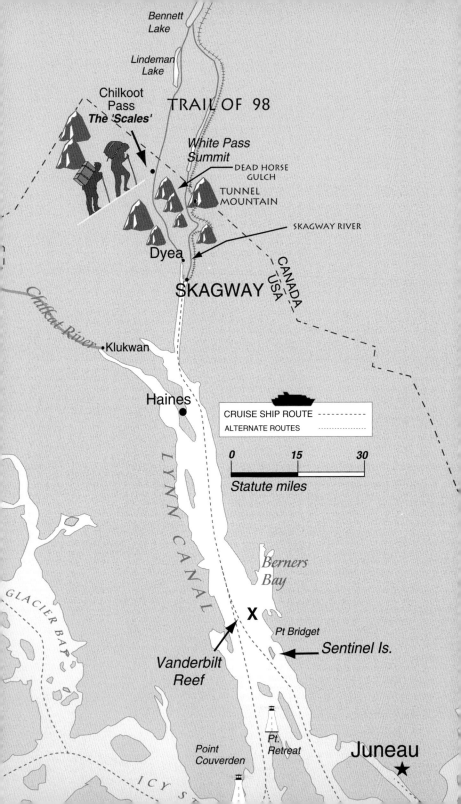

Bennett
Lake

Lindeman
Lake

Chilkoot
Pass
The 'Scales'

TRAIL OF 98

*White Pass
Summit*

DEAD HORSE
GULCH

TUNNEL
MOUNTAIN

SKAGWAY RIVER

Dyea

SKAGWAY

CANADA
USA

Chilkat River

• Klukwan

Haines

CRUISE SHIP ROUTE - - - - -
ALTERNATE ROUTES ·········

LYNN CANAL

0   15   30

Statute miles

*Berners
Bay*

X

Pt Bridget

*Vanderbilt
Reef*

Sentinel Is.

GLACIER BAY

Point
Couverden

Pt.
Retreat

Juneau

★

ICY ST

SKAGWAY

Captain Vancouver must have been particularly homesick while surveying **Lynn Canal**. Not only did he name Point Couverden at its western entrance for his ancestral home in the Netherlands, he also named Berners Bay and Point Bridget for his mother – Bridget Berners. The inlet itself is named for Vancouver's birthplace of King's Lynn in Norfolk, England. This nostalgic naming of landmarks took place in the summer of 1794, during Vancouver's third and last season on this coast. His health was failing and he no longer joined his officers in the open boats as they ventured up the last few winding channels and twisting fjords still unexplored in their search for an inland waterway.

Homesick as Vancouver and his men no doubt were by this point in their lengthy voyage, the Tlingits who lived here were quite at home. Their main village of **Klukwan** was located at the mouth of the **Chilkat River** near the head of Lynn Canal. Not only was the Chilkat River a fine salmon stream, its valley was also a trade route to the interior, where the vast Athapaskan region extended across much of the continent to Hudson Bay in northern Canada.

When explorers of Britain's Hudson's Bay Company began building forts on the western edges of Athapaskan territory, they came face to face with Tlingit tribes. Travelling upriver from their coastal villages, the Tlingits were not pleased to encounter white men invading their fur trade territory. Robert Campbell, a rugged Scotsman hired by the HBC to explore the rivers flowing westward, experienced his first taste of Tlingit hospitality on a tributary of the Stikine River in 1838. The Stikine Tlingits, under the leadership of Chief Shakes (one in a series of powerful leaders bearing that name), came close to murdering Campbell.

Ten years later, an undeterred Campbell took possession of lands at the junction of the Pelly and Yukon rivers by blazing "HBCo." on a tree. Here he built **Fort Selkirk** and found he no longer had to deal with the Stikine Tlingits but with an even more fearful tribe – the Chilkats of Lynn Canal, who finally attacked the fort in August, 1852. Campbell was again nearly murdered but managed to survive the brawl. The fort was not so lucky. Abandoned by Campbell and his handful of men, it was quickly demolished by the Chilkats for its nails and ironwork.

Skagway is beautifully situated in a valley at the head of Lynn Canal.

While Campbell and other HBC explorers were pushing westward into the **Yukon River** territory, the Russians were venturing inland from the river's mouth. Almost 2,000 miles in length, the Yukon River winds across Alaska, reaching the Arctic Circle before bending south-eastward through Canada's Yukon to culminate at Bennett Lake, 50 miles north of Skagway. The Russians, travelling east along this great river, never did reach its terminus. In fact, not until 1863 did a Russian trader penetrate inland as far as Fort Yukon at the junction of the Yukon and Porcupine Rivers.

As the fur trade began running out of steam, gold prospectors started trickling into the Yukon area. In 1874 a prospector/trader named Jack McQuestion built Fort Reliance, just north of where **Dawson City** would eventually sit at the junction of the Klondike and Yukon Rivers. Fort Reliance had its ups and downs as a trading post, controlled by fluctuations in local trade, but it became a reference point for tributaries

flowing into the Yukon River, i.e. Twelve Mile River, Sixty Mile River and Seventy Mile River. **Forty Mile**, which is actually 46 miles downstream from Fort Reliance, became the largest settlement in the Yukon when gold was discovered in near-by tributaries in 1886. Miners from Alaska and the Yukon converged on

Turn-of-the-century hotels and saloons attest to Skagway's gold rush history.

Vintage car tours and false fronted board-walk buildings are part of Skagway's colorful past.

Forty Mile, which was the main supply base for the area. The trickle of prospectors was now a steady flow but the flood was yet to come.

The miners' law of those times is reflected in a notice that was posted downriver at **Circle City**, Alaska :

TO WHOM IT MAY CONCERN: At a general meeting of miners held in Circle City it was the unanimous verdict that all thieving and stealing shall be punished by whipping at the post and banishment from the country, the severity of the whipping and the guilt of the accused to be determined by the jury.

Frontier justice worked well and peace generally prevailed. Bush cabins were left unlocked and stocked with firewood. Failure to replace this fuel was a major offense, for the next visitor might arrive so cold and exhausted that only an instant fire could save his life.

Miners' meetings were usually held in saloons and if a jail was needed at the conclusion of a hearing, one was quickly constructed. At Circle City, a notice on the jail's door stated that "All prisoners must report by 9 o'clock p.m., or they will be locked out for the night." When Judge James Wickersham arrived in the American part of the Yukon River valley and introduced himself to one old sourdough as

Arctic Brotherhood Hall, with a driftwood facade, was built in 1899.

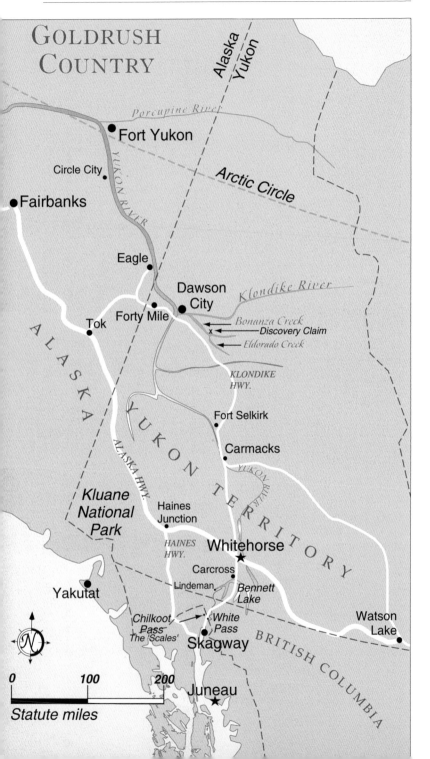

GOLDRUSH
COUNTRY

Alaska
Yukon

Porcupine River

● Fort Yukon

Circle City

Arctic Circle

● Fairbanks

YUKON RIVER

Eagle ●

Dawson
City ●

Klondike River

Tok ●
Forty Mile ●

Bonanza Creek
x
Discovery Claim

Eldorado Creek

KLONDIKE
HWY.

ALASKA

YUKON

ALASKA HWY.

● Fort Selkirk

● Carmacks

YUKON RIVER

Kluane
National
Park

Haines
Junction

TERRITORY

HAINES
HWY.

Whitehorse ★

Carcross ●

Yakutat ●

Lindeman ●
Bennett
Lake

Watson
Lake ●

Chilkoot
Pass
The 'Scales'

White
Pass

Skagway ●

BRITISH COLUMBIA

0   100   200

Statute miles

Juneau ★

"the district judge of the Territory of Alaska" the response was "Oh, the hell you are!"

While the boom towns of Forty Mile and Circle City attracted men and women in search of gold, a different sort of white man was roaming the Yukon River area. His name was **George Washington Carmack.** Born in California, he had witnessed gold fever as a teenager when his father joined California's stampede of 1849. When Carmack arrived in Alaska as a dishwasher on a Juneau-bound steamer, he did not pursue the riches of gold but instead adopted the native way of life.

The Yukon prospectors called him Siwash George. He married a native woman and lived off the land with her people. His closest companions were his brother-in-law, **Skookum Jim**, and another native called **Tagish Charlie**. Jim was a large and powerful man, skilled at hunting and trapping, while Charlie was of smaller stature but gracefully at ease in the wilderness.

In July of 1896, Carmack headed upstream from Forty Mile to the **Klondike River** to do some salmon fishing. There he was joined by Jim, Charlie and his wife Kate. The salmon run was poor, so the men decided to cut timber and sell it to the sawmill at Forty Mile. Jim headed up the Klondike to check out its timber, then turned off at a brook named **Rabbit Creek** which he followed until he found a good stand of spruce. He noticed flecks of gold in the stream and reported this to the others back at camp, but the matter was quickly forgotten.

A cairn marks the spot on Bonanza Creek where gold was found in 1896, triggering the Kondike Gold Rush. (Below) William Moore built Skagway's first cabin ten years before stampeders began arriving in July 1897.

Visitors to Skagway relive the excitement of the Klondike gold rush when they board the White Pass Railway and travel the Trail of '98 to the summit.

Then, a few weeks later, a veteran prospector named Robert Henderson (from Canada's east coast) arrived at Carmack's camp. He was prospecting an upstream tributary of the Klondike which showed promise. He shared this information with Carmack but displayed contempt for his native friends. When Carmack and his pals showed up at Henderson's camp a few days later, they weren't impressed with the stream's prospects nor Henderson's unfriendly attitude toward Jim and Charlie.

They soon left, but ran out of dried salmon on their return trip and stopped to hunt. Jim set off with his .44 Winchester and shot a moose which he butchered and cooked beside Rabbit Creek while awaiting the other two men. At one point he knelt beside the creek to take a drink of water and there in the creek bed's gravel was more raw gold than he had ever before seen.

When the other two arrived and Jim told them about his find, their reaction was in keeping with the occasion. Carmack, staring down at the glistening gold, first rubbed his eyes then reached down and picked up a dime-sized nugget which he put between his teeth and bit on. Charlie grabbed a pan and shovel and almost fell into the creek in his excitement. Carmack grabbed the shovel from Charlie and dug into the loose bedrock. He later described the raw gold as "laying thick between the flaky slabs, like cheese sandwiches." With a full pan of gold and gravel, Carmack set it on the ground and the three men danced around it, performing a combination of "Scottish hornpipe, Indian fox trot, syn-copated Irish jig and a sort of a Siwash Hula-Hula."

The next morning Carmack blazed with an axe this message on a spruce tree:

TO WHOM IT MAY CONCERN: I do, this day, locate and claim, by right of discovery, five hundred feet, running up stream from this notice. Located this 17th day of August, 1896.

G. W. Carmack

Under Canadian mining law, a prospector was allowed only one 500-foot claim per creek, except for the man recording the discovery who could stake two claims. All subsequent claims were then num-bered in relation to the discovery claim. At Rabbit Creek – promptly renamed **Bonanza Creek** by Carmack – the discovery claim was shared by Carmack and Jim, but registered in the former's name. Carmack also claimed Number One Below (downstream) while Jim claimed Number One Above (upstream) and Charlie claimed Number Two Below.

When Carmack returned to Forty Mile to register his claim at the mining recorder's office, he decided to stop first at Bill McPhee's saloon. He ordered a couple of drinks at the bar – to calm himself down – then turned to face the crowded, smoky room full of miners. "Boys," he said, "I've got some good news to tell you. There's a big strike up the river." This announcement fell on skeptical ears, for Carmack had a reputation for telling tall tales. In the words of some, he was "the all-firedest liar of the Yukon." But when he held up the gold he had just scooped from Bonanza Creek, everyone believed their eyes – if not their ears.

Carmack didn't bother telling Henderson – the prospector who had snubbed Jim and Charlie – about the Bonanza strike. By the time Henderson heard the news, the entire Bonanza Creek had already been staked by the miners from Forty Mile. Also staked was a smaller creek flowing into Bonanza Creek. This "pup" was christened Eldorado when its initial samplings showed promise.

Within a month of Carmack's discovery, 200 claims were staked on the Bonanza and its tributaries. But no one knew which claims would produce gold and which ones were "skunks." Luck determined whether a man struck it rich. A **cheechako** (newcomer) was as likely to hit pay dirt as a **sourdough** (seasoned miner). All each man could do was start working his claim and hope for the best.

Throughout the winter of 1896/97, men of varied backgrounds and nationalities dug into the Klondike's creek beds with picks and shovels. Malnourished and dirty, many suffered from scurvey. They slept in ramshackle huts where lice thrived in their unwashed bedding. But all were driven by gold fever as they scraped away the surface muck and burned fires to thaw the frozen ground to remove gravel covering the

***An Alaska Steamship, loaded with passengers bound for the
Klondike, heads up Lynn Canal.***

bedrock. Upon hitting bedrock, the pay gravel was removed by tun-
nelling into the side of the creek bank (drifting) and hauling the gravel
out with a hand-turned windlass. This was done in winter, when permafrost elminated the need to shore the shafts and drifts with timbers.
When warmer weather arrived and the ground softened, cave-ins
became a problem.

This dangerous and backbreaking work continued until spring when
meltwater was used for sluicing the piles of bedrock gravel. A sluice is
a series of inclined boxes with riffles on the bottom. As the water
washed the gravel away, the pieces of gold would fall to the bottom of
the boxes and remain trapped there by the riffles.

When the prospectors on Bonanza Creek and its tributaries finished
sluicing their claims in the early summer of 1897, many were rich men.
With their moosehide pokes and pickle jars filled with gold, they boarded two stern-wheelers in Dawson and headed down the Yukon to the
old Russian port of St. Michael. There they transferred onto two
steamships – the Excelsior bound for San Francisco and the Portland
bound for Seattle.

The Excelsior reached San Francisco one day before the Portland
pulled into Seattle – where a throng of spectators and news reporters
was waiting to greet the miners as they filed off the ship with their bags
and boxes of gold. People wanted to see and hear and touch these
stoop-shouldered, weather-beaten men who had struck it rich in the
Klondike.

During the winter of 1897-1898, thousands of stampeders ascended the Chilkoot Trail on their way to the Klondike. Above is the final part of the ascent known as 'The Scales'.

Gold fever swept the continent and the world. Men and women rushed to the Klondike, stopping at San Francisco, Seattle, Victoria or Vancouver to outfit themselves before heading north. Those who could afford the passage took a steamer to St. Michael, then a paddlewheeler up the Yukon. Others ascended the Stikine and Alsek Rivers or hiked from Edmonton, Alberta through boggy, mosquito-infested wilderness. The majority, however, headed up Lynn Canal to **Skagway**.

In the early summer of 1897, only one family lived in Skagway. William Moore, a former riverboat captain and prospector, had anticipated a gold rush to the Yukon and constructed a cabin and wharf here ten years earlier. But when the first shipload of prospectors arrived at the 'Mooresville' wharf on July 26, 1897, the surveyors who spilled off the steamer ignored Moore's homesteading claim and quickly laid out a new town which they called Skaguay. The spelling of this Tlingit name (its meaning open to interpretation) was changed to Skagway when a post office was established.

Saloons and brothels were quickly constructed and a boom town was born. Moore, who owned a sawmill and warehouse in addition to the wharf, prospered. However, **Soapy Smith** and his gang of con men soon controlled the town's activities and Superintendent Sam Steele of the Northwest Mounted Police called it "the roughest place in the world…little better than hell on earth."

Three miles away, at the mouth of the Taiya River, was a small trading post and village of about 250 Chilkoot natives. Called **Dyea**, it

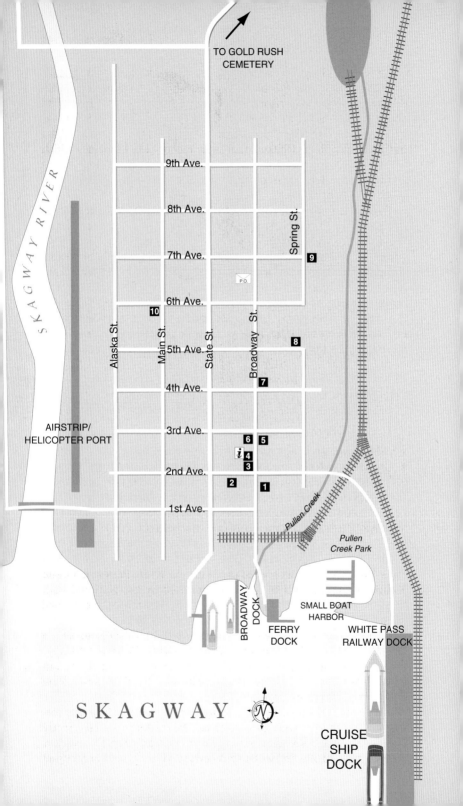

competed with Skagway for the gold rush trade. Most prospectors landed at Skagway but set off for the goldfields from Dyea via the 33-mile
Chilkoot Trail – the 'poor man's route' over the mountains to the
Yukon River's headwaters. The **White Pass**, which starts at Skagway,
was used by those who had could afford pack horses. The White Pass
trail links up with the Chilkoot trail at the foot of Lake Lindemen which
flows via a narrow rocky stream into **Lake Bennett**. It's estimated that
30,000 stampeders crossed the Chilkoot by these two routes, now
called the **'Trail of '98.'**

Overnight stops (tent cities) dotted the 30-mile Chilkoot trail, with
stampeders moving their goods in five-mile relays between caches. It
could take 20 trips back and forth to cover each leg of the journey. In
winter, sledges made hauling supplies a bit easier. At the **Summit**, the
stampeders crossed into Canadian territory. Those without a year's supply of food were turned back by the Mounties.

The majority of stampeders reached lakes Lindeman and Bennett in
the spring of 1898 where they waited for the ice to melt. When the ice
on Lake Bennett broke up on May 29, a flotilla of stampeders set sail
down the hazardous Yukon River on their makeshift rafts. A number of
these unseaworthy craft capsized and stampeders drowned in the cold
churning waters of **Miles Canyon** and **White Horse Rapids**. The
flotilla pressed on, traversing 500 miles of swift-flowing river to arrive,
in mid-June, at Dawson City. At last, they had reached the Klondike.

SKAGWAY ATTRACTIONS

A visitor to Skagway will have no trouble reliving the excitement of the
Klondike Gold Rush. Each summer, more than 300,000 people visit
this town, which has a year-round population of about 750. Some days,
four or five cruise ships are in port at the same time. A short walking
tour is a must in Skagway and, with an average annual precipitation of
less than 29 inches, a typical summer day here is warm and sunny –
perfect for strolling the town's historic streets.

Near the cruise ship docks, at the foot of Broadway, is the **National
Park Visitor Center 1** housed inside the old **White Pass and Yukon
Railroad Depot**, built in 1898 and restored by the National Park
Service. Here you'll find information on the town's attractions and
activities.

A block over from the Visitor Center is **Jeff Smith's Parlor 2** – a
saloon owned by Skagway's infamous Jefferson Randolph 'Soapy'
Smith, who led a gang of criminals that controlled the town. Smith was
killed in a shoot-out with surveyor Frank Reid on July 8, 1898. Reid
died later of his gunshot wounds.

On the next block you'll find the **Red Onion Saloon 3** at the corner of Broadway and 2nd Avenue. Next door is the **Arctic
Brotherhood Hall 4**, frequently featured in photographs. Its facade is
covered with 20,000 driftwood sticks collected and nailed to the front

*Skagway's
city hall
houses the
Trail of '98
Museum.*

of this 1899 building by an early lodge member. This restored building now houses a **Visitor Information Center** which is operated by the Skagway Convention & Visitors Bureau. Ask for a copy of their Walking Tour map which describes in detail the town's historic buildings and sites.

Some highlights of the walking tour are:

The **Mascot Saloon 5**, built in 1905 and restored for viewing by the National Park Service;

Golden North Hotel 6, built in 1908, and **St. James Hotel 7**, where in 1898 a British businessman and a Canadian railroad contractor hashed out a plan to build a railway over the White Pass;

Moore Cabin 8 – built by William Moore and his son in 1887;

Skagway City Hall 9 – built of stone in 1899 by the Methodist Church and now housing the **Trail of '98 Museum**.

A number of Skagway's old homes are also featured on the Walking Tour map, as is the **Blanchard Garden 10**. When the U.S. Army occupied Sitka during World War II, many of the local gardens were gravelled over but have since been revived, and every August the town holds a Gold Rush Garden Club contest.

Back on the waterfront, at the foot of State Street, is a marker showing where Frank Reid gunned down Soapy Smith on the evening of July 8, 1898. Reid and a few others were guarding the entrance to the Juneau Co. wharf where a mass meeting was being held to organize the townspeople against Soapy Smith and his gang of hoodlums.

On the east side of Skagway's waterfront is the **White Pass Railroad Dock**. Here passengers board the train's vintage parlor cars for a trip that retraces the 40-mile Trail of '98. Construction of this mountain-pass railroad was a massive challenge. Workers, suspended by ropes, chipped and blasted their way through the barriers of rock.

Accidents claimed lives and gold fever regularly swept through the work gangs, depleting their numbers.

Against tough odds, the narrow gauge railroad was completed in the summer of 1900 – after the big rush to the Klondike was over. The rail line transformed Skagway into a shipping port and during World War II thousands of army troops landed here during construction of the Alaska Highway. Shortly after the **Klondike Highway** (from Skagway to Whitehorse) was completed in 1978, the railroad was closed. However it was reopened in 1988 to provide summer passenger service.

The trip is a fascinating blend of dramatic scenery and history. As the train rolls out of Skagway, it passes the **Gold Rush Cemetery** – resting place of Soapy Smith and Frank Reid – then follows the river valley past glacier-fed waterfalls and overhanging rock ledges. The train slowly climbs from sea level to 2,865 feet at the Summit. Along the way, passengers get a close look at the **Glacier Gorge** chasm as the train steams across the abyss and into **Tunnel Mountain**. The ascent continues past **Inspiration Point** (with its mountaintop view of Lynn Canal) and **Dead Horse Gulch** (where 3,000 pack animals died of exhaustion from carrying heavy loads up the steep climb).

Another tunnel – Steel Bridge – is followed by a cliffside glimpse of the famous Trail of '98. Then it's over the **White Pass Summit**, where only those stampeders with a ton of supplies (enough for one

Canada's Mounties maintained law and order at Dawson City during the boom days of the Klondike Gold Rush. (Below) the grave marker of villain Soapy Smith, at the Gold Rush Cemetery.

A 'four ship' day at Skagway

winter) were waved on by the Mounties into Canada. This is the turn-around point for cruise passengers on a three-hour shore excursion.

On the other side of the Summit is **Fraser Station** where rail passengers bound for the Klondike clear Canadian Customs before the railcars continue their historic journey to Lake Bennett. Here, in the winter of 1897-98, close to 30,000 stampeders built rafts and, following the spring breakup, floated down the Yukon River to the Klondike gold fields.

Rail passengers bound for Whitehorse usually disembark at Fraser Station and transfer to motorcoaches. From here the Klondike Highway travels to **Carcross** – originally called Caribou Crossing – at the top of Lake Bennett where it flows into the Yukon River. The three natives with George Carmack when they discovered gold on Bonanza Creek – Skookum Jim, Tagish Charlie and George's wife Kate – are buried in the Carcross cemetery. **Whitehorse**, the capital of Canada's Yukon territory, takes its name from the nearby Whitehorse Falls. When stampeders travelled this treacherous section of the Yukon River, they said the frothy white water looked like a horse's mane.

From Whitehorse, the **Klondike Highway** continues along the Yukon River valley to **Dawson City**, which sprang to life in the summer of 1897. The Northwest Mounted Police, anticipating an onslaught of stampeders, built a fort here that first summer but in their haste they did a few things wrong. When clearing the land, they scraped away the moss covering the permafrost. This allowed the sun to melt the topsoil and the fort's foundations soon settled into a knee-deep morass. Also, green logs were used in construction and they began to shrink and warp. As buildings fell apart, the Mounties were kept busy reconstructing their fort when they weren't enforcing law and order among the 30,000 new residents of Dawson City.

Among these new arrivals was a young American prospector named **Jack London**. He lived only briefly in the Yukon but turned his experiences into masterful stories, including his famous novels *The Call of the Wild* (a bestseller in 1903) and *White Fang* (published in 1906). His cabin, built on Henderson Creek in 1899, has been moved to Dawson City and reconstructed to house the Jack London Interpretation Centre.

The Yukon's other famous writer was the British-born, Scottish-educated **Robert Service** who immigrated to Canada in 1894. He worked for the Bank of Commerce in Victoria and various branches in in British Columbia before he was eventually stationed at Dawson City. Service published his first collection of poems in 1907. Called *Songs of a Sourdough* (republished in 1916 as *The Spell of the Yukon*), this first volume included 'The Shooting of Dan McGrew.' His second volume – *Ballads of a Cheechako* – was published in 1909.

Service was heavily influenced by Rudyard Kipling and his poems about life as a gold prospector earned him a reputation as 'The Canadian Kipling' and 'The Poet of the Yukon.' His restored cabin is a major visitor attraction in Dawson City, where his poetry is recited twice daily throughout the summer.

Another popular attraction in Dawson City is **Diamond Tooth Gertie's Gambling Hall** – where the roulette wheel still spins and blackjack is played. At the **Palace Grand Theatre**, you can enjoy honky-tonk music and can-can dancing by the Gaslight Follies.

THE SOPHIA TRAGEDY

When the great gold rush died down in the Klondike, the prospectors gradually sold their claims to mining companies which continued mining the area's pay gravels with machinery. Each fall most of the miners, riverboat crew and others who worked in the Yukon would head south for the winter. On October 23, 1918, a full boatload of people coming out of the Klondike for the winter, boarded the ill-fated *Princess Sophia* (a CPR steamship) in Skagway.

Carrying 343 passengers and crew, the *Sophia* was heading down Lynn Canal in a snowstorm when, two hours past midnight, she grounded on **Vanderbilt Reef**. Her distress calls were answered by a variety of smaller vessels which stood by at dawn in choppy seas, waiting for the *Sophia* to transfer her passengers to the waiting vessels. But the seas were too rough to safely launch the small boats and the *Sophia*'s captain decided the passengers would be safer on board the stranded ship.

The next night, shrieking winds pushed the *Sophia* off Vanderbilt Reef and she plunged into the icy water. All 343 people on board drowned in the stormy seas. The only survivor was a dog that swam ashore. Most of the dead – their bodies found floating near the wreck or

Eight years before the tragic sinking of CPR's Princess Sophia *on Vanderbilt Reef, the* Princess May *grounded on nearby Sentinel Island but refloated with little damage.*

washed up on shore – were taken to Juneau, then shipped south to grieving relatives. Some were buried in Juneau's Evergreen Cemetery, including Walter Harper – the first man to set foot on Mount McKinley's summit.

HAINES (POP. 2,000)

While the Klondike gold rush was creating the boom towns of Dawson City and Skagway, another entrepeneur named **Jack Dalton** was trying to get a piece of the stampede action in Haines – 15 miles south of Skagway on the west side of Lynn Canal.

Haines was founded by the Presbyterian missionary Samuel Hall Young in 1880. He was given land for building a mission by the Chilkat natives whom he had visited with John Muir in 1879. So impressed were the Chilkat chiefs with Muir's brilliant oratory, they wanted him to run the mission but had to settle for Mr. Young, who named it after Mrs. F. E. Haines – chief fund raiser for the mission.

When Jack Dalton arrived at Haines, several canneries had been built and a wagon road wound its way from nearby Pyramid Harbor to the Yukon River, following roughly the route of today's Haines highway. He built a few posts along this trail, called it the Dalton Trail, and charged stampeders $2 per head of cattle and $2.50 per horse. Historic stops on the **Dalton Trail** include Glacier Camp – from which 26 glaciers can be seen – and the abandoned native village of Nasketahin, where traditional "spirit houses" stand in the local graveyard.

Haines may not have the colorful gold rush history of Skagway, but the town's beautiful setting – backed by the Cathedral Peaks of the Chilkat Mountains – attracted the movie producers of White Fang who filmed here in the winter of 1990. The local fairgrounds were converted into a gold rush town and locals were hired as extras.

The Chilkat tribe of Tlingits – once feared and respected by all – display their art, which includes the famous Chilkat blanket, at the **Center for the Arts** on the Fort Seward grounds. **Fort Seward** was built in 1903 during a border dispute with Canada. This U.S. army post was closed in 1946, then bought by a group of World War II vets who turned the white frame buildings and lawned grounds into private residences and commercial enterprises. Alaska's first ferry service was initiated in Haines in 1948 with a privately run landing craft connecting the ports of Haines, Skagway and Juneau.

The **Sheldon Museum and Cultural Center**, housed in the original Presbyterian mission, is located at the corner of Main and Front streets.

Northwest of Haines, several thousand bald eagles gather each fall along a five-mile stretch of the Chilkat River. They come here to feed on chum salmon where an upwelling of warm water prevents the river from freezing over in winter. In 1982, the **Alaska Chilkat Bald Eagle** Preserve was established to protect a 48,000-acre section of the river valley. The eagles can be seen from the Haines Highway, which runs parallel with the river, and the highest concentration of eagles occurs between Mileposts 17 and 22 from Haines.

The town of Haines is dwarfed by the Chilkat Mountains. The large white frame buildings in the background are part of Fort Seward.

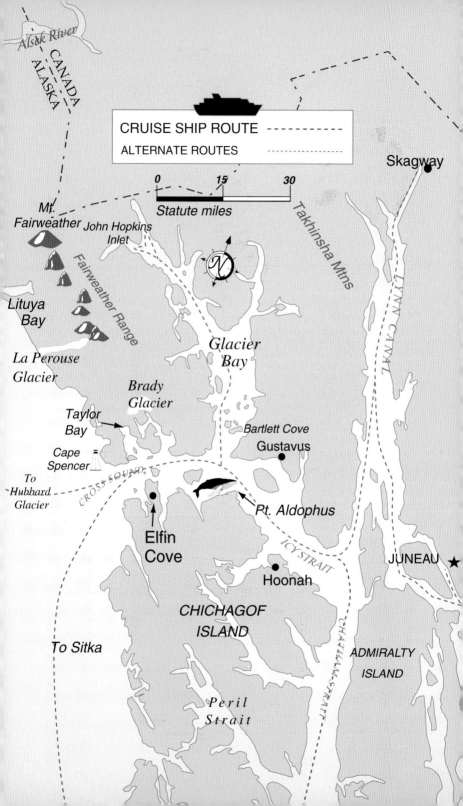

GLACIER BAY

When John Muir discovered Glacier Bay in 1879, it was – and still is – in the process of creation. Glaciers that had filled the entire bay a mere century before Muir's first visit, were now staging a drastic retreat, leaving behind a freshly exposed landscape of newborn islands and inlets.

Neither Muir nor his travelling companions fully believed Sitka Charley when he first described Glacier Bay – at least not the part about the absence of trees. After all, Charley hadn't visited this bay of 'ice mountains' since he was a boy on a seal hunt with his father, and none of them had ever seen a woodless shoreline in this land of rainforests. Nonetheless, they turned up Icy Strait, as directed by young Charley, to see this mysterious bay for themselves. It was the fall of 1879 and John Muir, with the help of Presbyterian missionary Samuel Hall Young, had convinced four native men (Toyatte, Kadachan, John and Sitka Charley) at Fort Wrangell to take him north to see the glaciers. Despite the imminent onset of winter, this brave party piled into a canoe and headed north.

They were just 20 miles from the entrance to Glacier Bay when they pulled into the Tlingit village of **Hoonah** on the southern shores of **Icy Strait**. They were spotted at a distance by the villagers who could tell by the shape and style of their canoe that they were strangers. The Hoonah canoe, designed for sea otter hunting, had a flared hull and moved faster through the water. Like many Tlingit canoes, it was carved out of Sitka spruce because the Western red cedar – a more durable wood – is not found in Tlingit territory west of Chatham Strait. The name Hoonah means 'protected from the north wind' and the village's two original clans had once lived in Glacier Bay until advancing ice forced them to abandon their homes. This likely happened during the Little Ice Age, which began about 3,000 years ago and generally ended in the mid-1700s. Prior to that, numerous advances and retreats of the glaciers took place as the climate fluctuated between cooling and warming.

During the height of the Great Ice Age, which began more than 12 million years ago in parts of Alaska, a massive ice sheet extended across half of Alaska's land mass and right across the northernmost Gulf of Alaska. Some of these mountains have never emerged from the Ice Age, supporting almost continuous glaciation for as far back as scientists can determine.

No one knows what the future holds for the glaciers still covering 30,000 square miles of Alaska. Should snowfall increase or the average temperature decrease only slightly, the glaciers could stage another major advance. On the other hand, a warm, dry trend would cause them to retreat. This happened in Glacier Bay where, in just over 200 years, the ice has melted back more than 65 miles.

In his book *Travels in Alaska*, John Muir describes how, upon arriving at the entrance to Glacier Bay, he could see little because of thick weather. Captain Vancouver's chart, "hitherto a faithful guide" was of no use because Glacier Bay had been completely clogged with ice when Vancouver's ships sailed through Icy Strait a hundred years previous. Only a small bay had indented the ice wall guarding Glacier Bay's entrance.

The wall of ice had now retreated more than 40 miles and this newly landscaped bay awaited discovery by John Muir, a man fascinated with glaciers and the way they sculptured the earth. At Glacier Bay he could see the glaciers in action and he no longer had to speculate on their movements as he had done in the Sierra Mountains of California. Here was a living science experiment, proof at last "that this is still the morning of creation." But first he had to convince his travelling companions of the wondrous opportunity before them.

They had come across a camp of Hoonah sealhunters near the entrance to Glacier Bay and Charley, who said the place had changed since he was last there, wanted one of the sealhunters to guide them into the bay. Meanwhile, the Hoonahs were curious about this motley crew "coming to such a place, especially so late in the year." They had heard of Reverend Young but wondered what a missionary was doing in this lonely, desolate bay. "Was he going to preach to the seals and gulls, they asked, or to the ice mountains?"

A wall of ice blocked the entrance to Glacier Bay when Captain Vancouver sailed past in 1794.

Muir's native guides explained everything to the Hoonahs and one of them agreed to join Muir's expedition as a guide. Next morning they sailed up the bay in cold, pelting rain and made camp just beyond Geikie Inlet. The next day, while the party stayed put due to bad weather, Muir climbed the mountain slopes above their camp for a cloud-fringed view of the bay. It was filled with icebergs and fed by many glaciers, five of which Muir could see.

When Muir returned to camp, Young took him aside and told him their guides were discouraged, fearing this expedition would end in disaster. They questioned Muir's desire to go mountain climbing in a storm and figured he "must be a witch to seek knowledge in such a place as this and in such miserable weather."

Rising to his reputation as an eloquent speaker, Muir addressed his demoralized crew. He reassured them that luck always followed him and told them to put away their childish fears. This pep talk worked wonders and, although it was still sleeting rain the next morning, they pushed on towards the head of the bay and the Hoonah sealing grounds.

They spent five days in Glacier Bay, visiting six glaciers and landing on three of them. The others were inaccessible because the fjords had started freezing. Muir was able to study how the rise and fall of the tide sent warmer seawater rushing in and out beneath the snout of the glaciers, gradually melting back the terminus. He climbed the mountainsides for an overall view, and made notes and sketches of the glaciers.

On his second visit to Glacier Bay the following summer, Muir was able to get close to his namesake glacier. After some urging, his native guides paddled within half a mile of its ice-cliff terminus to disembark

John Muir said the world was "still in the morning of creation" after entering the newly exposed waters of Glacier Bay in 1879.

A cruise ship glides close to an active tidewater-glacier in Glacier Bay.

Muir and Reverend Young on the fjord's eastern shore. A few minutes later, the natives' nervousness was justified as a large chunk of ice crashed into the water. They had to paddle furiously to flee the tossing waves. **Muir Glacier** is fed by the snow-covered slopes of the **Takhinsha Mountains** and, like other glaciers on the east side of Glacier Bay, has retreated since Muir's visit. On the west side of Glacier Bay, a few of the glaciers – fed by the **Fairweather Range** – are advancing.

The movement of glaciers is a complex process. No two glaciers are exactly alike and their unique anatomies – determined by the topography of the land they are carving and by localized weather conditions – cause them to often behave quite differently within the same general area. A good example of this is the **Brady Glacier**, which drains into Taylor Bay. This advancing glacier lies outside Glacier Bay but is fed by the same icefield as some of the retreating glaciers within the bay. The Brady Icefield covers much of the spectacular Fairweather Range, which separates Glacier Bay from the Gulf of Alaska.

John Muir hiked across Brady Glacier in 1880, accompanied by a small dog named Stickeen. While navigating the glacier's maze of

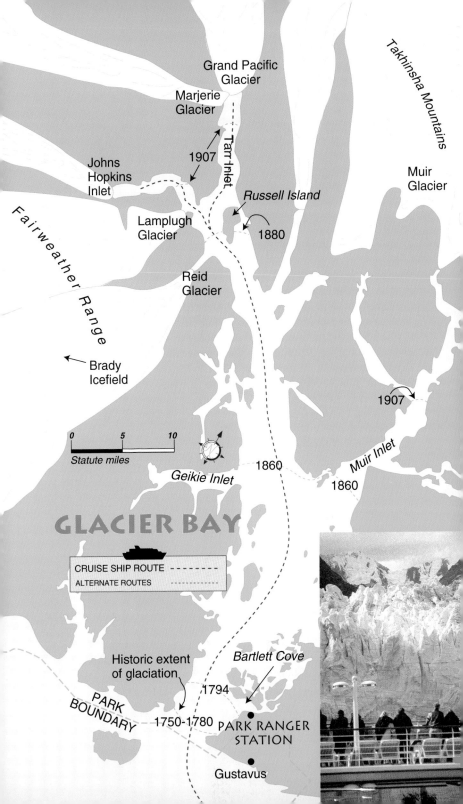

Takhinsha Mountains

Grand Pacific
Glacier

Marjerie
Glacier

1907

Tarr Inlet

Muir
Glacier

Johns
Hopkins
Inlet

Russell Island

1880

Lamplugh
Glacier

Reid
Glacier

F a i r w e a t h e r   R a n g e

← Brady
Icefield

1907

0   5   10
Statute miles

Muir Inlet

Geikie Inlet

1860

1860

GLACIER BAY

CRUISE SHIP ROUTE ------
ALTERNATE ROUTES ········

Historic extent
of glaciation

Bartlett Cove

1794

PARK
BOUNDARY

1750-1780

PARK RANGER
STATION

Gustavus

First surveyed by John Muir in 1879, Johns Hopkins Inlet, with its nine glaciers, is one of Glacier Bay's most dramatic inlets.

crevasses, they frequently crossed ice bridges the width of a knife edge. Muir would flatten these with his knife so that little Stickeen could follow him. "These I had to straddle," Muir explains in *Travels in Alaska* "cutting off the top as I progressed and hitching gradually ahead like a boy riding a rail fence. All this time the little dog followed me bravely, never hesitating on the brink of any crevasse that I had jumped . . ."

As darkness fell, the crevasses "became more troublesome" and they eventually found themselves stranded on an island of ice – completely surrounded by crevasses including one they had leaped over but could not leap back across because of the incline. So Muir cut steps in the steep ice down to a sliver of a bridge which he then inched across – hitching himself forward and flattening the top for Stickeen. When he reached the other side, he carved notch steps and finger holds in the wall of ice.

Meanwhile, little Stickeen was watching and "crying as if his heart was broken." He refused to come when Muir, now on the other side of the 75-foot-wide crevasse, coaxed him to follow. Muir pleaded and at last Stickeen "hushed his cries, slid his little feet slowly down into my footsteps out on the big sliver, walked slowly and cautiously along the sliver as if holding his breath, while the snow was falling and the wind was moaning and threatening to blow him off."

Stickeen made it to the other side where Muir crouched on the brink, ready to help him up onto level ice. But the dog "looked up along the row of notched steps" Muir had made "as if fixing them in his mind" and in one movement whizzed past Muir to safety where he "ran and cried and barked and rolled about fairly hysterical in the sudden revulsion from the depth of despair to triumphant joy."

INSIDE GLACIER BAY

Glacier Bay National Monument was established in 1924 and renamed **Glacier Bay National Park & Preserve** in 1980. The entire park encompasses 3.2 million acres and Glacier Bay lies in the middle of this huge preserve, its many inlets and fjords containing, in total, 16 active tidewater glaciers.

Park headquarters are located at Bartlett Cove, just inside the entrance to Glacier Bay on the eastern shore. A ranger station, lodge and campground are located in Bartlett Cove and cruise ships entering Glacier Bay often pause outside the cove to await the embarkation of two park rangers who explain the sights and wonders to the ship's passengers.

Vessel traffic within Glacier Bay is tightly regulated. There are strict limits placed on the number of cruise ships, sightseeing boats and private pleasurecraft allowed into the bay at any one time, and permits must be obtained beforehand. Commercial fishermen are not allowed to trawl in these waters or catch certain marine life, such as herring, shrimp and pollock. The reason for these restrictions is to protect the **humpback whales** that feed in Glacier Bay.

A sudden decline in the number of humpback whales feeding in the bay was recorded in July of 1978 and 1979. Recent studies indicate this may have been a normal seasonal decline, with the whales using Glacier Bay as their early summer feeding grounds. However, to be on the safe side, measures were taken to protect the whales from excessive disturbance to their feeding grounds.

Today the annual number of humpback whales in Glacier Bay varies from 10 to 32. This population is stable and possibly increasing. During the whale season in Glacier Bay – June 1st to August 31st – no vessel is allowed to come closer than a quarter of a mile to a feeding whale or allowed to follow a whale without maintaining a distance of at least one-half mile. Park hydrophones measure vessel noise and its effect on the whales.

Park rangers will come aboard to answer passengers' questions about the dynamics and beauty of Glacier Bay.

S tanding here, with facts so fresh and telling and held up so vividly before us, every seeing observer, not to say geologist, must readily apprehend the earth-sculpturing, landscape-making action of flowing ice.

John Muir
Travels in Alaska

A retreating tidewater glacier will leave behind a submerged end moraine of rock and gravel.

Johns Hopkins Inlet

Harbor seals are a common sight on the ice floes of Glacier Bay, while overhead you'll see gulls (both glaucous-winged and mew), black-legged kittiwakes and Arctic terns. On shore you may spot a brown bear or mountain goat.

As your ship proceeds up Glacier Bay, you will see a raw landscape of freshly exposed rock and soil. Lichens and mosses are the first forms of vegetation to reclaim deglaciated land. They break down the rock and enrich the soil so that small flowering plants and low bushes can grow. Thickets of alder and willow are the next to take hold. They build up the soil and are eventually replaced by spruce trees.

Forests at the entrance to Glacier Bay gradually give way to more recent stages of growth until, near the snout of each glacier, the immediate landscape is one of silt, sand and gravel. In **Tarr Inlet**, at the very head of Glacier Bay, the exposed rock on the northeast side of the fjord is over 200 million years old while that on the southwest side is about 90 million years old. They belong to separate terranes (fragments of the earth's crust) which nudged their way up the west coast and are now wedged between the Pacific Plate and the North American Plate.

At the head of Tarr Inlet is the **Grand Pacific Glacier** which retreated another 15 miles after Muir first sketched it in 1879, leaving Russell Island in its wake as it retreated up Tarr Inlet. The glacier crossed the border into Canada between 1913 and 1916, then stopped retreating in 1925. It is now back in Alaska, having readvanced, and is on the verge of rejoining the **Margerie Glacier**, from which it separated in 1912. Kittiwakes nest in rocky cliffs between the two glaciers. Here they wait for the glaciers to drop their ice into the sea; this churns up the water and brings baitfish – on which they feed – to the surface.

A glacier's dimensions are constantly changing but the Grand Pacific Glacier is presently, at tidewater, approximately 150 feet high (above the water) and 200 feet deep (below the water). It is 1-1/2 miles wide and about 25 miles long. The 14-mile-long Margerie is one mile wide, 180 feet high and 400 feet deep.

The adjacent inlet – **Johns Hopkins** – is 10 miles long and contains nine separate glaciers. From 1892 to 1929 the ice in Johns Hopkins retreated 11 miles but has been readvancing ever since. **Toyatte, Kadachan, John** and **Charley Glaciers** are all named for Muir's guides on his first trip to Glacier Bay in 1879. The **Johns Hopkins Glacier** is about 12 miles long and one mile wide, with an impressive terminus that is 200 feet high and 400 feet deep.

Reid Inlet's glacier is 160 feet high but shallow, so it calves very few icebergs and has a rounded profile – versus the sheer cliffs of blue ice seen at the snout of an actively calving glacier. The Reid Glacier is retreating entirely through melting and evaporation.

Muir Glacier, one of the retreating glaciers that carved **Muir Inlet**, was a big producer of icebergs when John Muir studied it in 1880 and again in 1890, camping in a hut on the shores of the ice-filled fjord near the face of the glacier which bears his name. One day he saw a huge blue berg – 240 feet long and 100 feet high – break off the glacier and sail past his camp. Muir noted 33 species of plants in flower in the glacial moraine, and he observed sandpipers on shore, loons and ducks in the water, gulls and eagles overhead. But his attention always returned to the glacier's "crystal wall...thundering gloriously."

Muir made himself a sled so he could travel across the glacier and study its tributaries. He camped at night on the glacier and awoke on the seventh day of this expedition to discover he was nearly blind from the glare of the ice. Everything he looked at had a double image. He kept a snow poultice bound over his eyes and dryly commented in his notes that this was the first time in Alaska he had gotten too much sunshine. His eyes recovered and a few days later, back at his hut, he stayed up all night watching an aurora borealis light the sky above his glorious world of ice mountains.

THE FAIRWEATHER COAST

Cruise ships proceeding through **Cross Sound** provide passengers with a fleeting view of Brady Glacier and its 175 square miles of ice and snow. Less easy to spot is the tiny community of **Elfin Cove** opposite Brady Glacier on the northern tip of Chichagof Island. Elfin Cove is a boardwalk community of about 50 year-round residents. In summer the population swells to 200 with fishboats coming and going to take on fuel, water and provisions. When the sun shines in Elfin Cove, the local shopkeepers sit outside on wooden benches and soak up the welcome rays. A post office, school, store, cafe and laundromat ring the inner harbor where fishermen ready their boats. Some of them head out into the Gulf of Alaska to fish the famous Fairweather Bank. Gentle ocean swells wash into Cross Sound and brown sea otters, floating on their backs, are often seen in these waters.

Cape Spencer marks the northern end of the Inside Passage and the beginning of the Gulf's mainland coast. A light is housed here in a white, square concrete tower atop a rocky islet, and is a welcome sight for fishermen returning from the Gulf to inside waters. Captain Vancouver named this cape in 1794 for an earl whose descendants would eventually include Lady Diana Spencer, the Princess of Wales.

Cruise ships proceeding north, toward Yakutat Bay or Prince William Sound, sail past the seaward portion of Glacier Bay National Park & Preserve, where an unobstructed view of the **Fairweather Range** is one of Alaska's most spectacular sights. Some of the highest coastal mountains in the world ring the Gulf of Alaska. Their upper slopes covered with ice and snow, they rise abruptly from the edge of the sea, their steep summits towering within 15 miles of the shoreline. Fishboats are dwarfed as they pass beneath the magnificent peaks of the Fairweather Range. The sprawling **La Perouse Glacier** – at the base of Mount La Perouse – is the only tidewater glacier in Alaska that calves icebergs straight into the open Pacific.

About 20 miles northwest of La Perouse Glacier is famous **Lituya Bay**, site of the largest wave ever recorded in Alaska. It was witnessed one July evening in 1958, when an Alaska fisherman was jarred awake by the sudden pitching and rolling of his boat at anchor in Lituya Bay. He rushed to the wheelhouse and looked out at a scene which drove all thought from his mind. The mountains at the head of the bay were moving. Mesmerized by this impossible sight, he watched the massive

(Above) A ship's officer eases the vessel past chunks of ice found floating near the snout of a tidewater glacier.
(Left) A tourboat gives its passengers a close look at a tidewater glacier.
(Below) A cruise ship slowly approaches the Grand Pacific Glacier at the head of Tarr Inlet.

Lituya Bay, on the outer coast of Glacier Bay Park, is plagued by recurring giant waves which are caused by earthquake-induced avalanches at the head of the bay.

mountains twist and shake, then heave an avalanche of snow and rock into the water. Up rose a 1700-foot wall of water which lashed against one mountainous shore and then another before roaring down the bay toward him at 100 mph. The fisherman and his battered boat somehow survived, but two other fishboats were swept from the bay, one of which vanished.

This was not the first giant wave to strike Lituya Bay, nor will it be the last. An active fault runs through the Fairweather Mountains at the head of Lituya Bay and another earthquake could hit at any time. Called everything from "bewitcher" to "death trap," Lituya Bay is breathtakingly beautiful. Mountains stand like snowy sentinels at the head of the bay, their rugged crowns and shoulders draped with glaciers, their lower portions consisting of exposed rock and stands of spruce timber. A line of demarcation between the light green of young trees and the darker green of old growth shows how high the 1958 wave surged up the sides of the bay, denuding the lower slopes.

Fishboats in the Gulf of Alaska are dwarfed by the Fairweather Range – among the tallest coastal mountains in the world.

La Perouse Glacier is the only tidewater glacier in Alaska that discharges its ice directly into the Pacific Ocean.

The Tlingits who once hunted here believed the bay's recurring giant waves were caused by an underwater sea monster who disliked people and occasionally threw a temper tantrum. They established summer villages near the bay's entrance, at what is now called Anchorage Cove, and hoped for the best. Unfortunately, Tlingit legends recall giant waves wiping out entire villages and canoe-paddling men drowning in churning seas at the entrance. This pincer-like entrance is guarded by a submerged bar – the end moraine of the glacier that carved Lituya Bay. The tide rushes in and out of this deep bay with hardly a pause and the tightly-squeezed currents at its entrance can be very treacherous.

In 1786, when the French explorer La Perouse sailed his two frigates through this narrow entrance, the wind shifted in mid-passage and he noted afterwards in his log that "during thirty years experience at sea, I never saw two ships so near destruction." Ten days later La Perouse sent three boats to survey the entrance. He issued explicit instructions to approach the bar only at slack and if no seas were breaking. However, La Perouse's officers were careless and all three boats were seized by an ebb current. One was swept through roaring breakers out to sea but somehow didn't sink or capsize. The other two were wrecked at the entrance and all 21 men died, their bodies never found. The only traces of the disaster were pieces of the boats that later washed ashore.

No one lives permanently in Lituya Bay, although for years a man named Jim Huscroft lived in a cabin on Cenotaph Island in the middle of the bay. He raised foxes and mined gold in the area. The only boats to pull in now are fishboats and the occasional pleasureboat. Floatplanes sometimes drop off or pick up mountaineering expeditions. A Canadian team of climbers –the first to ascend Mount Fairweather – was picked up at the head of Lituya Bay just hours before the 1958 earthquake struck.

Mount Fairweather – the tallest peak in the range at 15,300 feet – was named by Captain Cook when he sailed along this coast in 1778. Today it marks the border between Alaska and Canada. Northwest of Lituya Bay, the next bay to indent the remote Gulf Coast is Dry Bay, into which the Alsek River flows. This is the northern boundary of the Fairweather Range and of Glacier Bay National Park. The interior boundary of Glacier Bay National Park traces the Alaska/Canada border to the top of Muir Glacier then veers southeastward through the Takhinsha and Chilkat mountains to Icy Strait. Excluded from the reserve is the town of Gustavus, which sits near the entrance to Glacier Bay on a glacial outwash plain – produced when the bay was completely filled with ice.

The terrain here consists of sandy beaches, meadows and forest. Much of this is land that rebounded (lifted) when the ice retreated. The shoreline has risen about 20 feet since the ice started melting 200 years ago. In 1914 these flatlands were homesteaded as a farming community named Strawberry Point, because of the abundance of wild berries. The town's current residents (population about 200) still grow gardens and provide services to fishermen, sightseers and park visitors. Adjacent to the town is the Dude Creek Critical Habitat Area – a stopover each spring and September for thousands of migrating lesser sandhill cranes.

Elfin Cove
is a friendly fishing
port located off
Icy Strait.

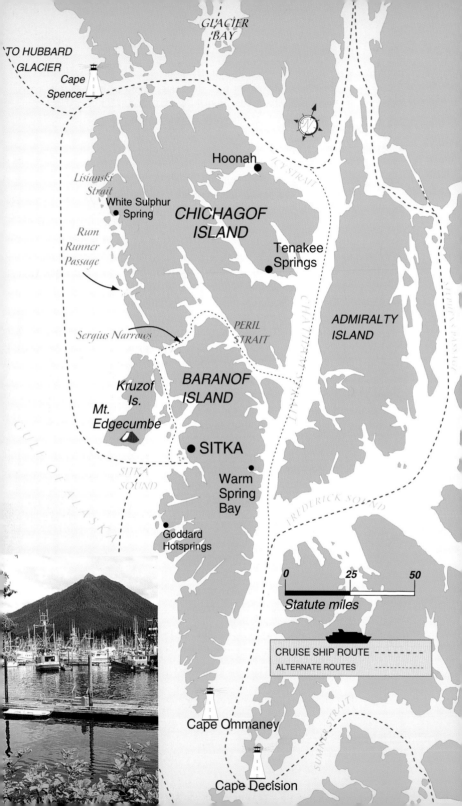

TO HUBBARD
GLACIER

GLACIER
BAY

Cape
Spencer

Hoonah

ICY STRAIT

*Lisianski
Strait*

White Sulphur
• Spring

*CHICHAGOF
ISLAND*

*Run
Runner
Passage*

Tenakee
Springs

Sergius Narrows

*PERIL
STRAIT*

CHATHAM STRAIT

*ADMIRALTY
ISLAND*

Kruzof
Is.

*BARANOF
ISLAND*

Mt.
Edgecumbe

• SITKA

*SITKA
SOUND*

GULF OF ALASKA

Warm
Spring
Bay

FREDERICK SOUND

Goddard
Hotsprings

0   25   50

Statute miles

CRUISE SHIP ROUTE - - - - -

ALTERNATE ROUTES · · · · · ·

Cape Ommaney

SUMNER STRAIT

Cape Decision

CHAPTER TEN

SITKA

T he Russians gained their first toehold in North America on the outer islands of the Aleutian chain. Following Bering's expedition of 1741, Russian frontiersmen, called *promyshlenniki*, set off in rickety ships from Siberia's Kamchatka Peninsula (only a few hundred miles distant) to reach this string of volcanic islands. Here lived the Aleuts – skilled hunters of the sea – who were forced by the promyshlenniki to hunt sea otters on a scale which quickly depleted their numbers.

Moving east along the stepping stones of the Aleutians, these Russian fur traders – accompanied by their Aleut hunters – eventually arrived at Kodiak Island and, in 1784, established their first sparse settlement at Three Saints Bay. A merchant's clerk named **Grigori Shelikof** led this eastward expansion. He had grand visions of establishing a fur trading company similar to Britain's Hudson's Bay Company. But, whereas the Hudson's Bay Company traded in beaver skins, Shelikof was pursuing the sea otter – whose fur pelts fetched exorbitant prices in Canton.

Shelikof hired a man named **Alexander Baranof** to manage his new settlement at Three Saints Bay. In 1791, at the age of 44, Baranof embarked on his first sea voyage to Russian America. The son of a storekeeper, Baranof couldn't resist the opportunity to escape both an unhappy marriage and his country's rigid class system. He was heading for a new land where social rank was secondary to ambition and hard work.

When Baranof arrived at Three Saints Bay in a baidara (a large, open boat), he was sick with pneumonia after enduring seasickness, a diet of raw fish and nights spent sleeping on wet beaches. Yet he was a tough and wiry man who learned the

Sitka celebrates its Russian roots in various forms, including traditional handicrafts.

basics of navigation in the course of the trip and within a few weeks he was back on his feet. His furious energy revived, Baranof set off with 900 natives in 450 baidarkas (kayaks) on a tour of the Kodiak coastline to visit the local villages, meet the chiefs and bargain for sea otter pelts.

When a tsunami all but wiped out the Russian settlement at Three Saints Bay, he took this opportunity to move everyone to a new site at the present-day city of Kodiak. From here he continued his preliminary explorations of the region, setting off with a fleet of 90 baidarkas to visit the mainland. While visiting a tribe of southern Eskimos in Prince William Sound, Baranof promised to marry the chief's daughter. This was apparently a pleasant task, for she was young and pretty and Baranof gave her the Russian name of Anna.

In the summer of 1795, Baranof sailed to **Sitka Sound**. He had heard much about the beauty of this natural harbor. It was inhabited by a powerful Tlingit clan – the **Kiksadi** – who lived in a village called Shee Atika, atop a hill overlooking Sitka Sound. Backed by mountains and fronted by sea, this Tlingit stronghold was a popular port of call for British and American merchant ships. In exchange for sea otter pelts, these fur traders provided the Tlingit with rum and firearms.

When Baranof journeyed to Sitka Sound four years later with 1,100 men – 100 of them Russian, the rest Aleut or Eskimo – they were attacked along the way by Tlingits. But this did not deter Baranof who, upon arrival at Sitka, bargained with the local chief for a piece of land six miles north of the village. There, using timbers two feet thick, he built a Russian fortress protected by high watch towers. A stockade encircled its outbuildings and the new settlement was placed under the patronage of **Saint Michael Archangel**.

Baranof returned to Kodiak and an uneasy co-existence pervaded Sitka Sound. For the Kiksadi, it was one thing to trade with white men who came and went by ship, but it was quite another to let these Russians steal the family business by settling on their doorstep with a troop of Aleut hunters. Antagonism erupted into violence in 1802 when the Tlingits attacked the Russian fort and massacred or enslaved about 400 inhabitants. A handful escaped through the woods and were rescued by merchant ships lying at anchor in Sitka Sound.

A British merchant ship took the survivors back to Kodiak where Baranof was informed of the tragedy. Determined to retake Sitka and make it the headquarters for his company, Baranof returned two years later with a fleet of two sloops, two schooners, 300 baidarkas and a Russian frigate, the *Neva*, commanded by Captain-Lieutenant Yuri Lisianski (who had sailed to Sitka Sound from Hawaii).

A bloody battle ensued in which the Tlingits, led by their fearless warrior **Katlian**, withdrew from their village to a fort on the far side of the harbor. Baranof led one of the first charges and took a bullet in the arm for his efforts. Eventually he left Lisianski in charge of military strategy and, under a steady bombardment of cannon fire from the *Neva*'s guns, the Tlingit depleted their ammunition and quietly abandoned their fort in the middle of the night.

Baranof and his men burned the deserted village to the ground and in its place, on the hill overlooking the harbor, a fortified town was built. It was called **New Archangel** and, by 1809, close to 50 ships a year were pulling into port to trade for furs. Baranof hosted the commanders of these merchant ships at his castle on the hill and these banquets became legendary for the amount of food and liquor consumed.

By the end of his tenure as manager of the Russian-American Company, Baranof was known far and wide as the 'Lord of Alaska.'"He was not without enemies, however. Many considered him a tyrant. The Orthodox clergy did not approve of Baranof's lifestyle, especially his common-law marriage to Anna and this union's two illegitimate children. Russian fur traders under his employ at times objected to Baranof's crude management skills and in 1809 a plot to murder him and his family was uncovered.

Baranof sent his wife and children to Kodiak, wrote out his will, then drank his way through the long, dark winter. A man predisposed to black moods, he was now thoroughly demoralized. He resigned his position, but when two of his replacements died en route to New Archangel, he read this as a sign that he was destined to carry on as 'Lord of Alaska.' He turned pious and sent for his wife and children. His son and daughter returned but Anna chose to remain in Kodiak.

Baranof's Castle, standing atop Castle Hill, overlooked Sitka Sound during the days of the fur trade.

(Above) Sitka Pioneers Home. (Left) Aspiring musicians can listen to international artists perform at Sitka's Summer Music Festival. (Bottom) Kayakers enjoy a waterborne view of Sitka Sound.

By 1818, the 70-year-old Baranof was no longer needed by the Russian-American Company. Officials had decided the navy should run the company and two frigates were sent to New Archangel to relieve Baranof of his duties. After running the colony for 27 years, Baranof was ordered to hand over his books. It was rumored that he had embezzled company funds, but an audit revealed the books were in perfect order. Baranof, far from having accumulated great personal wealth, was almost penniless. He had, over the years, paid for improvements to the colony – such as schools – out of his own pocket while making the Russian-American Company the most profitable fur dealer in the world.

It was an emotional farewell for Baranof when the time came to board a ship bound for Russia. His daughter had fallen in love with a Russian naval officer stationed in New Archangel and would remain there for the time being. Longtime friends bid Baranof farewell, including his Aleut hunters, many of whom were devoted to the hard-drinking old Russian. Baranof never made it back to his homeland. He caught a fever during a stopover in Indonesia and died at sea. While a smooth transition to naval rule was taking place back at New Archangel, his body was commited to the Indian Ocean.

Baranof had successfully built the fur trading colony envisioned by Shelikof, but now a different type of management was required to keep it running smoothly. Under naval rule, education and religion were advanced and public health became company policy. The wives of

Castle Hill, a former Russian bastion, was the site of the October 18th, 1867, transfer ceremonies at which the Russian flag was lowered and the Stars and Stripes was raised.

The Bishop's House was built by shipwrights of the Russian navy in 1841 and has been meticulously restored by the Park Service.

naval officers accompanied their husbands to Russian America and brought with them the culture and fashion of St. Petersburg, which earned New Archangel the epithet 'Paris of the Pacific.'

The Tlingits were invited to return to Sitka and they settled at the foot of Castle Hill. The Russian clergy, led by such missionaries as **Bishop Innocent**, built a bridge with the natives by learning their languages and encouraging them to retain their own customs so long as they didn't clash with Orthodox doctrine. Bishop Innocent moved to Sitka from the Aleutians in 1834 and, an accomplished linguist, he quickly learned the Tlingit language. He produced written instructional material in both Russian and Tlingit so the native children could be taught to read and write. The navy built an imposing residence for him. Completed in 1842, it also housed a chapel and seminary for native and creole children.

Bishop Innocent was eventually transferred to Siberia. He left Sitka a few years before the dwindling fur trade prompted Russia's Imperial Government, under Czar Alexander II, to sell its North American colony to the the United States in 1867. New Archangel's name was changed back to Sitka, and a period of decline and lawlessness followed as Russian residents returned to their homeland. Gold was discovered near Sitka in1872 but this was overshadowed by the larger strike in 1880 at Juneau (which eventually became the territory's new capital).

America's purchase of Russian America also brought a change in missionaries arriving in Alaska. The Protestants, led by Sheldon Jackson, had a well-intentioned but different approach to converting the natives, who were no longer encouraged to retain their language and customs, but to adopt those of the country now governing them. However, the presence of the Orthodox church did not vanish with the transfer of political power, and to this day it remains a strong force among the native population – a living legacy from Alaska's Russian era.

Neither did the Russian place names disappear. When the United States conducted a survey in 1867 of its newly acquired territory, many of the Russian place names were retained. Islands bear such names as Chichagof, Mitkof, Kupreanof, Wrangell and Zarembo – all naval officers who served in Russian America.

St. Michael's Cathedral, a legacy from Alaska's Russian past, is today a Sitka landmark.

Captain Lisianski, whose survey is responsible for many of the Russian place names, is remembered by an inlet and a strait bearing his name. Grigori Shelikof is honored by a bay named for him on Kruzof Island opposite Sitka. And the island on which Sitka stands is, fittingly, named Baranof.

The islands of Southeast Alaska are called the **Alexander Archipelago,** named this in 1867 by the U.S. Coast Survey to honor Alexander II – the current czar. In Sitka itself, much of the architecture and art from its Russian era is preserved. Cruise ships drop anchor in Sitka Sound, where square-rigged schooners once lay at anchor to take on furs for shipment to China. These waters, at one time busy with baidarkas and dugout canoes, now bustle with tenders ferrying cruise passengers ashore.

SITKA SIGHTS

The **Centennial Building**, which houses the **Sitka Convention & Visitors Bureau**, is right on the waterfront and a short stroll from the cruise tender dock. Built in 1967 to commemorate Alaska's statehood

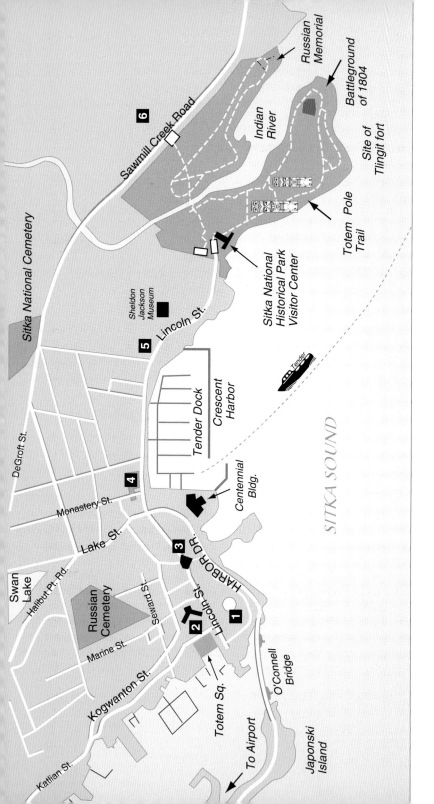

Russian Memorial

Battleground of 1804

Indian River

Site of Tlingit fort

Sawmill Creek Road

6

Sitka National Cemetery

Totem Pole Trail

Sheldon Jackson Museum

Sitka National Historical Park Visitor Center

Lincoln St.

5

DeGroff St.

Tender Dock

Crescent Harbor

Tender

SITKA SOUND

Monastery St.

4

Lake St.

Halibut Pt. Rd.

Swan Lake

Russian Cemetery

Seward St.

HARBOR DR.

3

Lincoln St.

Centennial Bldg.

Marine St.

2

1

Kogwanton St.

Totem Sq.

O'Connell Bridge

To Airport

Kattlan St.

Japonski Island

centennial, it also contains the **Isabel Miller Museum** which is run by the Sitka Historical Society. Museum exhibits include a scale model of Sitka as it looked in 1867 (the year Alaska was transferred from Russia to the United States), and items from Vitus Bering's historic voyage of 1741 during which Russians first set foot on Alaskan soil. Local handicrafts can be purchased in the gift shop.

The stage of the Centennial Building's auditorium is backed by windows overlooking Sitka Sound. This waterfront view of passing fishboats and gliding eagles so impressed the violinist Paul Rosenthal when he performed here in the late '70s with the Arctic Chamber Orchestra, that he founded Sitka's Summer Music Festival. Held each year in the first three weeks of June, these classical concerts attract distinguished artists from around the world.

Sitka's **New Archangel Dancers** also perform their Russian folk dances in the Centennial Building. An all-women dance troupe which was formed in 1969, they wear authentic costumes for their crowd-pleasing show.

Between the Centennial Building and the library is a 50-foot **ceremonial canoe** carved by local artist George Benson in 1940. The 70-foot cedar log from which it's carved was towed by a fishboat from Port Renfrew at the southern tip of British Columbia's Vancouver Island.

From here, Harbor Drive winds in a southwesterly direction toward **Castle Hill** **1** which can be reached by a spiral path leading from a parking lot off Harbor Drive. (Stairs off Lincoln Street beside the old post office also provide access.) The sweeping view from this hilltop takes in Mount Edgecumbe – a dormant volcano visible across Sitka Sound on Kruzof Island. This mountain was named in 1778 by Britain's Captain James Cook.

The hilltop was originally occupied by Tlingit natives until they were driven out in 1804 by the Russians, led by Alexander Baranof – manager of the Russian-America Fur Trading Company. Baranof lived here in a wood house filled with fine furnishings, paintings and books until he was asked to retire in 1818. This house was eventually replaced with an enormous two-story log mansion called **Baranof's Castle**. Company officials held gala balls in Baranof's Castle until 1867, when Russia sold its North American colony to the United States. Prince and Princess Maksoutoff were the last occupants of the castle, which later burned to the ground. Its encircling stone walls and mounted Russian cannons are reminders of the past dramas which unfolded on this hilltop.

Stairs lead from Castle Hill down to Lincoln Street where, directly opposite, is the **Sitka Pioneers Home** **2**. It was built in 1934 – the first such facility for elderly Alaskans – and visitors are welcome to stroll the lawned grounds where flower gardens contain native Alaskan plants. A shop in the basement sells handicrafts.

Across the street from the Pioneers Home, on the waterfront, is **Totem Square**. The totem pole displayed here was carved by local artist George Benson. One of the pole's crests is the doubled-headed eagle of Imperial Russia. Traditionally, a clan would symbolize an enemy's defeat by borrowing its emblem. Also on display at Totem Square are a Russian cannon and some salvaged anchors from British and American fur trading ships.

Standing prominently in the middle of Lincoln Street like a mid-channel island is **St. Michael's Cathedral 3**. This is a splendid replica of the original church which was built from 1844 to 1848, shortly after Sitka (then called New Archangel) became the diocesan seat of the Russian Orthodox Church in Alaska (then called Russian America).

A fire destroyed the cathedral in 1966, but Sitka residents managed to save most of its valuable icons – religious works of art dating as far back as the 17th century. Many were painted on boards that were gilded with gold and other precious metals, and embellished with jewels. These magnificent icons, and the beautiful domed and spired architecture of the church itself – which took 10 years to rebuild from blueprints – draw thousands of visitors each summer.

Heading east of St. Michael's Cathedral on Lincoln Street, you'll pass the Shee Atika (a Westmark Hotel) and MacDonald's Bayview Trading Company (with a postal substation on the main floor) before reaching the **Russian Bishop's House 4**. Built in 1841-42, this heritage building served as a hospital, school, rectory and place of worship. The first bishop to live here was Father Innocent, who arrived at New Archangel (Sitka) in 1834 as Reverend Veniaminof, after spending 10 years as a missionary in the Aleutians. When his wife died in

Lincoln Street, in downtown Sitka, is lined with inviting shops and galleries.

Sheldon Jackson Museum is located on the college campus and contains an impressive collection of native artifacts.

1840 he took monastic vows and was consecrated a bishop. He resided here for the next 18 years before moving to a new diocese in Siberia. In 1868 he became Metropolitan of Moscow – the highest rank in the Russian Orthodox Church – and in 1977 he was canonized a saint.

When the Park Service acquired the Bishop's House, a 15-year restoration project was undertaken to fix its sagging structure and restore the interior furnishings. Hundreds of experts were consulted as the painstaking work was carried out. Blackened icons were sent to an iconologist for cleaning, and teams of specialists at the Park Service's Harper's Ferry Center in West Virginia restored the house's furnishings. The first floor now contains historical and architectural exhibits. In 'The Room Revealed' a cutaway section of the building shows the sturdy scarf joints and other shipbuilding techniques used by Finnish shipwrights during construction. Upstairs is the beautiful chapel where Bishop Innocent and his fellow missionaries spent time in prayer each morning.

From the Bishop's House, the walk heading east on Lincoln Street couldn't be more pleasant. Along the waterfront are lawns, walkways and benches which overlook Crescent Harbor. Across the street, a sidewalk leads past **St. Peter's By-the-Sea** (a pretty stone church with a gift shop out back), followed by the campus of **Sheldon Jackson College 5**, which hosts summer workshops, conferences and events such as the Sitka Summer Music Festival and the Writer's Symposium. In 1983 the college's president, Dr. Michael Kaelke, read that James

The trails of Sitka National Historical Park provide visitors the opportunity to view skillfully carved totem poles in a lovely forest setting.

Michener was interested in writing a book on Alaska but was reluctant to spend time in a cold climate at his age. Dr. Kaelke promptly wrote the famous author, explaining that winter in southeastern Alaska is quite mild with temperatures generally above freezing. Michener accepted the college's invitation to use it as a base from which to research and write his book *Alaska*.

The **Sheldon Jackson Museum** is an octagonal-shaped concrete building located on the college campus. It contains a fine collection of Eskimo, Aleut and Indian artifacts collected by Dr. Sheldon Jackson, a presbyterian missionary and General Agent for Education, who travelled Alaska by boat, dogsled and on foot in the late 1800s. Sleds, umiaks and other watercraft hang from the museum's ceiling. Haida argillite carvings, a Chilkat blanket and the Raven's Head Helmet worn by Sitka Chief Katlian during the 1804 battle with the Russians, are just a few of the fascinating items on display.

At the end of Lincoln Street is the **Sitka National Historical Park**. A visitor center, located at the park's entrance, displays Tlingit exhibits and presents a recorded slide presentation on Sitka's history. Available at the visitor center is a booklet called *Carved History*, which explains each of the totem poles standing along a 1/4-mile section of the park's two miles of trails. Many are replicas of poles collected from various villages throughout southeastern Alaska for the 1904 Louisiana Purchase Exposition. They were brought to Sitka the following year and the deteriorating originals are now being preserved in storage.

Just beyond the totem poles is the site of the 1804 battle between the local Tlingits and the conquering Russians. Nearby is the site of the Tlingits' fort to which they retreated under steady Russian bombardment and from which they fled in the middle of the night when their ammunition ran out. From there the trail follows the shores of the salmon-spawning Indian River to a footbridge. Across it are more trails which lead to a Russian memorial for the men who died in the 1804 battle.

An eagle receives rehabilitative care at the Alaska Raptor Center.

Yet another trail connects with the Sawmill Creek Road. A short distance north, at 1101 Sawmill Creek Road, is the **Alaska Raptor Center 6**. Sick or injured birds of prey are brought here for treatment and rehabilitation before they are returned to the wild. Open houses, demonstration tours and eagle exercise sessions in a nearby muskeg field are held regularly.

Another scenic walk can be taken along the Sheldon Jackson College Forest Trail which follows the Indian River through the college grounds.

OUT-OF-TOWN EXCURSIONS

With the Pacific Ocean at its doorstep, the waters off Sitka offer some of Southeast Alaska's best wildlife viewing. Sea otters are especially abundant and humpback whales are frequently sighted. Boat cruises out of Sitka are a good opportunity to see marine mammals up close as well as such seabirds as the colorful puffin.

Nearby Silver Bay is a favorite fjord for sightseeing cruises. Here you can view not only the area's wildlife but also an old gold mine, a modern pulp mill and a salmon hatchery.

Sportfishing is also fruitful in the bountiful waters off Sitka. Salisbury Sound, 20 miles north of Sitka, is especially good for catching halibut – a prize bottom fish with delicate white meat

Mount Edgecumbe, a dormant volcano on Kruzof Island, can be seen from Sitka.

OUTLYING PORTS

Sitka is steeped in Russian history but visitors to outlying ports will find themselves soaking in something quite different – the region's hot springs. Long used by natives, then by hunters and trappers, these scattered hotsprings later became winter retreats for fishermen and gold prospectors.

The **Goddard Hotsprings,** 16 miles south of Sitka on the outer coast of Baranof Island, was one of the first to be developed in the mid-1800s when a few cottages were built to house invalids from Sitka. In the 1920s a hotel was built, which was then turned into an overflow facility for Sitka's Pioneers Home in 1939. Today two cedar bathhouses stand on the hillside and capture the hot mineral waters for visitors arriving by boat.

At beautiful **Warm Spring Bay**, on the other side of Baranof Island, a once-thriving bathhouse with change rooms and hose-fed tubs has fallen into disrepair. But farther up Chatham Strait, on the east side of Chichagof Island, a community has formed around the local springs. Called **Tenakee Springs**, this hamlet is the former site of crab and salmon canneries, but is now inhabited by retirees and young families. Juneau and Sitka residents arrive by ferry for weekend retreats.

Tenakee's existence centers around the hotspring-fed bathhouse where bathing hours for men and women are posted on the outside door. Visitors soon know them by heart, however, because the bathing hours are promptly told to any strangers arriving in town (it's presumed) for a soak in the springs. The local bathhouse is a more popular

The former cannery town of Tenakee Springs is now a mecca for people seeking relaxation in a hot mineral bath.

topic of conversation than even the weather. It's not unusual to over-hear one resident asking another if he or she has bathed yet that day. Anywhere else this might seem a somewhat personal question, but not in Tenakee Springs.

There are no cars here, but a 2-mile road called Tenakee Avenue runs the length of this waterfront village. Only four feet wide in places, the road is travelled by foot, bicycle or three-wheeled motorbike. Near one end of town is a hotel and post office; at the other end is a school. The bathhouse and an old-fashioned general store are in the center of town, just up the road from the ferry dock.

The Alaska State Ferry pulls into Tenakee Springs on its way from Juneau to Sitka. The ferry route includes **Peril Strait** – a twisting chan-nel that separates Chichagof and Baranof Islands. This strait was origi-nally named Pernicious by Russia's Captain Lisianski, in remembrance of 200 Aleut hunters who died from eating toxic mussels at its entrance in 1799. They were part of Baranof's expedition who established a gar-rison at Sitka and who were returning to Kodiak. The site of the initial Russian settlement – a few miles north of the present downtown – is now referred to as Old Sitka and the Alaska State Ferry docks nearby.

Another hotsprings, called **White Sulphur**, exists on the ocean side of Chichagof Island. Some gold prospecting took place on Chichagof, followed by whiskey smuggling when prohibition took effect in 1918. Piehle Passage (also known as Rum Runner Passage) was named for an adroit smuggler who apparently used this tortuous, rock-strewn passage to evade a Revenue cutter.

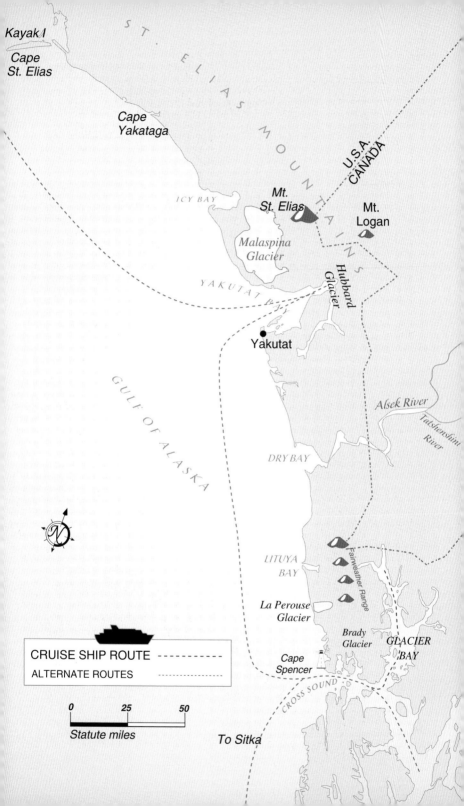

CHAPTER ELEVEN

HUBBARD GLACIER
and Yakutat Bay

Some of the most spectacular scenery in the world is found along Alaska's Gulf coast on the way to Yakutat Bay. Standing on the edge of the sea are some of the world's tallest coastal mountains, their slopes blanketed by North America's largest glaciers.

Few people live along this coast, where the overall landscape is one of looming mountains and sprawling glaciers. There are but three or four sheltered anchorages for mariners to pull into and Yakutat Bay offers the only harbor for large ships. The bay's entrance, 16 1/2 miles wide, is visible from great distances because it is marked by Mount Saint Elias, which is 18,008 feet tall and growing. Yes, growing. A piece of the earth's crust – called a terrane – is sandwiched here between two tectonic plates. This terrane (called the Yakutat Block) broke away from the edge of the Continental Plate about 25 million years ago and, riding on the Pacific Plate, was pushed 330 miles northwest along a fault until it reached the top of the Gulf of Alaska.

About 100,000 years ago, the Pacific Plate began shoving the Yakutat Block (360 miles long and 120 miles wide) against the Continental Plate at a rate of about 2 1/2 inches per year. Something must budge as the dense oceanic plate pushes underneath the more buoyant continental plate and, in this case, part of a mountain range is being forced upward. At a growth rate of 2 1/2 inches per year, it will take Mount Saint Elias quite a while to surpass 20,320-foot Mount McKinley as the tallest mountain in North America. Saint Elias also faces competition from 19,850-foot Mount Logan (only 25 miles away) which is presently in Canada's Yukon but could eventually be pushed across the border into Alaska. All this bumping and grinding of terranes and plates is invisible to the human eye until an earthquake gives the area a good jolt, which happened at Yakutat in September 1899. Living at this remote village on the shores of Yakutat Bay were native Tlingits, a few missionaries and some mining prospectors.

The tremors and shocks began on September 3rd and lasted four weeks. No lives were lost, even though at least one of the quakes was of the same magnitude as the 1906 San Francisco quake. The small community of Yakutat was at first alarmed and then terrified when, on September 10th, the strongest of these quakes sent people rushing from their creaking and groaning homes, while the trees outside swayed like stalks of grass.

Mount Saint Elias was the first point on North America sighted by Vitus Bering in 1741, and for decades it served as a navigational marker for European explorers venturing into the Gulf of Alaska.

An eyewitness report, by a civil engineer camped at the time in Yakutat, was published in the San Francisco Examiner. He described natives of the village pleading with the missionary to hold church services that morning (a Sunday) to pacify their god, who was obviously "angry at the earth and shaking it." They were horrified when the mission church "rocked until the church bell rang," perceiving this as an omen. When the earthquake ceased, three great waves (tsunamis) rolled in from the ocean and filled Yakutat Bay with whirlpools. Lowlands were flooded as the water level rose 15 feet. The eyewitness engineer reported that "the earthquake was undoubtedly a magnificent sight, but hardly one a fellow would hunt up for the sake of looking at it."

The U.S. Geological Survey sent a team to inspect the aftereffects of the earthquake six years later, and they found that a former tidal zone of beach and barnacled rocks had been raised as much as 47 feet above the high-tide line. This uplifting was felt most dramatically by a group of prospectors camped beside Russell Fjord at the head of Yakutat Bay, not far from **Hubbard Glacier**.

When the September 10th quake hit that morning, the men ran from their tents. The glacial moraine under their feet was undulating and the Hubbard Glacier was surging forward. As if that weren't enough, a lake behind the beach spilled from its bed and swept across their abandoned camp. Tons of rock came pouring down as the men fled along the beach. Four days later they made it to Yakutat where they found the residents camped in tents on Shivering Hill, given this name right after the September 10th earthquake.

The **Harriman Expedition** had visited Yakutat just 11 weeks prior to the September earthquakes. The scientific party on board the steamer *George W. Elder*, chartered by their host Edward H. Harriman, would have had much to observe and record had they been exploring the shoreline of Yakutat Bay a few months later. As it was, the narrow inlet of **Disenchantment Bay** (at the head of Yakutat Bay) was thick with ice floes when the *Elder* arrived at its entrance and waited for the ice to disperse before proceeding. Meanwhile, some Tlingits paddled along-side in canoes filled with furs and skins for sale. This welcome was similar to that given another scientific expedition a hundred years earlier when the Spanish explorer **Alejandro Malaspina** visited Yakutat.

Malaspina was a talented mariner of grand vision, who wanted to lead a scientific expedition that would rival those of Britain's Cook and France's La Perouse. He presented his plan to King Carlos III, Spain's great bourbon ruler, who gave it his stamp of approval. Not only was Spain's dominance in the Pacific being challenged by other seafaring nations, but a French geographer had recently endorsed the credibility of an obscure manuscript, claiming there existed the 'Strait of Anian' – a northwest passage. The King of Spain sent Malaspina to the North Pacific to check out this rumor.

Turner Glacier is overshadowed in size and dynamics by Hubbard Glacier. However, during the July 9, 1958 earthquake (centered at Lituya Bay), massive sections of ice broke away from Turner's tide-water terminus. This excessive calving was likely caused by submarine landslides undermining support beneath the ice mass.

In the summer of 1791, Malaspina headed north from Mexico, setting a course that took his two ships directly to Yakutat Bay. When he saw the bay's wide opening at the latitude substantiated by the Academy of Sciences in Paris as being the Strait of Anian's location, Malaspina figured he was onto something.

The Tlingits living at Yakutat had already dealt with Russian, French and British ships, and they anticipated a brisk trade with this new batch of white men. The Spaniards, however, seemed preoccupied with setting up a base camp and preparing two launches to explore the Strait of Anian. Others were busy collecting specimens and sketching the scenery.

Eventually the Tlingits engaged the Spaniards in barter. By the time the men in the two launches returned with disappointing reports of a huge glacier blocking their way, the mood on the waiting ships had also soured. The Spanish were not getting along with the Tlingits and tensions reached a climax when a pair of trousers went missing. A chief was detained and trading was halted until the trousers were returned. The expedition's artist captured the reconciliation scene on canvas – natives approaching in a canoe, one with his arms outstretched in a gesture of friendship, another holding up the stolen trousers.

Disappointed but convinced that the 'Strait of Anian' theory was false, Malaspina left. The name he gave the ice-filled inlet at the head of Yakutat Bay reflects his dashed hopes – Disenchantment Bay.

By the time the Harriman Expedition pulled into Yakutat Bay, the wall of ice that had stopped the Spaniards dead in their tracks was now retreating up the inlet. The *Elder* was able to pick its way through the ice floes and it became the first ship to enter Disenchantment Bay. On board was a Yakutat Tlingit named James who had impressed Harriman with his detailed knowledge of the area and was invited to join the elite party of scientists as a consultant to the ship's pilot.

Harriman's scientific party included **John Muir** (described in the guest list as 'Author and Student of Glaciers'), John Burroughs, (Ornithologist and Author) and Dr. William H. Dall (Paleontologist of the U.S. Geological Survey). Dall had made several trips to Alaska and his keen observance and recording of what he saw resulted in various animal species receiving his name, such as the Dall porpoise and Dall sheep.

Grove Karl Gilbert was the scientist who produced one of the most insightful volumes for the Harriman Reports, published at the conclusion of the expedition. As glaciologist and chairman of the expedition's Committee on Geology, Gilbert made careful empirical studies of each glacier they visited, drawing dozens of maps and taking plenty of his own photographs in addition to those taken by the expedition's two official photographers. He studied each glacier's topography and the eroded fjords, valleys and rutted plains left behind by receding glaciers. He also conducted experiments to find out if a tidewater glacier rests on

A cruise ship pulls within a quarter mile of Hubbard Glacier's massive snout at the head of spectacular Yakutat Bay.

the sea bottom, and he concluded that their partly submerged snouts float on a thin film of water. Gilbert's work was a major contribution to the emerging science of glaciology which today measures the thickness of ice with radar and uses aerial photography to monitor a glacier's movements.

The **Hubbard Glacier** at the head of Disenchantment Bay is the longest tidewater glacier in North America. Its total length is 76 miles, and its ice-cliff face is six miles wide. At one time, perhaps as as recently as 600 years ago, the glacier completely covered Yakutat Bay. When the Harriman expedition examined the glacier in 1899, it had just finished retreating and was starting to readvance.

The sheer cliffs of Hubbard's terminus are typical of an actively calving glacier.

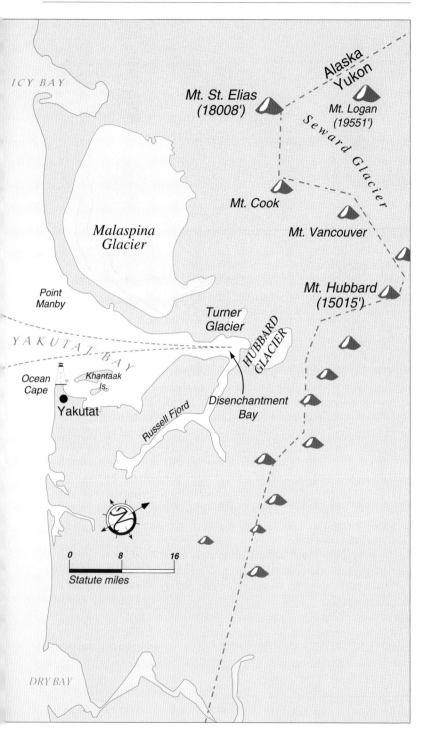

Hubbard Glacier, longest tidewater glacier in North America, begins its 76-mile journey to the sea on the slopes of Mount Logan, the tallest mountain in Canada and part of the largest non-polar icefield in the world.

Hubbard received widespread attention in the summer of 1986 and was dubbed the 'Galloping Glacier' when it advanced hundreds of feet within a few weeks. The glacier's snout over-ran a small island and dammed the entrance to Russell Fjord, trapping seals inside what became a huge lake. Its water level rose 83 feet and threatened to over-flow, the runoff potentially pouring into the Situk River where salmon would be washed away in a flood of debris. Then, on October 8th, the ice dam ruptured and 3,500,000 cubic feet of water per second was dumped into Disenchantment Bay. Shrimp lying on the bottom of this deep fjord were lifted by the turbulent water and thrown onto shore. Scientists speculate that an equivalent discharge of water last took place near the end of the Great Ice Age, when Lake Missoula emptied into the Columbia River.

Surging glaciers are still not completely understood but it's surmised that faulty plumbing is the culprit. A healthy, slow-moving glacier slides on its base while its top layer flows steadily forward, transferring ice from its source (where snow accumulates) to its snout (where the ice melts). When a glacier isn't flowing smoothly, its upper end becomes clogged with accumulated snow and ice. Then, in a year of high runoff due to heavy rain or spring thaw, the glacier's motion is suddenly eased and the glacier is pushed forward as its top-heavy mass of ice surges down the slope.

Hubbard Glacier was a major media attraction in the summer of 1986 and the fishermen of Yakutat found themselves chauffeuring

Swells off the Gulf of Alaska break on the outer shores of Khantaak Island at the entrance to Yakutat Bay. Stretching across the northern horizon are the icefield-covered Saint Elias mountains .

reporters and camera crews to the head of the bay. One resident recalls loading a group into his fishboat for a trip to the Galloping Glacier. The two things he remembers are that the reporters didn't like being charged $200 each and that they all held their microphones pointed toward the glacier to record its rumbling noises.

Yakutat is an important port for Alaska's fishing fleet, being the only one with dock facilities between Juneau and Cordova (in Prince William Sound). Most of Yakutat's 500 residents run fishboats or work in fish processing plants, and many will tell you that Yakutat is the most beautiful port in Alaska. The town overlooks **Monti Bay**, on the southeast shores of Yakutat Bay, with Khantaak Island lying opposite and acting as a breakwater to the swells which roll into Yakutat Bay off the Gulf of Alaska.

Beautiful beaches ring much of the area's shoreline and, stretching across the northern horizon, is a breathtaking vista of mountains and glaciers, including **Malaspina Glacier.** It is the largest piedmont (foot-of-the-mountain) glacier in North America, measuring 45 miles from east to west and 30 miles from north to south. Its fan-like terminus is almost 60 miles in circumference and ends within three miles of the Pacific Ocean.

Malaspina Glacier is fed by more than two dozen tributary glaciers. As these smaller glaciers merge with the main glacier, they bring along rock and gravel eroded from valleys. These dark stripes of moraine run in parallel lines like feeder lanes joining a main highway. From the air

*Mount Saint Elias looms above the small fishing port of Yakutat,
located near the mouth of Yakutat Bay.*

the Malaspina Glacier looks like an abstract painting with its parallel
moraine stripes twisted into swirls or folded into zigzags by surges
within the glacier.

Cruise ships pass fairly close to Malaspina Glacier when entering
Yakutat Bay. Few pleasure boats visit this remote Gulf of Alaska port,
but in the summer of 1992 a Canadian sailboat pulled into Yakutat Bay.
The fellows on board wanted to see a glacier up close, so they motored
to the head of Disenchantment Bay and were suitably impressed with
massive Hubbard Glacier. After retrieving some pieces of floating ice
and stuffing them in the freezer as souvenirs, they returned to Monti
Bay – near the entrance of Yakutat Bay – for the night. They awoke the
next morning to find a layer of fine gritty sand on the decks of their
boat and were baffled until they turned on the radio and heard that
Mount Spurr in Cook Inlet had erupted the previous evening. Prevailing
winds had carried the volcanic ash hundreds of miles east. So, having
come to see a glacier, the Canadian yachtsmen also slept through a volcanic eruption.

Jet planes land daily at Yakutat on regularly scheduled flights. For
travellers approaching Yakutat by ship, the landscape looks so uninhab-
ited that the sight of a jet plane coming in for a landing looks completely out of place. These planes touch down on Alaska's longest runway –
built during World War II when 15,000 troops were based at Yakutat.

For most of this century, Yakutat's main industry has been the commercial catching and processing of salmon, cod, halibut and crab. The

Cape Saint Elias is a feared cape and a famous landmark, being the first place in Alaska visited by Europeans when the Bering expedition stopped here for a few hours in 1741.

town's first cannery was built in 1904. Timber harvesting is also under-way on Tongass National Forest lands between Yakutat and Dry Bay.

Dry Bay lies at the mouth of the **Alsek River** and is slowly being turned into a huge delta. The Alsek River drains 9,500 square miles of Alaska and Canada while carving its way through the Saint Elias Mountains, past glaciers and through canyons, to reach the Gulf of Alaska. Canada's **Tatshenshini River** flows into the upper Alsek. In 1993 it was declared a Wilderness Park by the British Columbia gov-ernment after environmentalists opposed an open-pit mine planned for the summit of Windy Craggy Mountain. The Tatshenshini-Alsek water-shed, considered North America's wildest river, is now completely pro-tected. Intrepid kayakers occasionally paddle the white waters of this river but it is normally not well travelled. The natives used the Alsek ('Raven's River') as a trade route until a burst ice dam wiped out a riverside village. Afterwards, they restricted their settlements to the river's headwaters and its mouth at Dry Bay.

During the Gold Rush, some prospectors tried to reach the Klondike via the Alsek River. In the spring of 1898 more than 300 men arrived at Yakutat Bay and hauled their mining outfits 50 miles across Hubbard Glacier to Alsek River. At this point most turned back, but those who ascended the river set up their winter camp in a desolate area almost devoid of fuel. Freezing and sickness took its toll, with only a handful surviving the ordeal. That spring the survivors reached Dalton Post on the Tatshenshini River. Had they taken a different route from the coast, they would have reached Dalton Trail after a few days of travel.

Some prospectors tried to cross the massive Malaspina Glacier to reach the Yukon. Those who made it were in bad shape – both mentally and physically. When the *George W. Elder* stopped at Yakutat, members of the Harriman Expedition met groups of bedraggled and penniless miners who were hoping to catch the next steamer home. A few were panning for gold in the creeks around Yakutat.

Specks of gold lie in the black sand beaches of **Cape Yakataga** – about 70 miles west of Yakutat Bay. To this day, the residents of Cape Yakataga work their claims by hauling sand and running it through sluice boxes. These modern-day prospectors are mainly summer residents, with about a dozen people living year-round at this remote cape. They grow small gardens in summer, make preserves from wild berries, can or smoke fish and wild game, and collect firewood for their stoves. Stands of spruce and hemlock grow right to the beach, and alder, willow and cottonwood flourish along the river banks. Leisure time is spent beachcombing to see what the Gulf has thrown onto the exposed shores of the Cape. On clear nights the northern lights can often be seen. In spring and fall thousands of migrating birds – swans, geese, cranes and ducks – stop here briefly.

Cape Yakataga is backed by mountains and flanked on either side by massive icefields – Malaspina to the east, Bering to the west. Lying at the base of Bering Glacier is Cape Suckling. Offshore, jutting into the Gulf like a sore thumb, is **Kayak Island**. In July of 1741 a Russian ship under the command of the Danish captain Vitus Bering anchored in the lee of Kayak Island. The ship remained there for only a few hours, just long enough for naturalist Georg Steller to go ashore to sketch and name a few plants and animals, such as the Steller's jay. He was thus the first European to step on Alaskan soil.

Kayak Island rises from the water like a wedge of rock. **Cape Saint Elias** – one of the most feared capes on this coast – is located at the south end of Kayak Island where it is connected by a low, narrow strip of land to Pinnacle Rock. Fishermen give this stark cape a wide berth. Strong winds funnel off its sheer cliffs and turbulent currents create erratic waves. This is one of the most dramatic capes of the entire Alaskan coastline and well worth the effort to spot during your cruise.

The seas south of Cape St. Elias were considered perilous until a manned light station was installed in 1916 and later automated by the U.S. Coast Guard in 1974. Today the only inhabitants of Kayak Island are brown bears and foxes.

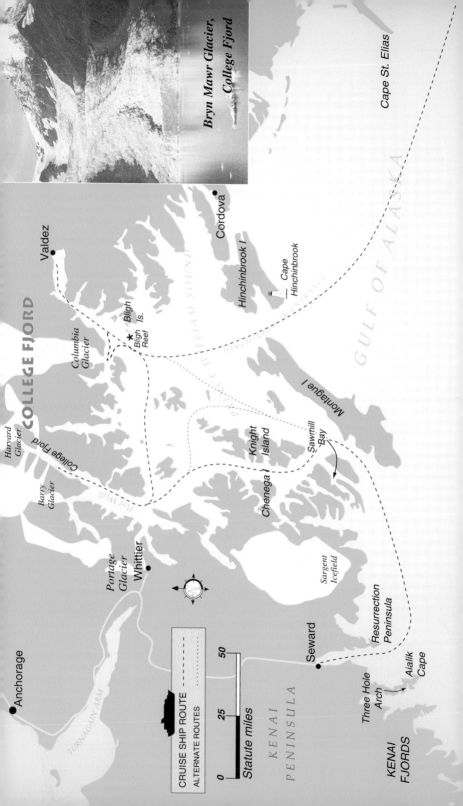

Bryn Mawr Glacier, College Fjord

Anchorage

TURNAGAIN ARM

KENAI PENINSULA

Portage Glacier
Whittier

Harvard Glacier
Barry Glacier
College Fjord
Port Wells

COLLEGE FJORD

Columbia Glacier

Valdez

PRINCE WILLIAM SOUND

Bligh Is.
Bligh Reef

Cordova

Hinchinbrook I

Cape Hinchinbrook

HINCHINBROOK ENTRANCE

Knight Island

Chenega

Sawmill Bay

Montague I

GULF OF ALASKA

Cape St. Elias

Sargent Icefield

Seward

Resurrection Peninsula

Alalik Cape

Three Hole Arch

KENAI PENINSULA

KENAI FJORDS

CRUISE SHIP ROUTE
ALTERNATE ROUTES

Statute miles
0   25   50

CHAPTER TWELVE

PRINCE WILLIAM SOUND
and Kenai Peninsula

P rince William Sound is the crowning glory of coastal Alaska. Situated at the top of the Gulf of Alaska, its mainland shores are surrounded by a lofty barrier of mountains and snow, and are indented with dozens of glacier-carved fjords that wend their watery way inland. These fjords contain Alaska's greatest concentration of tidewater glaciers – 20 of which are active.

Glaciers are not the only feature found here in abundance. The numerous forested islands are habitat for Sitka blacktail deer, black and brown bears, wolves, red fox, river otters, mink and other fur-bearing animals. Marine mammals thrive in waters rich with salmon, halibut, red snapper, crab, clams and shrimp. Each summer, thousands of sea otters, Dall porpoises and harbor seals frequent the Sound, along with killer whales and about 50 humpback whales. Overhead bald eagles fly, numbering 5,000 during the summer months, and about half a million marine birds take up residence at the 88 seabird colonies.

Human habitation of Prince William Sound has always been sparse compared to the animal life it supports. About 3,000 Pacific Eskimos (Chugachs and Eyaks) were living in this area when the first European seafarers arrived. Britain's Captain Cook named Prince William Sound in 1778, and when Spanish explorers surveyed part of Prince William Sound in 1790, they left behind such place names as Valdez and Cordova. In 1791 Russia's Baranof visited Prince William Sound and departed with a new wife – the daughter of a native chief.

Sea lions are among the many marine mammals that inhabit Prince William Sound.

Seabird colonies thrive in Prince William Sound, such as this one at Porpoise Rocks near Hinchinbrook Entrance.

A century later, salmon canneries dotted the Sound and herring processing had become a going concern. To compete with European processors, Scottish and Norwegian experts were brought in to teach the locals how to cure and pack herring. A salmon cannery was in operation at **Cordova** when the Harriman Expedition stopped for a visit in the summer of 1899. American railway magnate Edward H. Harriman had chartered the steamship *George W. Elder* for his family's vacation and he invited an impressive collection of scientists to join him in exploring Alaska's coastline. This elite expedition put their time to good use in Prince William Sound. Not only did they name **College Fjord** and its numerous glaciers for the various colleges and universities with which the scientists were affiliated, they also discovered a newly formed fjord.

The *Elder's* captain was using U.S. Coastal Survey charts which showed the navigable waters of Port Wells ending at **Barry Glacier**, located in an inlet adjacent to College Fjord. But when Harriman's expedition pulled up to Barry Glacier, they discovered a narrow passage leading past the glacier's snout. Its wall of ice had retreated since it was last surveyed.

Tidewater glaciers line the slopes of College Fjord.

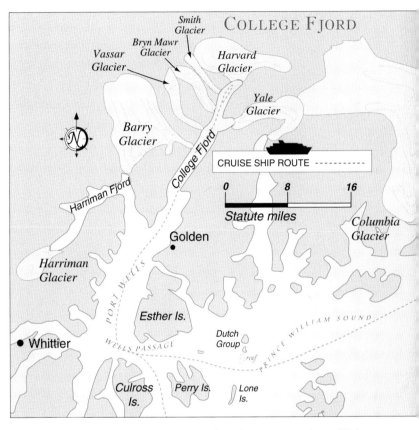

Few white people had ever ventured into the upper reaches of Prince William Sound, and none had ever seen this unknown inlet, which was now visible beyond the snout of Barry Glacier. Harriman was a risk taker and he saw this open sliver of water as a window of opportunity. "We shall discover a new Northwest Passage!" he declared. His captain was opposed to taking the ship into uncharted waters where a submerged rock might pierce a hole in the *Elder*'s hull. But Harriman took full responsibility and ordered that they proceed.

Harriman's gamble resulted in their discovery of **Harriman Fjord**. His scientific guests were ecstatic at the sight of more than a dozen glaciers, and expedition members such as John Muir and Grove Karl Gilbert could hardly wait to set up camp on shore and survey these new rivers of ice that flowed into the fjord. Between that summer of discovery and 1914, the Barry Glacier retreated a further four miles. Since then, it has slightly readvanced. The fjord's other glaciers have also retreated, except for Harriman Glacier at its head, which has slowly readvanced. Surprise Glacier was so named because it was the first glacier the Harriman party saw when they entered the fjord.

(Top) A cruise ship lingers near the snout of a tidewater glacier in College Fjord.
(Bottom) An on-board naturalist provides glacier commentary.

Today, fishing is the mainstay for most residents of Prince William Sound. In addition to the annual herring and salmon runs are abundant harvests of crab, clams and shrimp. The clam industry suffered a setback when the 1964 Good Friday earthquake raised clam beds 10 feet above the water. The town of **Valdez**, sitting on silt, was shaken so violently that the entire town swayed as if riding ocean waves. Cracks formed in the ground, and began opening and closing, spurting water in the process. Then huge blocks of land slid out to sea, and waterfront buildings and docks collapsed. The final blow came from the tsunamis. Four of these giant, earthquake-generated waves swept ashore, devastating what was left of Valdez.

The town of **Whittier**, on the west side of Prince William Sound, was closer to the quake's epicenter but, unlike Valdez, it was built on bedrock and the ground didn't collapse. The port was, however, hit by a huge harbor wave. A native village on **Chenega Island** was destroyed in the Good Friday earthquake by a tsunami, and was rebuilt at **Sawmill Bay** on Evans Island, on a former saltery site. Valdez was also rebuilt at a new location, about four miles from the original townsite.

In the early '70s, Prince William Sound experienced three bad fishing years in a row, due to poor pink salmon runs. To counteract the cyclical nature of salmon fishing, an aquaculture corporation was formed and over the next few years several large fish hatcheries were built in the western part of the sound. The one at Sawmill Bay, near the

Morning breaks at the scenic port of Valdez.

native village of Chenega, is one of the largest of its kind in the world in terms of fry released. Salmon runs became so predictable that by the late '80s local fishermen said that catching pink salmon in the sound was more like ocean ranching than fishing.

Meanwhile, a new concern had arisen for fishermen – the presence of oil tankers in their pristine fishing grounds. When oil was discovered beneath the tundra of Alaska's far north, Valdez was chosen as the southern terminus for an 800-mile-long pipeline. Enormous storage tanks were built at Valdez, along with a maze of feeder lines and valves, tanker berths and giant incinerators.

Starting in 1977, crude oil was regularly loaded into tankers and shipped south to refineries. The men and women who fished in local waters were largely opposed to these massive ships traversing the intricate waterways of their fishing grounds. However, measures were taken to ensure their safe movement and for years the transport of oil through the Sound ran smoothly, with no major accidents occurring. Escort tugs and harbor pilots safely saw these tankers (the length of three football fields) through the narrow entrance of the Port of Valdez, past Middle Rock (dubbed the 'can opener') and into open waters. Then, in 1986, things began to change. Budget cutbacks resulted in decreased Coast Guard staff at Valdez, and their radar system was downgraded. Tanker crews, with a proven track record of safety, were no longer required to have a pilot on board past Rocky Point.

Oil tankers in Prince William Sound are now subject to stringent safety measures, including tug escorts and travel restrictions in weather too severe to contain a spill.

Complacency is a mariner's worst enemy and this lesson was learned the hard way in the early hours of March 24, 1989, when the *Exxon Valdez* ran onto **Bligh Reef** and spilled 11 million gallons of crude oil into the pristine waters of Prince William Sound. Currents quickly spread the oil in a southwest direction for 1,200 miles towards the Kenai Fjords, Kodiak Island and the southern tip of the Alaska Peninsula.

Reporters and photographers from around the world converged on Valdez and local residents turned their spare bedrooms into hotel rooms to meet the demand for accommodations. Others arriving at Valdez came to help, and thousands of workers were employed by Exxon to clean the oiled beaches – either by hand or with power hoses. An Alaska state ferry became a floating dormitory for workers.

Fishing fleets were hired to install, clean and repair booms used to corral the spilled oil. As the slick rode the prevailing currents toward the south-western entrance of Prince William Sound, boats rushed to Sawmill Bay to protect its hatchery with booms. While Alaskans scrambled to keep the spreading oil off their local shores, waterbirds died by the thousands – many so coated in oil they were unidentifiable. Hardest hit of the mammals were the sea otters.

Snug Harbor, on Knight Island, was heavily oiled from the 1989 spill and its streams are still being monitored for lingering after-effects.

Unlike other marine mammals, sea otters retain their body heat not with blubber but with an insulating fur coat. If this thick fur becomes coated with crude oil, it quickly loses its ability to trap warm air next to the skin and the animal dies of hypothermia. Many of these oil-coated creatures climbed out of the frigid water in an attempt to stay warm. Others inhaled toxic fumes or ingested oil as they groomed their fur.

Exxon spent millions of dollars rescuing the area's wildlife, and extraordinary efforts were made to save the afflicted sea otters. Rushed to emergency headquarters, they were stabilized and sedated before enduring repeated washings with a soap solution. Local swimming pools became holding pens for the cleaned otters while they groomed themselves (which restores natural oils) and regained their strength before being returned to the wild. Some were flown to city aquariums for treatment.

Sea otters, which depend on their thick coats for warmth, are especially vulnerable to oil spills.

The majority of Prince William Sound's shoreline was untouched by the oil spill, and attempts were made to clean the islands and beaches that were in the slick's path. The verdict is still out on the success of this clean-up operation, with a recent government study concluding that lingering oil remains in many streambeds and is dispersed into waterways by tidal action. This residual oil will, according to scientists with the National Marine Fisheries Service, continue to kill or stunt Alaska's pink salmon stocks for generations to come. However, visitors who come to view the pristine beauty and abundant marine life of Prince William Sound will not be disappointed.

The massive Columbia Glacier (largest in Prince William Sound) is one of Alaska's most active tidewater glaciers, calving large quantities of ice as it beats a steady retreat.

One of the Sound's most impressive natural sights also played a major role in the 1989 oil spill. **Columbia Glacier**, largest in Prince William Sound, was named by the Harriman Expedition in 1899. It is over 40 miles long, covers about 440 square miles and terminates at the head of Columbia Bay, a fjord with depths reaching 2,300 feet. The snout of this glacier is six miles across and varies from 160 to 260 feet in height above sea level. The Columbia Glacier has retreated almost a mile in recent years, and scientists predict a drastic retreat of about 20 miles in the next 50 years. This will cause an increase in iceberg production which could potentially block the entrance to the nearby Port of Valdez. Ice discharged from the Columbia has already proven to be a hazard, for the ill-fated *Exxon Valdez* had altered its course to avoid some large ice floes when it hit Bligh Reef. The cruise ships usually keep their distance from Columbia's towering terminus, which is often congested with floating ice, bobbing seals and numerous birds attracted to the fish that feed here on plankton.

Valdez (population 4,000) is the most northerly ice-free port in the Western Hemisphere and is connected to the rest of mainland Alaska by the Richardson Highway. Nestled at the base of the Chugach Mountains, Valdez has been called Alaska's Little Switzerland because of its scenic alpine setting. Attractions include a tour of the Alyeska Pipeline Terminal, the local museum, and a visit to the retreating Valdez Glacier, located about four miles above the pre-1964 townsite.

The **Richardson Highway**, running parallel with the pipeline, leads north to Fairbanks. It winds past the Worthington Glacier (accessible on foot) and past the Black Rapids Glacier, which became international news in the 1930s when it began surging up to 200 feet per day. As it advanced toward the highway, a radio announcer was there waiting to

Three Hole Point is one of several dramatic landmarks viewed by visitors to Kenai Fjords National Park.

provide play-by-play action to his listeners. With a true sense of dramatic timing, the wall of ice stopped just short of the highway and the announcer was left with no destruction to report.

KENAI PENINSULA

Seward, headquarters for Kenai Fjords National Park, is 127 highway miles from Anchorage. Located at the head of Resurrection Bay at the foot of the Kenai Mountains, Seward was established in 1903 as an ocean terminal for the planned Alaska Railroad. Named after Secretary of State William Seward (who arranged the purchase of Alaska in 1867), the town of 2,500 is today a cargo and fishing port.

The waters in and around Resurrection Bay are prime fishing grounds, with huge salmon runs and halibut weighing over 300 pounds. The Seward Silver Salmon Derby, held each August, is Alaska's most prestigious fishing event, drawing thousands of anglers. Halibut, a seafood delicacy, is served fresh from the sea in Seward's modern, waterfront restaurants overlooking the bustling boat harbor.

At the south end of town is the new **Alaska SeaLife Center**, a research and educational complex operated by the University of Alaska-Fairbanks. Sick, injured or stranded sea mammals and birds are brought to the Center to be cared for by a team of veterinarians. Those animals unable to return to the wild will find a permanent home at the Center where rookeries are designed to mimic the region's natural habitat, featuring pools of clear sea water and secluded areas where animals can mate and rear their young.

The **Park Visitor Center** provides information on **Kenai Fjords National Park**, which was established in 1980 and is best seen from the water. Seward's sightseeing boats take visitors to see the park's rugged

The cruise ships dock at the head of Resurrection Bay opposite Seward's bustling boat harbor.

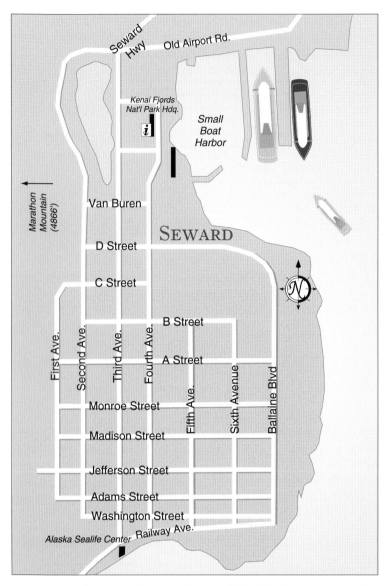

capes, sea arches and tidewater glaciers. (**Exit Glacier**, about 10 miles outside Seward along Exit Glacier Road, is the easiest of the park's glaciers to reach by land.) The massive **Harding Icefield** covers an area of 30 by 50 miles and is a remnant of an icecap that completely covered the Kenai Mountains at the end of the last ice age. As recently as 1909, the Kenai Fjords were still ice-filled bays. Fifty years later these glaciers had staged a major retreat, leaving in their wake fjords which contain new islands and cliffs freshly scoured by ice.

In addition to this dramatic glacial action, tectonic plates are colliding in the area. The Kenai Mountains rest on the subsiding edge of one plate and, as they are pulled under, glacial-carved cirques become half-moon bays and former peaks are reduced to craggy islands. The Kenai coast is slowly slipping into the sea. All this happens very slowly of course, except when an earthquake hits.

When the 1964 Good Friday Earthquake struck, the ground underneath Seward – perched on the edge of a submarine slope – lost its shear strength and became part of a massive underwater slide. The Seward shoreline dropped six feet within 30 seconds, taking with it the town's harbor and fuel docks. This was followed by a series of tsunamis that wiped out the remaining waterfront industries, including the railroad docks. Seward's death toll was 13 and a plaque in remembrance of these victims rests in the center of town near the rebuilt harbor.

The natural forces at work along the Kenai coast are manifested in dramatic landmarks that compete for sightseers' attention. First there is **Aialak Cape**, a granite intrusive formed 60 million years ago, which looks like a huge boulder shoved skyward from the earth's crust. Then there is **Three Hole Point** – a towering sea arch formed by wave erosion. And of course there are the glaciers, many of which are still unnamed. Sea mammals thrive in these waters and more than 200,000 seabirds – including horned and tufted puffins – nest on the rocky islands and capes of the Kenai Peninsula. The **Chiswell Islands** are also used by sea lions, and **Barwell Island**, off Cape Resurrection, is a murre colony. In Resurrection Bay, sea otters are a common sight.

Resurrection Bay was once used by Russian fur traders for ship building. Before that it was inhabited by a small population of Southern Eskimos called Unegkurmit. In 1918, the artist and adventurer Rockwell Kent lived with his son and a fox farmer on **Fox Island**. His book *Wilderness: A Quiet Adventure in Alaska* describes his winter experiences here.

On the western shores of Resurrection Bay, six miles south of Seward, is **Caines Head State Recreation Area**. This steep headland, with its strategic view of the bay, was chosen by the United States Army for building a Harbor Defense System during World War II. Seward was an important wartime port, being Alaska's only year-round transportation center before completion of the Whittier Tunnel and Alcan Highway. A half-dozen other locations were also chosen for guarding Resurrection Bay, and boat tours often take passengers past an iron bunker installed opposite Fox Island near the bay's eastern entrance.

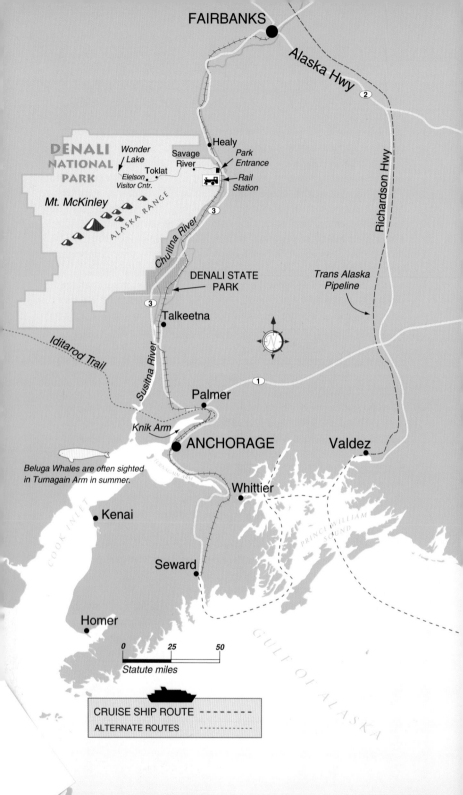

CHAPTER THIRTEEN

ANCHORAGE
Denali National Park and Fairbanks

Anchorage, 'Air Crossroads of the World,' is also the crossroads of Alaska. Not only does its busy international airport handle over 200 flights per day, the city's Lake Hood Air Harbor is the world's busiest floatplane base – handling more than 800 take-offs and landings on a peak summer day. Anchorage is also connected by road and rail to Seward and other communities on the Kenai Peninsula, to Prince William Sound (via Whittier), to Alaska's interior, and to the rest of North America.

As transportation hub of Alaska, Anchorage is the state's distribution center. Fish and other Alaskan products pass through Anchorage before being shipped elsewhere, and more than 80% of Alaskans depend on Anchorage for incoming freight. In addition to being a major cargo port, Anchorage is the commercial center of Alaska. The city's highrises house the offices of large oil corporations, as well as federal, state and local government agencies. Yet, even with a population of a quarter million, Anchorage remains refreshingly Alaskan.

Like most Alaskan ports, Anchorage is dominated by the surrounding scenery. The city is situated on the eastern shores of Cook Inlet and backed by the Chugach Mountains, which wrap around Prince William Sound and eventually join another coastal range – the Saint Elias Mountains. To the south of Anchorage are the glacier-carved and ocean-lapped fjords of the Kenai Peninsula, and to the north is the Alaska Range, home of Mount McKinley and Denali National Park.

On a clear day, the distant peak of Mount McKinley can be seen from downtown Anchorage.

The wilderness surrounding Anchorage also makes its way into the city. In winter, moose often show up in the suburbs looking for food, and each spring Anchorage hosts a large population of nesting loons. The city celebrates its close ties to the wilderness with such events as the annual Moose Dropping and Bear Paw Festivals. Best known is the Iditarod Trail Dog Sled Race, an 1,100-mile race from Anchorage to Nome which is held each March. Since the first race in 1977, trained dog teams have mushed their way across two mountain ranges and the pack ice of Norton Sound to reach the finish line at Nome. The race commemorates a heroic rescue mission carried out in 1925 when an outbreak of diphtheria threatened the residents of Nome. A life-saving serum was relayed by sled dog mushers who followed an old dog-team mail route that had been blazed in 1910.

Amid the outdoor activities and festivals of Anchorage, there exists the refinement of luxury hotels, gourmet restaurants, and a center for the performing arts. In addition to a resident symphony orchestra, the city has hosted an impressive list of international artists which includes the famous cellist Yo-Yo Ma, Russian pianist Alexei Sultanov, soprano Dawn Upshaw, and The Chieftains.

About the only thing lacking in Anchorage is a fishing fleet. The reason is its location at the head of Cook Inlet, where the tidal range is the second largest in the world – second only to Atlantic Canada's Bay of Fundy. Tidal fluxes in Turnagain Arm can surpass 33 feet, and surface waters are in constant motion – travelling at speeds of five to seven knots – with incoming tides often creating a tidal bore (a standing wave) in Turnagain Arm. From November to April, the upper inlet is often frozen or packed with floe ice, and the water's high content of glacial silt is damaging to the saltwater pumps and shaft bearings of fishboat engines.

The water's high silt content was likely a factor in Captain Cook's assuming the inlet was a river when he sailed into this uncharted and boulder-strewn body of water in 1778. His survey was also hindered by recurring thick fog. When Captain Vancouver retraced Cook's route in 1794, he determined that "Cook's River" was actually an inlet and renamed it Cook Inlet.

At one time, the ice in Cook Inlet was 3,000 feet thick. When the ice retreated up Knik and Turnagain Arms at the head of the inlet, shallow estuaries formed as glacial silt was deposited by the retreating glaciers. Upon these shores human presence appeared in about 6000 BC when Southern Eskimos first arrived. They inhabited upper Cook Inlet until about 1650 AD, then moved to Prince William Sound when Tanaina natives migrated into the area. Russian fur traders were the next to frequent the region, followed by Russian priests who established a mission near Knik, close to present-day Anchorage, in 1835.

When gold was discovered in 1882 at Crow Creek, about 40 miles of where downtown Anchorage would eventually stand, prospec-

The Alaska Railroad joined Seward and Anchorage in 1918 and still provides summer passenger service.

tors began moving into the area. Then, in 1914, President Woodrow Wilson authorized construction of the Alaska Railroad, with Anchorage the mid-point of a line connecting the coal and gold fields of the interior with the port of Seward. Job seekers flocked to the area and a tent city sprang up on the banks of Ship Creek.

A grid pattern of streets and avenues was laid out by army engineers and a land auction was held, with 655 lots selling for an average price of $225 each. A month later, in August 1915, a poll was held to choose a name for the budding railroad town. The voters chose Alaska City but the federal government decided to keep the existing name of Anchorage. Three years later, the arrival of the first train from Seward marked the completion of the southern line.

World War II brought the next boom to Anchorage. In 1940, Fort Richardson and Elmendorf Air Force Base were built. This military buildup continued with construction of the Alaska Highway in 1942 and, by the end of the war, Anchorage's population had increased five and a half times to 43,000 residents.

In 1951, Anchorage opened its international airport to transpolar air traffic between Europe and Asia, as well as domestic and inter-state airlines. Seven years later, on June 30, 1958, the Statehood Act was passed and Anchorage celebrated with a 50-ton bonfire. 'North to the Future' was the new state's motto, and the future looked promising for Anchorage. Then, on March 27, 1964, a massive earthquake – the largest ever recorded in North America – hit the city. Situated on glacial silt deposits, downtown Anchorage was devastated. Amid violent shaking, the ground beneath buildings slid into the sea. Sections of

A view of downtown Anchorage as seen from across the waters of
Knik Arm at Earthquake Park.

3rd and 4th Avenues collapsed, dropping as much as 10 feet. In the Turnagain area, 75 homes were destroyed, some of them sliding 2,000 feet. Despite such destruction, the city wasted no time rebuilding.

The discovery of North Slope oil in 1968 brought the most recent boom, as oil and construction companies set up headquarters in Anchorage. In 1979, oil revenue began providing the city with such facilities as a new sports arena, a convention center and the Alaska Center for the Performing Arts. The Anchorage Museum of History and Art was expanded and, in 1985, Anchorage was a contender for hosting the 1992 Winter Olympics. The future has arrived for the former tent city of Anchorage.

DOWNTOWN ATTRACTIONS

A tour of downtown Anchorage usually begins at the **Visitor Information Center ▋**. Housed in a rustic log cabin with a sod roof, the center is a much photographed sight, with a milepost out front showing directions and flying distances to various cities around the world. Outside the entrance stands a 5,144-pound jade boulder. (Jade, ᵗʰe state gem, is mined around the Arctic Circle.) Across the street from Information Center is a mural that was commissioned in 1990 to ᵉmorate Anchorage's 75th anniversary.

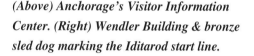

(Above) Anchorage's Visitor Information Center. (Right) Wendler Building & bronze sled dog marking the Iditarod start line.

The city's grid pattern (streets running north and south, avenues running east and west) makes downtown Anchorage an easy place to navigate on foot. Hour-long city trolley tours depart every hour on the hour from in front of the 4th Avenue Theater.

Many of Anchorage's original buildings are found on 4th Avenue, and the **4th Avenue Theater 2** is a city landmark. Built in the art deco style, it first opened in 1947. Completely refurbished in 1992, the theatre contains floor-to-ceiling bronze murals and a ceiling decorated with twinkling lights in the shape of the Big Dipper. This heritage building also houses a restaurant and gift shop. Across the street, at the corner of 4th Avenue and F Street, is the **Alaska Public Lands Information Center 3**. It was completed in 1939 and is included in the National Register of Historic Places. Formerly the location of a post office and Federal District Court, the building is now a source of park information for visitors planning trips to various regions of Alaska.

Stewart's Photo Shop 4 (one block east) is the second-oldest downtown building and its pressed tin ceiling dates from its earlier days as Oscar Anderson's Meat Market. Continuing east along 4th to D Street, you will come across the North Pacific Arc Mural, a huge painting depicting the route of the Anchorage-to-Nome Iditarod Trail Sled Dog Race. On the opposite corner is the Wendler Building **5** (Club

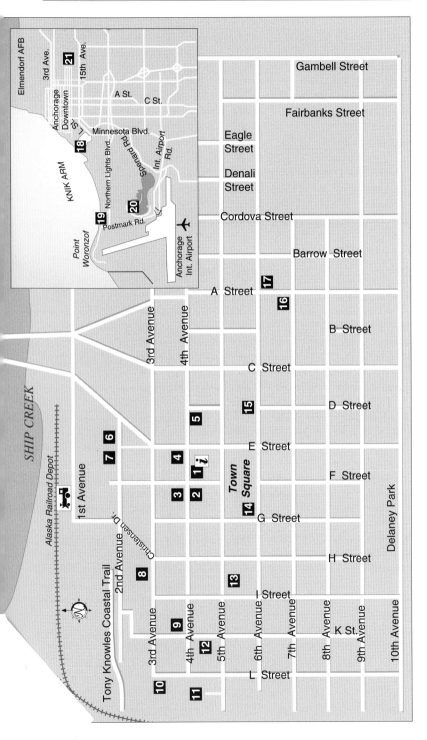

25). Built in 1925 by an early resident, this turreted building was moved here (from the corner of 4th and I Street) in 1984 and is on the National Register of Historic Places. The annual Iditarod Trail Dog Sled Race starts in front of this building and is commemorated with a large, bronze sculpture of a sled dog. Next door, at 446 W. 4th Avenue, is the **National Bank of Alaska** where tapestries depicting Alaska's history are displayed in the lobby. Another lobby worth visiting is that of the Hilton Hotel, at 3rd Avenue and F Street, where a stuffed brown bear and polar bear are on display.

If you head north on E Street to 2nd Avenue, you arrive at the **Alaska Statehood Monument** **6**, erected in 1990 to commemorate Anchorage's 75th anniversary and the 100th anniversary of President Eisenhower's birth. To the west of the monument is the **Ship Creek Overlook** **7**, providing views of the Alaska Railroad Depot to the north and of Ship Creek itself – site of a former fish camp of the Tanaina natives, then a tent city of railroad workers. Today the creek is a popular salmon fishing stream for Anchorage residents. West of the Ship Creek Outlook, on 2nd Avenue, are some of Anchorage's historic homes, built in 1917 when the railroad was being developed.

A few blocks west, near the end of 2nd Avenue, is the start of the **Tony Knowles Coastal Trail** – eight miles of paved trail which winds along the coast. One block south of the trail's starting point, at the top of Christensen Drive, is the **Port of Anchorage Viewpoint** **8**. This overlooks Knik Arm and the mouth of Ship Creek, where gold rush steamships once anchored while unloading passengers and supplies.

Turning off 3rd Avenue at K Street, you come to the **Boney Memorial Courthouse** **9**, with lobby artwork which includes a totem pole depiction and 19th century Eskimo motifs carved in teak wall panels. Across the street is the 'Last Blue Whale' statue, designed by Joseph Princiotta.

Returning to 3rd Avenue and proceeding west one block to L Street, you arrive at **Resolution Park** **10** and the Captain Cook Monument, commemorating the 200th anniversary of Captain Cook's third and final voyage on board his ship, the *Resolution*. Across the inlet stands Mount Susitna (the Sleeping Lady), its rounded shape carved by glacial ice that once flowed across its summit and lay 3,000 feet deep in Cook Inlet.

Three of Alaska's four tallest active volcanoes are also found on the western shores of Cook Inlet – Mount Spurr (11,070 feet), Mount Redoubt (10,197 feet) and Mount Iliamna (10,016 feet). On an island within the inlet stands Mount St. Augustine (4,025 feet) which erupted in 1986, sending ash eight miles high and disrupting air traffic in south-central Alaska. Mount Redoubt erupted in December 1989, lightly dusting Anchorage with ash and disrupting holiday air travel. A more recent eruption came from Mount Spurr in August 1992, with prevailing winds carrying the ash west to Prince William Sound and Yakutat Bay.

The Alaska Statehood Monument commemorates Alaska's 75th anniversary.

Directly south of Resolution Park is **Elderberry Park 11**, which contains the Oscar Anderson House – Anchorage's first wood frame house built in 1915 and now a museum, open daily in the summer.

A walk east along 5th Avenue will take you past the **Three Ships Sculpture 12**, which depicts the voyages of Captain James Cook who, in 1778, searched the Alaska coast for a northwest passage.

Other points of interest along 5th Avenue are the **Holy Family Cathedral 13**, transported from the town of Knik by horse and sleigh in the early 1920s; the **Imaginarium**, a science discovery center; and the **William A. Egan Civic & Convention Center**, named for Alaska's first governor elected after statehood.

On 6th Avenue between F and G Streets, is the **Alaska Center for the Performing Arts 14**. In the same block is the Town Square Municipal Park – an outdoor amphitheater. At 343 W. 6th Avenue is the **Reeve Aviation Picture Museum 15**, with over a thousand photos on display featuring famous bush pilots of Alaska.

At 121 W. 7th Avenue is the **Anchorage Museum of History and Art 16**, an impressive museum housing Alaskan and northern art – from prehistoric to contemporary times. A gift shop and cafe are also on the premises. Across the road, at 605 A Street is the **TAHETA Art & Culture Group Co-Op 17**, where you can watch native artisans at work and purchase their craftwork, including baskets and soapstone carvings.

In summer, flowers fill the streets of downtown Anchorage, blooming in park beds and spilling from baskets along 2nd Avenue (left).

OTHER ANCHORAGE ATTRACTIONS

Delaney Park is a strip of parkland running east/west from A to P Streets between 9th and 10th Avenues. Named for a former mayor, it was originally a firebreak for the townsite. Called 'Park Strip,' it now contains flower gardens, picnic tables, sports fields and was the location of Pope John Paul II's open air mass – attended by 50,000 people – when he visited Anchorage in 1981.

Ship Creek Salmon Overlook & Waterfowl Nesting Area 🔟, at the mouth of Ship Creek, is where you can watch salmon swimming upstream from June through September. At the nearby Westchester Lagoon Waterfowl Sanctuary, wild geese and ducks live year round.

Earthquake Park 🔟, located between Northern Lights Boulevard and the shores of Knik Arm, is the site of Anchorage's worst destruction during the 1964 earthquake. Here buildings were leveled by landslides. Rather than rebuild in this area, Anchorage residents decided to turn it into a park with an interpretive display. The Tony Knowles Coastal Trail runs along the park's shoreline.

The Captain Cook Monument overlooks the water at Resolution Park.

Lake Hood Air Harbor [20], located between Earthquake Park and the International Airport, is the world's largest and busiest floatplane base. A shoreside park offers visitors a view of the lake and its aerial activity. **Alaska Aviation Heritage Museum** on the south shore of Lake Hood (4721 Aircraft Drive) contains an observation deck and fascinating displays featuring historic aircraft and pioneer aviators.

North of downtown is the **Elmendorf Air Force Base Wildlife Museum**, **Elmendorf State Fish Hatchery**, and the **Russian Jack Springs Park**, containing golf links, hiking/biking trails and picnic areas.

One mile east of downtown is **Merrill Field** [21], named in honor of a pioneer pilot who was the first to fly a commercial flight west of Juneau and the first to attempt a night landing in Anchorage. He also discovered, in 1927, a key pass in the Alaska Range which bears his name. With half of Alaska's licensed pilots living in Anchorage, Merrill Field is a busy small plane base.

Some of Anchorage's most popular attractions are located south of downtown. The **Alyeska Resort & Ski Area** offers world-class alpine skiing in the winter and sweeping views from atop alpine meadows in the summer. The **Wetlands Observation Platform** provides excellent birdwatching opportunities and a view of Twenty-Mile Glacier at the end of the valley.

The scenic Matanuska Valley is fertile farming country.

PORTAGE GLACIER

One of the most-visited sites in Alaska is the Portage Glacier. The highway leading to **Portage Lake** passes the former townsite of Portage – a railroad town which was once part of a natural trading route between Cook Inlet and Prince William Sound, used by natives, Russian fur traders and gold prospectors. The land underneath Portage sank during the 1964 earthquake and, flooded by Turnagain Arm, the town was abandoned. The marshy land is now ideal habitat for waterfowl. There is no road connection between Portage and Whittier (on Prince William Sound), but in summer the Alaska Railroad runs a daily train from Portage to Whittier, with vehicles riding on flat cars through mountain tunnels.The turnoff to Portage Lake is about three miles past the former townsite, and it follows eight miles of paved highway to the **Portage Glacier Recreation Area**. In addition to a visitor center providing information on glaciers, there are boat tours available on Portage Lake. Your sightseeing vessel will wind past floating icebergs to the face of Portage Glacier. A number of glaciers can be viewed from the Recreation Area, as well as mountain goats and other wildlife. The area also supports a thriving moose population.

MATANUSKA VALLEY

This lush valley is 40 miles northeast of Anchorage and was settled in the 1930s by midwest farmers. The growing season here is only four months but the long daylight hours produce giant vegetables – turnips over seven pounds and 70-pound cabbages. Palmer is the valley's trading center and home of Olympic champion skier Tommy Moe.

*Regular bus excursions into the tundra of
Denali National Park offer travellers a
chance to spot moose, bear or sometimes,
as shown above, caribou.*

The rail connection to Denali stops right at the park entrance.

DENALI NATIONAL PARK AND PRESERVE

Denali is a native word meaning 'high one' and it refers to **Mount McKinley** (named after President McKinley) – a mountain that rises 15,000 feet above the surrounding countryside. Its twin peaks stand in isolation, often shrouded in clouds that collect around the tallest mountain in North America. The north summit is 19,470 feet high and the south peak rises to 20,320 feet. The Denali National Park and Preserve is huge and, at six million acres, is larger than Massachusetts.

Mount McKinley is part of the six-hundred-mile long **Alaska Range** and its massive size is likely due to its location in a bend of the Denali fault system, where one crustal block has shoved against another. McKinley is an impressive sight and a challenging climb for mountaineers, who first reached the North Peak in 1910 and the South Peak in 1913. Summer weather on Mount McKinley is cool, wet and windy.

The Alaska Range was a natural barrier between native groups living for centuries in this area – north of the range were the interior Athabascans and to the south were the Cook Inlet Athabascans. Both groups hunted the abundant wildlife (especially caribou and moose) which thrived along the alpine slopes of the range.

The Park was created to protect these large mammals and came about largely through the efforts of naturalist and conservationist Charles Sheldon who first visited the Denali region in the summer of 1906. As chairman of the Boone and Crockett Club of New York, Sheldon led a campaign for ten years to preserve the Denali wilderness and finally, in 1917, Congress approved a bill to establish a national park. Although Sheldon wanted the name of Denali for the new park, it was called the Mount McKinley National Park from 1917 until 1980. In that year the boundary of the park was tripled in size from 1.9 million acres to six million acres and became the Denali National Park and Preserve.

The Park is located 240 miles north of Anchorage (120 miles south of Fairbanks) and can be reached by road, rail or plane. The park contains habitat for 37 species of mammals (caribou, grizzly bear, moose, wolf and Dall sheep among others) and 155 species of birds, including golden and bald eagles. These animals live in the taiga (white and black spruce intermingled with aspen, birch and poplar) and tundra (willow, dwarf birch, sedges and grasses), alongside the lakes, rivers, canyons and alpine glaciers of the park. A 90-mile road traverses the park, providing visitors with breathtaking sights of **Wonder Lake**, **Savage River Canyon** and **Muldrow Glacier**, which descends 16,000 feet from the upper slopes of Mount McKinley.

The Park is the highlight of land tours available to cruise passengers embarking or disembarking in Seward and gives a traveller first-hand experience with Alaska tundra. The main area staging area for Park visitors is just south of the town of Healey where a number of hotels and

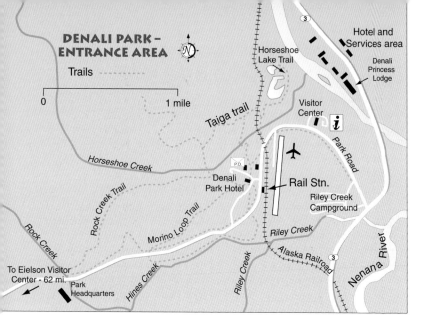

services are situated. Cars are restricted within the Park and regular bus shuttles take visitors to various points throughout the Park where one can wander and observe this beautiful landscape.

If you arrive at Denali with a cruise line land tour, you will have the option of numerous excursions into the Park organized by the hotel or the cruise line. The buses move along the park gravel road at a leisurely pace, stopping at the various viewpoints along the way. The Eielson Visitor Center is the most common turnaround point and is an eight-hour round trip providing spectacular views of Mt. McKinley and the surrounding tundra. Longer day excursions extend to Wonder Lake, about 170 miles or 11 hours round trip. Although there are restrooms and drinking water available at the park centers, there is no food service. So, in addition to warm clothing, you should be sure to pack a lunch if it is not being provided on the excursion.

If you arrive at Denali by car, be aware you will have to leave your vehicle at your hotel and reserve a seat on a bus to take you into the further reaches of the park, as private vehicles are restricted beyond Savage River. It is recommended you reserve seats on the bus at least two days in advance. There is regular bus shuttle service to the entrance areas of the park where there are well maintained trails.

If you are considering overnight camping in the backcountry of the park, permits must be obtained in person at the visitor center.

WHAT TO LOOK FOR IN DENALI PARK

There are many species of wildlife you will be able to see from roadside vantage points. Caribou and moose can sometimes be seen feeding within a few miles of the road and occasionally a brown (grizzly) bear might be spotted foraging near a lake or along a slope. The Park is also home to wolves, but during summer months they generally hunt individually and usually at night so a sighting is not common.

The Park also supports a variety of birds, some of which have migrated great distances, including the arctic tern (from Antarctica) and jaegers which have arrived from southern oceans. More common are the ptarmigan (a small goose-like bird), grouse and jays. Some birds of prey can also be seen in the Park, such as golden eagles (second-largest of all hawks) which ride the updrafts along ridgetops in search of food.

The area near the hotels is taiga forest and the vegetation includes small white and black spruce as well as birch, larch and aspen.

> ## SAFE HIKING
> When hiking in Denali, especially in backcountry areas, bear in mind weather conditions can change quickly and sturdy footgear is a must. Never approach a wild animal or attempt to feed it and be especially wary of grizzly cubs – the sow is usually nearby and can become very aggressive. Crossing glacial rivers can be dangerous. Check with the visitor center for information on trails for longer hikes or to obtain an overnight permit.

FAIRBANKS

Situated on a flat river plain, Fairbanks is a sprawling city – the second largest in Alaska with a borough population of 75,000. Named for the Indiana Republican Senator Charles W. Fairbanks (who became Vice President to Theodore Roosevelt), the town was founded during the gold rush. Enjoying a strategic position on the banks of the Chena River, Fairbanks became a major trading center for miners.

During World War II, the military built airfields and roads around Fairbanks, and this construction boom produced jobs for the local civilians. Fairbanks also benefited from the Cold War Era when renewed defense spending expanded the area's existing bases, and radar systems and missile sites were installed. Today its airforce base serves as the site of a joint American-Canadian-Russian training program for coordinating search and rescue operations in the Arctic.

In 1967, the Chena River overflowed and flooded Fairbanks. With the help of federal aid, local businesses were rebuilt and homes were restored. A year later, oil was discovered near Prudhoe Bay, and Fairbanks was once again in a strategic position for the proposed pipeline. When construction began in 1974, the population surged. The heyday ended in 1978 and Fairbanks plummeted into a recession with widespread unemployment.

The hot and cold nature of Fairbanks' economic past is also reflected in its climate. Located just 90 miles south of the Arctic Circle, winter days are short and bitterly cold. In contrast to the dark chill of winter are the long, hot, sunny days of summer with daylight in June and July lasting about 21 hours. The aurora borealis is regularly seen in the skies over Fairbanks.

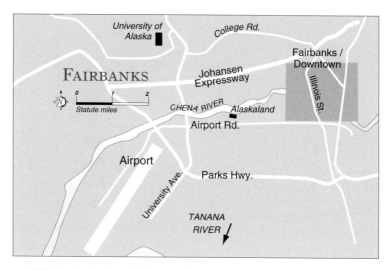

With its local sites fairly spread out, Fairbanks is best seen by car or coach tour, although guided walking tours are offered by the Fairbanks Convention & Visitors Bureau.

The following are a few popular attractions.

Alaskaland Pioneer Park

Established in 1967 to commemorate the centennial of Alaska's purchase, this 44-acre park is encircled by its own small-scale railroad to provide transportation for visitors. Admission is free and sites include the Gold Rush Town, where shops and cafes are housed in relocated pioneer cabins; Palace Theater & Saloon which holds summer musical reviews; the sternwheeler Nenana which is drydocked in the middle of the park; the Pioneer Museum; and Northern Inva, where native athletes demonstrate their heritage sports.

University of Alaska Fairbanks (UAF)

In 1915, Congress set aside 2,500 acres of land in the Tanana Valley upon which an agricultural college was built, opening in 1922 with six students and six faculty. Enrollment steadily climbed and for decades the University of Alaska Fairbanks was the main institution for higher learning in Alaska. In recent years, other university campuses (and private colleges) have been established, but the University's statewide administration remains in Fairbanks.

The Office of University Relations provides guided tours of campus attractions throughout the summer. On campus is the University of Alaska Museum – one of the state's top 10 visitor attractions – containing displays of Alaska animals, plants, natural history, native culture and gold rush history. Also popular is the Geophysical Institute – a center for earthquake research – and the **Large Animal Research Station** where you can view musk-ox, reindeer and caribou from raised platforms.

The **SS Klondike,** *on permanent display in Whitehorse, was the largest sternwheeler to ply the Yukon River when riverboats were the main source of transportation for the region.*

Sternwheeler Cruises

Extremely popular is the four-hour-long, narrated cruise of the Chena and Tanana Rivers aboard an authentic sternwheel riverboat. A local family with 90 years of Alaskan riverboating heritage runs these river cruises. From the decks of a sternwheeler you will see log cabins, fish wheels and the 'Wedding of the Rivers' where the Tanana – carrying 100,000 tons of glacier sediment – meets the mouth of the Chena. Stops along the way include a dog sledding demonstration and visits to a native village and a trapper's cabin.

OUT-OF-TOWN ATTRACTIONS

A few miles outside of Fairbanks is the **Cripple Creek Resort** (also known as the Ester Gold Camp). Listed on the National Register of Historic Places, its authentic gold rush buildings include the Cripple Creek Hotel and the famous Malemute Saloon.

Proceeding west along the Park Highway, travellers arrive at **Nenana** where the local railroad depot houses the official State of Alaska Railroad Museum. Built in 1923, it too is listed on the National Register of Historic Sites.

An hour's drive east of Fairbanks along the Chena Hot Springs Road culminates at the **Chena Hot Springs**. Rustic cabins provide accommodation and soaking facilities include two jacuzzis, a hot tub and a swimming pool. The springs here circulate through fractures in the granite to depths of two miles where the rock is hotter than the surface boiling point of water.

Circle Hot Springs, discovered by a prospector in 1893, are reached by the Steese Highway which leads in a northeast direction from Fairbanks. **Manley Hot Springs** are located a 45-minute flight north-

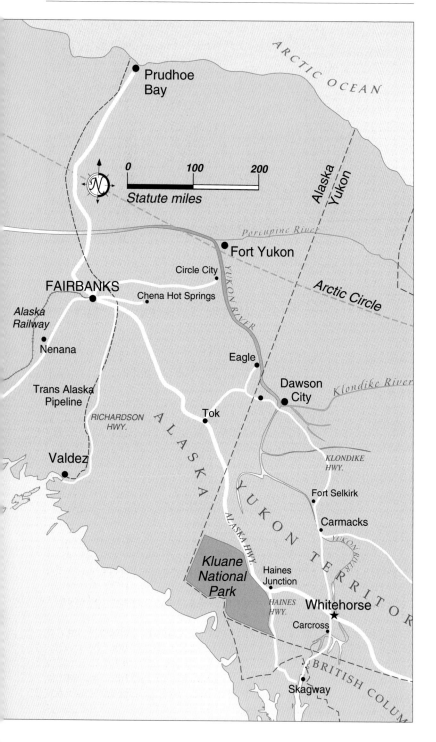

Visitors can pan for gold at Gold Dredge Number 8, which operated in the Goldstream Valley near Fairbanks from 1928 to 1959.

west of Fairbanks or via a detour off the **Dalton Highway**, which leads north to Prudhoe Bay. A trip along the Dalton takes you across the Yukon River, the Arctic Circle, the rugged Brooks Range, rolling foothills and a vast, tundra-covered plain. Called the "Haul Road," it was a supply route for trucks serving work camps during construction of the **Trans-Alaska Pipeline**.

Construction of the pipeline was Alaska's most important economic boom since the Gold Rush. Built by a conglomerate of oil companies, called Alyeska Pipeline Service Company, it was a major engineering feat and was designed to prevent thawing of the permafrost which covers much of Alaska's interior. Other factors in construction were the region's drastic temperature range (from 90° F to -60° F) and high earthquake activity. Last but not least were concerns that the pipeline would damage the region's fragile ecosystem and disrupt migration of caribou and other animals.

The discovery of oil in 1968 set a series of events into motion. In 1971, the Native Claims Settlement Act resolved the grievances of Alaska's natives who felt that neither the Alaska Purchase nor the Statehood Act had established their land rights. The 1971 Act established 13 native-owned corporations, and granted the native peoples $1 billion in revenue and 40 million acres of land.

In November 1973, Congress passed the Pipeline Authorization Act and construction of the 800-mile pipeline began. About half of its length was raised on stilts joined in a zig-zag pattern for flexibility when the pipeline expands and contracts with drastic temperature changes. The accordion-like pattern also allows the pipeline to absorb earthquake waves without damage.

The oil started to flow in 1977, with friction from the pumping pressure keeping the oil at about 140° F. To absorb this heat rather than transfer it into the ground (and melt the permafrost), the stilts supporting the pipeline contain a special liquid that absorbs the oil's high temperature and releases it into the air through radiator fins. The pipeline is buried underground at regularly spaced intervals to allow for crossings by caribou, which reportedly will not pass beneath a raised structure. The caribou herds which migrate across the North Slope appear to be unaffected by the pipeline's presence and are flourishing.

The oil discovered at **Prudhoe Bay** was a long time in the making. Its source is a rich shale deposited during early Jurassic time, which was eventually covered with 6,000 feet of sandstone and other rock during the geological formation of Alaska. A chemical process (not yet fully understood) transforms organic material into oil which, being lighter than water, will float through available pores and fractures in the rock above and collect in reservoirs.

ALASKA HIGHWAY

Another major engineering project which changed the landscape of Alaska was the construction of the Alaska Highway. Built during World War II, it was hastily completed during the Japanese occupation of the Aleutian Islands. The highway starts at **Dawson Creek** (Mile 0) in northern British Columbia and winds through 1,520 miles of forests, mountains, muskeg and rivers to Fairbanks.

Construction began on March 9, 1942, with the U.S. Army Corps of Engineers bulldozing from either end. They met at Soldiers' Summit, near Kluane Lake in the Yukon, on November 20, and a pilot road,

Watson Lake is a popular milepost, its colorful collection of place names started by a homesick American soldier during construction of the Alaska Highway.

passable by army jeeps and trucks, was opened. The following year a permanent road was completed and was named the Alcan Military Highway. After the war, the highway was turned over to civilian contractors and was regraded, widened and opened to unrestricted travel. Today most of the highway is asphalt-surfaced, but improvements and repairs are ongoing.

Points of interest along the highway include **Tok**, known as the dog mushing capital of Alaska; **Burwash Landing**, founded as a gold rush trading post; **Whitehorse**, a gold rush boomtown; and the **Liard Hotsprings**, where construction workers soaked their tired muscles in 1942. Nearby **Watson Lake** (Mile 635) is well known for its wall of sign boards. The first signpost was carved by a homesick G.I. in 1942, and hundreds of signs, license plates and other paraphernalia now line the roadside. **Summit Lake Pass** marks the highest point of the Alaska Highway, where it traverses the northern Rocky Mountains.

The Alaska Highway also marks the eastern boundary of **Kluane National Park**. Kluane is a native name for 'place of many fish' and this wilderness park contains the most extensive non-polar icefields in the world. The Saint Elias Mountains run through the park and feed such rivers of ice as Hubbard Glacier, which terminates in Yakutat Bay on the Gulf of Alaska. A Visitor Centre is situated at Haines Junction and offers visitors an impressive multi-image, audiovisual slideshow of the park's spectacular scenery, much of it hidden behind a front range of mountains. The Kluane Range is visible from the Alaska Highway, as is Kluane Lake, which parallels the highway for 35 miles. The more distant Icefield Range lies west of the Kluane Range and contains Mount Logan, Canada's highest peak.

Spectacular scenery abounds in Kluane National Park, part of Canada's Yukon Territory and a World Heritage Site.

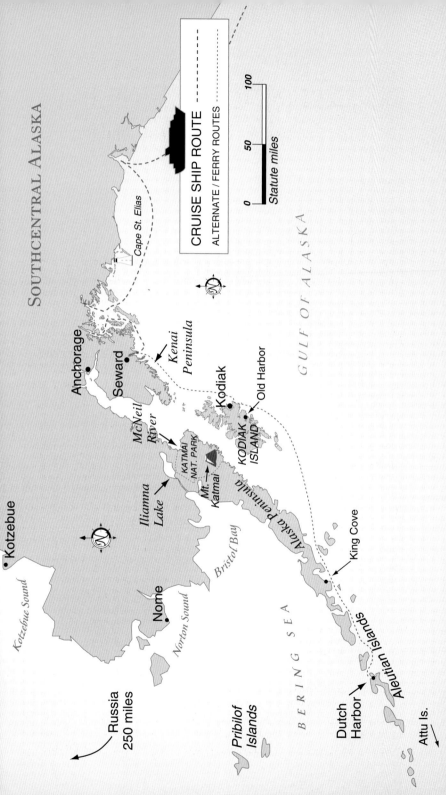

SOUTHCENTRAL ALASKA

CRUISE SHIP ROUTE
ALTERNATE / FERRY ROUTES

Statute miles

0   50   100

Cape St. Elias

Anchorage

Seward

Kenai
Peninsula

McNeil
River

Kodiak

Old Harbor

KATMAI
NAT. PARK

Mt.
Katmai

KODIAK
ISLAND

Iliamna
Lake

Alaska Peninsula

Bristol Bay

Kotzebue

Kotzebue Sound

Nome

Norton Sound

Russia
250 miles

Pribilof
Islands

BERING SEA

King Cove

Dutch
Harbor

Aleutian Islands

Attu Is.

GULF OF ALASKA

CHAPTER FOURTEEN

EXPEDITION CRUISING
Kodiak, The Aleutians and Beyond

Although most ships conclude a Gulf of Alaska 'Glacier' cruise at Seward or Anchorage, there are still thousands of miles of spectacular coastline to explore west of Cook Inlet. Beyond is the Alaska Peninsula and such famous places as the McNeil River – where brown bears congregate each fall to feed on salmon runs – and Katmai National Park & Preserve containing 2.5 million acres of volcanic mountains, caldera lakes, caribou herds and the largest unhunted population of brown bears in the world. Few places are more remote than Katmai Park, except perhaps the outer islands of the Aleutian chain which stretches for 1,000 miles along the edge of a deep-sea trench separating the Gulf of Alaska from the Bering Sea.

Alaska's state ferries journey the waters west of Cook Inlet, with stops at Kodiak Island; at Chignik, Sand Point and King Cove on the Alaska Peninsula; and at Dutch Harbor in the Aleutians. A few cruise companies also offer adventure expeditions to the Bering Sea where isolated islands contain Eskimo and Aleut villages, as well as huge populations of seabirds and sea mammals. Here is a sampling of what awaits visitors to the more remote waters of coastal Alaska.

KODIAK ISLAND

As a cruising destination, Kodiak Island remains undiscovered. Called "Alaska's Emerald Isle", this mountainous island is covered by a dense growth of grass, berry bushes, alder thickets and wildflowers. At the island's southernmost end, heath and tundra cling to the thin topsoil. Some adjacent, smaller islands contain spruce forests, but most of Kodiak Island itself is devoid of trees, the land scoured by glaciers in the last ice age. From the water, Kodiak's verdant slopes look like manicured golf links. However, upon stepping ashore, visitors quickly discover that the grass is chest high.

The lush vegetation of Kodiak Island (second largest island in the U.S. after Hawaii) is also prime habitat for the largest carnivorous land mammal in the world – the Kodiak brown bear. A salmon diet and mild climate allows this grizzly subspecies to grow as large as 10 feet (when

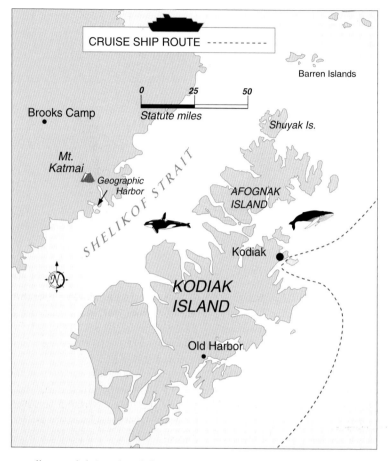

standing upright) and weigh as much as 1,500 pounds. Roads here are found only in the port towns, leaving the mountainous interior the sole domain of bears and other wildlife.

The waters around Kodiak are also rich with animal life. Humpback whales, Dall porpoises and sea otters are frequent sights as are colorful puffins. In the Port of Kodiak, where the state ferry docks, Steller sea lions are regular visitors. These large mammals swim near the fishboat docks, scavenging for fish scraps. Several summers ago, a local fisherman was squatting on the dock when a sea lion grabbed him by the backside and pulled him into the water, dragging him six feet under before letting him go. Such tales don't endear sea lions to fishermen, but Steller sea lions are a protected species in Alaska, having suffered a drastic population decline in recent years.

Kodiak is a colorful fishing port – one of the largest in America – and it attracts college kids each summer in search of lucrative deckhand jobs. Many of the greenhorns, however, end up working in

Glacial erosion shaped Kodiak and its neighboring islands, which are a geological extension of the Kenai Peninsula.

the canneries. At Larsen Bay, site of Kodiak Island's oldest operating cannery, summer workers are housed in wooden dormitories set on pilings and joined by boardwalks to the cannery buildings. When the fish tenders pull in loaded with salmon, the assembly lines roll – regardless of the hour.

Alaska's Russian history is closely tied to Kodiak, which was the colonial capital of Russian America before Alexander Baranof moved it to Sitka. Kodiak's Baranof Museum is the oldest Russian structure remaining in Alaska, built by the Russian-American Company in 1808 for storing fur pelts. Of solid log construction, it overlooks a stone wharf once used by sailing ships of the fur trade.

Behind the museum a sweep of lawn leads to the local Russian Orthodox Church – a vital presence in Kodiak since 1784 and a moderating influence on Russian fur traders who were often brutal in their treatment of natives. The Orthodox missionaries helped the natives preserve their traditions and the church has retained a faithful following among the indigenous population. Native fishermen display icons on their vessels and often ask the local priest to bless their boats before heading out.

In summer, the weather is generally placid, warm and pleasant. In winter, however, Kodiak is exposed to tremendous storms rolling in from the Aleutians and sea conditions around Kodiak Island can be treacherous when steep seas build on offshore banks. Nature is in control here, and people must tred lightly along this often stormy edge of the world.

The town of Kodiak has a history of adversity. When Mount Katmai erupted in 1912, falling ash blackened the skies for two days and resi-

Larsen Bay Cannery is a summer home for college students from the Lower 48 who work here during the salmon season.

dents could barely breathe. The ground shook and homes collapsed under the weight of ash that piled 18 inches thick on level surfaces and many feet deep in slides. During the 1964 earthquake, part of the town dropped two feet and seismic sea waves washed boats in the harbor onto shore. Outlying ports were also hit by tsunamis. At the native village of Old Harbor, residents climbed up the mountainside and watched a series of huge waves wash away their homes. The village church stood its ground against waves surging past its windows and the people of Old Harbor say it was a miracle that the church survived. It served as a refuge until outside help arrived, and to this day the church – with its resident priest Father Sergius – plays a major role in the community.

In recent years Old Harbor has attracted much attention from historians, geologists, archaeologists and conservationists. The first Russian settlement in Alaska was established just a few miles away at Three Saints Bay. The year was 1784 and an important battle took place near Old Harbor at which the invading Russians defeated the native Koniags (Southern Eskimos) on a site that has undergone careful excavation. The Koniags had inhabited Kodiak Island for some 7,000 years before the arrival of Russian fur traders. They spoke a Yup'ik language called Alutiiq, and one of their traditions was to partake of a banya (more commonly called a sauna). This tradition is still practised in Old Harbor, and visitors are often invited to the home of Sven Haakanson, the town's former mayor, for a steam in the family's banya.

Kodiak's Baranof Museum, the oldest Russian structure in Alaska, was built for storing furs.

Prominent visitors to Old Harbor include James Michener (while researching his book Alaska), singer John Denver (who arrived here in the wake of the 1989 oil spill), and David Rockefeller (who pulled into port in the summer of 1991 as the leader of a sailing expedition). In early 1994, the National Geographic Society aired a television documentary on the brown bears of Kodiak Island that was filmed in and around Old Harbor.

KATMAI NATIONAL PARK

Lying 25 miles across Shelikof Strait from Kodiak Island is the Alaska Peninsula. The Aleutian Range of snowcapped mountains forms the backbone of this peninsula and runs its entire length, from Cook Inlet to the Aleutian Islands. Best known of these peaks is Mount Katmai, around which a national park has been established.

Mount Katmai erupted on June 6, 1912, and drastically altered the surrounding valleys, lakes and rivers with material spewed from its volcanic core. For a week before Katmai's massive eruption, the surrounding area was rocked by earthquakes that were felt 130 miles away. When Katmai erupted through a vent in its base, the sound explosion was so deafening that, had it taken place in New York City, residents of Chicago would have heard it plainly. Glowing hot lava, ash and gas burst skyward from a vent in the base of Mount Katmai, its summit collapsing as the mountain's magma chamber emptied. Residents of Kodiak Island, 100 miles distant, were rained with ash so thick that for two days a person couldn't see a lantern held at arm's length.

It was one of the greatest volcanic eruptions in recorded history, but, because of Katmai's remote location, no human lives were lost. However, plant and animal life was destroyed as molten material flowed over the surrounding terrain. For several days the skies over much of the Northern Hemisphere were darkened by a haze of ash and gas that continued spewing from Novarupta – the new cone that had

The native fishing village of Old Harbor is located near the site of the first Russian settlement in Alaska.

formed over the vent at the base of Mount Katmai. In the end, hot ash covered an area of 40 square miles to depths of 700 feet.

Four years later, the National Geographic Society sent a scientific expedition, led by Robert Griggs, to study the aftermath of this cataclysmic event. They were awestruck at the sight of a valley completely filled with ash and thousands of smoking fumaroles, their steam still soaring 500 feet into the air. It was named the Valley of Ten Thousand Smokes and on September 24, 1918, President Wilson established Katmai National Monument to preserve this unique area of historical and scientific interest. In 1931 the monument was enlarged to protect its significant population of brown (grizzly) bears and other animals, such as moose and caribou. Presidents Roosevelt and Johnson each enlarged the preserve further and, in 1980, President Carter gave the area National Park status.

A mainly roadless region, Katmai Park is not the most accessible national park in America, but it does attract visitors from around the world who specifically research and seek out this unique corner of the globe. Brooks Camp – located inland on Naknek Lake, about 300 air miles southwest of Anchorage – is the hub of the park with a Visitor Center and a road leading to the Valley of Ten Thousand Smokes. Adventure cruise expeditions pull into Geographic Harbor for a close look at the volcanic ash which lies on the park's rugged slopes and

Fishboats often anchor in the numerous bays of Geographic Harbor – part of Katmai National Park – where large brown bears wander the isolated beaches.

beaches. The local beachcombers here are brown bears, which are frequently seen ambling along the foreshore in search of food.

THE ALEUTIANS

Extending westward from the Alaska Peninsula, the Aleutian chain is a lonely stretch of submerged mountains, their peaks marking the edge of a deepsea subduction zone called the Aleutian Trench. The weather here is an ongoing battle between the Bering Sea's cold Arctic air and the Gulf of Alaska's warmer Pacific air. Vicious winter storms are replaced with the dense fog of summer.

Japanese troops invaded the Aleutians in June 1942, the first foreign occupation of American soil since the war of 1812. The United States had anticipated such a move and installed two secret airfields (disguised as canneries) on either side of Dutch Harbor. The Japanese, thinking the nearest American airfield was at Kodiak, were repelled in their attack on Dutch Harbor but did land on the islands of Attu and

Kiska. When American military pilots attempted to retake the occupied islands, violent gales and poor visibility were more of a hazard than enemy fire.

Throughout the winter of 1942/43, Japanese troops defended their positions against relentless American air attacks. Dashiell Hammett, author of *The Maltese Falcon* and *The Thin Man*, was stationed at the Aleutians during the war and wrote about this northern battlefield in *The Capture of Attu, Tales of World War II in Alaska.* "Modern armies had never fought before on any field that was like the Aleutians," he wrote. "Bad weather fought against us there. Air reconnaissance was almost impossible."

Finally, on May 11th, 1943, 11,000 American troops landed on Attu and, after 18 days of fighting, 2,600 Japanese troops were reduced to 800. In the end, only 28 were taken as prisoners – the rest died in combat or committed suicide to save their honor. About 550 American soldiers were killed retaking Attu, and several thousand were wounded. On Kiska, east of Attu, the Japanese had secretly abandoned the island under cover of dense fog. When American and Canadian troops landed on Kiska's shores after weeks of heavy shelling, they found the place deserted.

An earlier invasion of the Aleutians took place in the 1700s, when Russian fur traders subjugated the Aleuts as hunters of sea mammals. The islands' Russian history is evident in the onion-domed, wooden churches that still grace the native villages dotting the green slopes of these misty islands. One of the Aleuts' oldest settlements was at Dutch Harbor, where the Russian fur traders based their operations. Today Dutch Harbor is a major fishing port – consistently ranking at the top of U.S. ports for value of commercial fish landed.

During the king crab boom of the 1980s, hundreds of fishboats passed through Dutch Harbor on their way to the Bering Sea. In 1987, they bought a total of 80 million gallons of fuel. Strategically located between the Bering Sea and the North Pacific Ocean, and with a geographic proximity to the Orient and the U.S. Northwest, this busy harbor is a major service center for the harvesting and processing of groundfish and crabmeat.

THE PRIBILOFS

The largest Aleut population exists not on the Aleutian Islands but on the Pribilofs, which lie to the north in the Bering Sea. The ancestors of these people were brought here by Russian fur traders to harvest seals. The islands' huge fur seal colonies still bring visitors to the Pribilofs, but now they come to discreetly watch these animals from special blinds. On St. Paul Island, hundreds of thousands of fur seals spend the summer at 14 different rookeries and haul-out locations. Large males – "beachmasters" – arrive in late May and establish their territories. The females arrive in June to bear their young.

Cruise passengers are taken ashore in Zodiac landing craft at Boxer Bay on St. Lawrence Island, located in the Bering Sea.

Other island residents are reindeer and the frequently sighted Arctic blue fox. The tundra-covered Pribilofs also host more than two million seabirds each summer, some migrating from as far away as Argentina. Species commonly sighted include horned and tufted puffins, rock sandpipers, red-legged kittiwakes and crested aukluts.

During World War II, Aleuts living on the Pribilofs were evacuated by the U.S. Navy after Japanese troops invaded the western Aleutians. These Aleuts were moved to Funter Bay on Admiralty Island in southwestern Alaska where they were interned for two years, living in the bunkhouses of an old cannery and an abandoned mine. Post-war reforms led to self-government for Pribilovians, as well as acting parts in such movies as Walt Disney's *The Seal Islands* and *The World In His Arms*, which starred Gregory Peck and was filmed on the Pribilofs in 1952.

Adventure cruises don't end at the Pribilofs, but carry on across the Bering Sea to the Diomede Islands (where both the Alaskan and Siberian mainlands are visible in clear weather) and to St. Lawrence Island, where the natives are Yu'pik-speaking Eskimos whose dialect is similar to the natives of Provideniya on the nearby Siberian coast. At least one cruise expedition crosses the International Dateline and lands in the Russian Far East, then cruises north through the Bering Strait and above the Arctic Circle. Polar bear sightings and tours of Eskimo villages are all part of expedition cruising in the remote waters of coastal Alaska.

ABOARD – Referring to being physically on a ship and not ashore.

ABEAM – off to one side of the ship at a right angle to its length.

ABAFT – or "aft" towards the rear of the ship. Anyone or anything closer to the stern than the speaker is aft.

AHEAD – area in front of the ship's bow as in "all ahead slow" .

ALOFT – anything which is overhead.

ALONGSIDE – when a ship is being maneuvered to a pier or another vessel.

AMIDSHIPS- the middle of the ship.

ANCHOR – cruise ships normally use a variation of a Danforth or Navy Stockless anchor while in harbor to hold the ship securely if it is not tied to a dock. Anchors dig in the seabed to hold the ship fast.

ASTERN – at or near the rear or stern of the ship.

BEAM – the widest part of the ship at about midway of its length.

BELLS – Thirty-minute time units. There are six watches to a 24 hour day, each watch being four hours. A crew on their watch would always know the time by the number of bells sounding.

BELOW – to indicate area below the main deck.

BILGE – lowermost spaces of the ship where water and oil will collect.

BOAT STATIONS – an area of the ship assigned to each passenger where they must be during lifeboat drill.

BOW – the front of the ship.

BALLAST – if you wonder how tall cruise ships stay upright without capsizing – it's because of ballast. All the machinery and fuel and water tanks near the bottom of ship help to dampen the motion of the sea and keep the ship upright and steady.

BRIDGE – navigational and controlling area of the ship.

BULKHEAD – a wall on a ship.

CHART – a detailed three-dimensional map used for navigation.

COMPASS – Single most important navigation instrument on board. A compass is a round card with 360 degrees which normally aligns with magnetic north and thus indicates the ship's course by reading the degrees the ship's bow is from north.

COURSE – direction in which the ship is travelling as measured in compass degrees.

COURTESY FLAG – the flag of the host country a visiting vessel will fly from the starboard side of the ship. Normally, the Canadian flag will be flown while in British Columbian waters.

DAVIT – small crane-like device to raise or lower lifeboats.

DECK – the outside flooring of ship. The inside flooring is referred to as a sole.

DRAFT – a vertical measurement from the waterline to the bottom of the ship.

FATHOM – measurement, usually of water depth, equal to six feet.

FLOTSAM – items which are

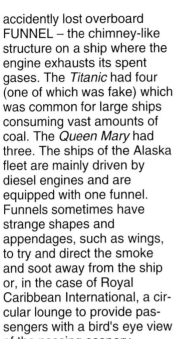

accidently lost overboard
FUNNEL – the chimney-like structure on a ship where the engine exhausts its spent gases. The *Titanic* had four (one of which was fake) which was common for large ships consuming vast amounts of coal. The *Queen Mary* had three. The ships of the Alaska fleet are mainly driven by diesel engines and are equipped with one funnel. Funnels sometimes have strange shapes and appendages, such as wings, to try and direct the smoke and soot away from the ship or, in the case of Royal Caribbean International, a circular lounge to provide passengers with a bird's eye view of the passing scenery.

GALLEY – the kitchen.

GANGWAY – this is the ramp or stairway by which you are able to board a ship.

HEAVE – this can mean to pull on a line and can also refer to a sudden upward or downward motion of a ship.

HEEL – to momentarily lean over to one side as when the ship is making a turn in its course.

HELM – the device by which to steer the ship.

HULL – the outside shell of the ship including its sides, upper decks and bottom.

JETSAM – items which are deliberately thrown overboard.

KEEL – the centerline along the bottom of the ship.

KNOT – a term expressing speed calculated by distance travelled, in nautical miles, in the space of an hour. A nautical mile is equal to 1.15 land miles.

LEEWARD – the side of the ship sheltered from the wind. (pronounced loo-ward.)

LIST – the inclining of a ship to one side or the other due to a shift of ballast or cargo. It is a more lasting situation than a heel.

NAUTICAL MILE – a unit of measurement at sea, equal to 1/60th of a degree if measured at the equator. It is 6076 feet.

PITCH – the rise and fall of the bow and stern.

PORT – the left side of the ship when facing forward.

PROPELLER – the bladed part of a shaft providing drive to the ship.

QUARTER – the two after-parts of the ship, one on each side of the centerline.

RUDDER – a paddle or finlike appendage at the stern of the ship, below the waterline and often aft of the propellers. The rudder is used to steer the ship.

STARBOARD – the right side of the ship when facing forward.

TENDER – Small boat used to ferry passengers from ship to shore.

WAVES – oscillations of the sea caused by wind. Water rolls on itself moving in the direction of the wind.

WINDWARD – the side of a ship where it feels windy.

YAW – a tendency to make a ship twist away from its course caused by a following wind or sea.

(Ship's ratings are quoted from various industry publications.)

Spirit of Alaska – 97 tons

ALASKA SIGHTSEEING / CRUISE WEST: The person often cited for popularizing cruises – and holidays – to Alaska is chairman of this company, Chuck West. The original founder of Westours (now part of Holland America Line), he worked for various airlines before opening a travel agency in Fairbanks specializing in sightseeing tours of the state. His company, Westours, was purchased in 1971 and West started Seattle-based Alaska Sightseeing two years later, offering land tours and small ship cruises that take passengers off the beaten path along less-travelled channels and pristine fjords of both the Canadian and Alaskan Inside Passage. The ships, all with outside cabins, carry 70 to 100 passengers. Their crew and officers are American.

CARNIVAL CRUISE LINES: The largest cruise line in the world returned to Alaska in 1996 and, in 1998, it brought the mainstream veteran *Jubilee* north. Carnival ships are popular with young people and attract a high number of first time cruisers. The itineraries offered are good value with stops at most ports and glaciers. Officers are Italian and service staff is international.

CELEBRITY CRUISES: Founded in 1990 as an offshoot of the Greek line Chandris Inc., Celebrity Cruises introduced its first ship to Alaska in 1996 and now uses two new megaships. Recently purchased by Royal Caribbean International as its premium brand, Celebrity remains

Galaxy, 1996 – 77,000 tons

an upscale cruise line offering fine cuisine, sophisticated service and a quality finish throughout its ships. Celebrity introduced it's new *Mercury* to Alaska in 1998 to complement the 77,000-ton *Galaxy* which has a huge observation lounge and wraparound windows which are 14 feet high. Both ships are scheduled for seven-day loop cruises out of Vancouver with the *Mercury* also offering seven-day line cruises between Vancouver and Seward. Officers are Greek and service staff are international.

CRYSTAL CRUISES: This luxury cruise line offers 12-day loop cruises out of San Francisco, with stops at Victoria and Vancouver, on the 50,000-ton *Crystal Harmony*. Launched in 1990, this spacious ship is finely appointed, carries only 960 passengers and features all outside cabins. Its Alaska itineraries include famous glaciers, ports of the Inside Passage and tailor-made shore excursions to suit individual preferences. The ship's officers are Scandinavian and service staff are international.

Crystal Harmony, 1990 – 48,000 tons

HOLLAND AMERICA LINE: This company's connection with Alaska began with the acquisition of Westours in 1971, which had operated cruises and tours to Alaska since 1947. HAL has a totally integrated operation for its customers and owns many support services such as tour coaches, rail cars, and hotels. This cruise line currently has six ships in Alaska and all are rated upscale mainstream. The *Noordam, Statendam* and *Ryndam* are working the seven-day glacier cruises between Vancouver and Seward. The *Veendam, Westerdam* and *Nieuw Amsterdam* offer Inside Passage itineraries of seven-day loop cruises out of Vancouver as well as three- and four-day one-way cruises that connect with an Alaska land

Statendam, 1993 – 55,000 tons

Noordam, 1984 – 34,000 tons

tour in Skagway. In business since 1873, HAL operated a successful transatlantic service from Rotterdam to New York for decades before turning to cruises in the late 1960s. Holland America's Dutch officers and staff of Indonesians and Filipinos have built a solid reputation of well-run, clean ships with a high level of friendly service. Holland America Line ships cut a fine profile and, with their distinctive sheer and blue hull, have a traditional look. Many of the ships contain extensive artwork to complement the ship's thematic decor and all have full wrap-around teak decks wide enough for joggers and those who prefer to stroll. The line recently retired the venerable flagship and perennial

*Norwegian Wind, 1993 –
39,000 tons*

Alaska favorite, *Rotterdam,* to make way for the new and much larger *Rotterdam VI* which will be cruising in Europe during the 1999 summer season.

NORWEGIAN CRUISE LINE: This company is credited as one of the first lines to invent modern cruises with three- and four-day trips from Miami to the Bahamas in the mid-1960s. NCL also revived the classic liner *SS France* (now the *Norway*), extensively refitting and rebuilding this grand ship for seven-day Caribbean cruises. The line currently positions the upscale mainstream *Norwegian Wind* (launched as the *Windward* in 1993) and *Norwegian Dynasty* on its Alaska cruises. *Norwegian Wind* was stretched in 1997 to over 1700 berths and cruises on seven-day Inside Passage roundtrips from Vancouver. The ship is often touted as being designed for Alaska with large picture windows throughout the ship. *Norwegian Dynasty* is the former 20,000-ton *Crown Majesty,* a popular ship with families, and offers seven-day line cruises between Vancouver and Seward with a slight variation in itinerary on north and south trips. Officers are Norwegian and service staff are international.

PRINCESS CRUISES: This company has had many years experience in Alaska since *Princess Italia* first steamed north in 1969. P&O, which bought Princess Cruises in 1972, also has a history in Alaska and was the first cruise company to send a large 'ocean liner' to Alaska when the *Arcadia* toured the Inside Passage. At its inception in the mid-1960s, Princess relied on chartered ships and took its name from one of these – Canadian Pacific's *Princess Patricia.* From the start, Princess Cruises established a reputation for a high standard of service and experienced phenomenal growth in the 1970s when the company permitted the television series *The Love Boat* to use its ships for onboard settings (a series now reprised). Princess currently operates six ships in Alaska each summer, including its new superliners the *Sea, Sun and Dawn Princess* – well designed 77,000-ton sister ships carrying 1,950 passengers each. They, along with the *Crown Princess,* offer seven-day one-way cruises between Vancouver and Seward. This itinerary takes in either Glacier Bay or Hubbard Glacier as well as the

Sun Princess, 1995 – 77,000 tons

many glaciers in College Fjord. These line cruises begin or end in the 'Far North' cruising area of Alaska with Seward as the northern terminus. The *Regal* and *Sky Princess* are the only Princess ships cruising Inside Passage loops in 1999. Princess Cruises' integrated tourist services include hotels (including lodges in Denali National Park), coaches and rail cars. Officers and service staff are international.

Crown Princess, 1990 – 70,000 tons

ROYAL CARIBBEAN IN'T: In 1995 RCCL introduced the largest ship ever to ply the waters of Alaska with the arrival of *Legend of the Seas*. Power lines across Seymour Narrows, a major pass of the Inside Passage, had to be raised 20 feet to accommodate this 70,000-ton, 1,800-passenger ship which comes equipped with a golf course. The new *Vision of the Seas* – launched in April 1998 and carrying 2,000 passengers – joins her sistership, *Rhapsody of the Seas*, for the 1999 season on Inside

Vision of the Seas, 1998 – 75,000 tons

Passage loop cruises out of Vancouver. Some itineraries are a little out of the ordinary with Hubbard Glacier and Haines included in the cruise. These handsome megaships have spacious and impressive public areas such as a multi-deck atrium with glass elevators and the company's hallmark Viking Crown Lounge – a glass-wrapped observation lounge located on the highest deck to provide passengers with a panoramic view of the passing scenery. RCCL officers are Scandinavian and service staff are international.

WORLD EXPLORER CRUISES: For some, this cruise company is synonymous with Alaska and for many years operated the *SS Universe,* built in 1953. World Explorer retired this ship in 1995 and now has a 23,000-ton leased vessel, the *Universe Explorer,* offering a casual atmosphere on 14-day Glacier Cruises from Vancouver to Seward and back. This cruise is unique in that the company offers a number of in-depth lectures about Alaska. Passengers can gain college credits from these lectures by registering when arriving onboard. Officers and crew are Chinese and Filipino.

A

Admiralty Island, 220,221
Alaska
    Chilkat Bald Eagle Preserve,
251
        Highway, 54, 328-329
        history of, 48-56
        Range, 321
        Railroad, 305, 311
        State Ferries, 209
albatross, 83
Alert Bay, 168-169
Aleuts, 50
Aleutians, 92-93, 331, 337-338
Alsek River, 294
Anchorage, 30, 62, 308-318
Annette Island, 191
Athapaskans, 93
aurora borealis, 63, 65

B

Ballantyne Pier, 150
Banff National Park, 21-23
Baranof, Alexander, 269-73
Bartlett Cove, 257, 259
bear, 83-85, 337
Beaufort Sea, 54
Behm Canal, 49, 202, 204
Bella Bella, 179-180
Bering Sea, 331, 337-339
Bering, Vitus, 51,
birds, 79-83
Blind Channel, 167
Bonanza Creek, 239-241
British Royalty, 134-135,160, 210
Brooks Range, 327
Burroughs, John, 192
Burwash Landing, 329
Butchart Gardens, 112, 117

C

Caines Head State Recreation
Area, 307
Calvert Island, 176-177
Campania Island, 183
Campbell River, 162-163
Campbell, Robert, 235-236
Canada Place Cruise Ship
Terminal, 133, 148-151
Canadian Pacific, 21, 111, 147
Cape
    Caution, 175
    Decision, 210
    Fox, 191
    Lazo, 160

    Mudge, 162
    Saint Elias, 294, 295
    Spencer, 263
    Suckling, 295
    Yakataga, 295
Capilano Suspension Bridge, 142,
146
Captain Cove, 183
caribou, 87,88
Carmack, George Washington, 239-
2w41
Carr, Emily, 115, 116, 137, 180
Chatham Strait, 219
Chilkat River, 235
Chilkoot Trail, 243, 245
Chugach Mountains, 304, 309
Circle City, 237
Coast Salish natives, 99
Coffman Cove, 208
College Fjord, 17, 298-300
Cook Inlet, 310
Cook, James, 51, 52, 99, 310, 315
Cordova, 298
Coronation Island, 210
Craig, 209
cruise ships - see ships
currents, ocean, 67
currents, tidal, 153

D

Dall, William H., 56, 288
Dalton, Jack, 250
Dalton Trail, 250
Davidson, Robert, 103
Dawson Creek, 54
Dawson City, 236, 248-249
deer, Sitka blacktail, 87
Denali National Park, 20, 21, 309,
320-323
Desolation Sound, 160
Diomede Islands, 339
Disenchantment Bay, 287
Dixon Entrance, 189
dolphins, 74
Douglas, James, 116
Dry Bay, 294
Duncan, William, 191-193
Dutch Harbor, 54-55, 337-338
Dyea, 243-245

E

eagle, 80-81, 251, 281
earthquakes, 60-62, 263, 265, 285-
286, 287, 300, 311-312, 317, 334
Egg Island, 175-176

Elfin Cove, 263, 267
Endicott Arm, 222, 223
Eskimos, 93, 334
Exxon *Valdez*, 302, 304
F
Fairbanks, 323-325
Fairweather Coast, 263-267
fish and fishing, 54-55, 77079, 162-163, 177
Fitz Hugh Sound, 176-178
float plane, 24, 25, 54, 203, 204
forest (see rainforest)
Frederick Sound, 217
Funter Bay, 339
G
Gastineau Channel, 224, 226-227
geese, 87
Geographic Harbor,
Georgia, Strait of, 56, 151
Gibsons, 156
Gilbert, Grove Carl, 288-289
Glacier Bay, 252-263, 264
Glacier cruise, 16-17
glaciers, 49, 57-60,222-223, 232-233, 254, 256, 288-292
    Brady, 256
    Columbia, 303, 304
    Hubbard, 31, 286-292
    La Perouse, 104-105, 263, 266
    Le Conte, 217
    Malaspina, 292-293
    Mendenhall, 232
    Portage, 319
gold rushes, 53, 212-213, 224-225, 235, 239-245
Grenville Channel, 181, 186
Grouse Mountain, 145, 146
Guinness family, 146
Gulf Islands, 119
Gulf of Alaska,
gull, 83
Gustavus, 267
H
Haida, 97-98, 101, 102-103
Haida Gwaii - see Queen Charlotte Islands
Haines, 250-251
Hakai Pass, 177
halibut, 78-79
Hammett, Dashiell, 338
Harding Icefield, 306
Harriman Expedition, 191, 287, 288-289, 298-299

Harriman Fjord, 299
hatchery, salmon, 194
Hays, Charles, 185, 186
Hecate Strait, 184
Holkham Bay, 222
homesteading, 207-208
Hoonah, 253
Hoonahs, natives, 254, 255
hotsprings, 66, 282-283, 325
Howe Sound, 144, 155-156
Hubbard Glacier, 31, 286-292
Hudson's Bay Company, 211-212, 235-236
Hydaburg, 209
Hyder, 190
I
Ice Age, 49, 224, 253
Icy Strait, 253, 254
Iditarod Trail Dog Sled Race, 86, 310, 311
Inside Passage, 14-15, 95, 152-187
J
Jackson, Sheldon, 53, 213, 275, 280
Jasper National Park,21-23
Johns Hopkins Inlet, 258, 260, 262
Johnstone Strait, 53, 165-167
Juan de Fuca, Strait of, 109
Juneau, 29, 224-233
Juneau Icefield, 219, 223
Juneau, Joe, 225
K
Katmai Nat'l Park & Preserve, 63, 64, 331, 335-337
Kayak Island, 294
Kenai Fjords, Nat'l Park, 304, 305-307
Kenai Peninsula,58
Kent, Rockwell,207
Ketchikan, 26, 28, 193
Khantaak Island, 292,
King Cove, 331
king crab, 79
Klondike Gold Rush, 53, 120, 160, 239-249
Kluane National Park, 31, 329
Kodiak Island, 331-335
Kotzebue, 330
Kupreanof Island, 217
Kwagiutl, 95, 98-99, 141, 168-169
L
Lake Louise, 22
Lake Hood, 309, 318

land tours, 20-24
La Perouse,explorer, 266
Lituya Bay, 263, 265-267
London, Jack, 175, 249
Loring, 205
Lynn Canal, 235, 249-250
M
Mackenzie, Alexander, 178
Malaspina, Alejander, 287
Marble Island, 210
Matanuska Valley, 319
McNeil River, 331
Mendenhall Wetlands, 82
merganser, 82-83
Metlakatla, 191-192
Michener, James, 279-280, 335
midden, 96
Misty Fjords, 49, 190, 202, 204-205
Moore, William, 239, 243
moose, 87, 88
Mount Edgecumbe, 64
    Fairweather, 267
    Katmai, 63, 64, 333-334, 335
    Logan, 285
    McKinley, 309, 321
    Roberts, 226, 228, 229
    Saint Elias, 285, 286, 292, 293
mountain goat, 86
Muir, John, 56, 191, 192, 213, 220,
253-258, 260

N
Namu, 77
Nanaimo, 159
natives, 50, 51-52
native art, 100-103
native culture, 92-103
Nenana, 325
New Archangel, 271
New Metlakatla, 191-192
Ninstints, 184, 185
Northern Lights - see Aurora
Borealis
Northwest Passage, 109, 139
Nome, 24, 56, 86, 310
Nootka Sound, 52
Nootka (West Coast natives), 98-99
O
Oil spills, 301-303
Olympic Peninsula, 127
Old Harbor, 334-335, 336
otter, river, 77

otter, sea, 76-77, 303
P
Palmer, 319
Petersburg, 215-217
petroglyph, 97
photography,37
pilotage, 43-45, 173-174
Pipeline - see Trans Alaska Pipeline
porpoise, Dall, 73-74
Port Hardy, 171
Port McNeill, 169
Port Protection, 210, 211
Portage, 319
Portland Canal, 190
Pribilofs, 338-339
Prince of Wales Island, 207, 208-
210
Princess Louisa Inlet, 157-158
Princess Royal Island/Channel, 181
S.S. Princess Sophia 249-250
Prince Rupert, 185-187
Prince William Sound, 296-305
Prudhoe Bay, 328
puffin, 81-82
Puget Sound, 127
Q
Queen Charlotte Islands, 184-185
Queen Charlotte Sound, 175
Queen Charlotte Strait, 173, 174
R
rainforest, 89-91
Rattenbury, Francis, 110-113, 136
Reid, Bill, 103, 142
Reid, Frank,
Resurrection Bay, 305
Richardson Highway, 304
Richter, Charles, 60
Ripple Rock, 164
Robson Bight, 161, 168
Rocky Mountains, 21-23
Roosevelt, Theodore, 190-191
Russia/Russians,
Russian-American Company, 211-
212
Russell Fjord, 290, 291
S
salmon, 77-78, 162-163
Saint Elias Mountains, 292
Sawmill Bay, 300
Saxman Village, 98, 192, 200-201
seal, 75
sea lion, 75,76, 298

sea otter - see otter, sea
Seattle, 108, 109, 120-127
Sechelt Peninsula, 156
Service, Robert, 249
Seward, 30, 305-306
Seward, William, 53, 305
Seymour Narrows, 153, 163-165
Shakes, Chief, 211, 213, 214
sheep, Dall, 87
Shelikof, Grigori, 269
ships, cruise, 17-19, 34-36, 38-47, 342-345
shore excursions, 25-27
Sidney, 118
Sitka, 29, 268-282
Skagway, 29, 31, 236, 237, 240, 243-248
Smuggler Cove, 156
sled dogs, 85-86
Soapy Smith, 243-247
Sointula, 169
Spanish explorers, 128, 155, 286, 295
Stanley Park, 140-141
St. Paul Island, 338
Steel, Sam, 243
Steller, Georg, 295
Stephens Passage,65, 221
Steveston, 143, 145
Stewart, 190
Stikine Icefield, 219
Stikine River, 210-212
Summit Lake Pass, 329
Sumner Strait, 210

T

Takhinsha Mountains, 256
Taku Harbor, 65
Taku Inlet, 223-224
Tanana River, 325
Tarr Inlet, 262, 264
Tatshenshini River, 294
tectonic plates, 48-49, 61, 285
Telegraph Cove, 168
Tenakee Springs, 66, 282-283
Tides - see Currents
Three Saints Bay, 52, 269, 334
Thorne Bay, 207, 208
Three Hole Point, 304, 307
tidal wave - see tsunami
Tlingit, 97-98, 100, 200-201, 211-213
Tok, 329

Tongass National Forest, 190-191, 207
Totem Bight State Park, 201
totem poles, 100, 141, 200-201
Tracy Arm, 65, 222-223
Trail of '98, 243, 245
Traitors Cove, 205
Trans Alaska Pipeline, 327-328
Tsimshian, 97-98
tsunami, 61-62

U

University of Alaska, 305, 324

V

Valdez, 30, 300, 301, 304
Valley of Ten Thousand Smokes,
Vancouver,City of, 128-151
Vancouver, George, 130-131, 133-134, 162, 165, 224, 235, 254
Vancouver Island, 152, 153
Victoria, City of, 28,108-118
Vickers, Roy Henry, 103
volcano, 63-64, 282, 315, 335-336

W

Watson Lake, 328, 329
weather, marine, 66-67
whales, 68-75, 168
    humpback, 69-71, 221, 259
    killer (orca) 71-72, 168
Whistler, 23, 145, 146
White Pass, 31, 240, 245, 246-248
White Horse Rapids, 245
Whitehorse, 248, 325
Whittier, 300
Wickersham, James, 231, 232
Wiks, Margaret Bell, 208
wildlife, 68-88
wolf, 85
World War II, 187, 307, 311, 328, 337-338, 339
Wrangell, 212
Wrangell Narrows, 208, 215

Y

Yakutat Bay, 285-295
Yukon River, 236, 325
Young, Samuel Hall, 213, 220, 250, 253-256

PHOTO CREDITS:

Alaska State Tourism, page 214, 303b
Alaska State Tourism, Robert Angell, page 80b, John Hyde, page 81
Anchorage Museum, Alaska Stock, © 1998 page 62a, 243
Buchart Gardens, page 112d
Canadian Hydrographic Service, page 62b,163, 164
Canadian Hydrographic Service, Richard Thomson, page 165
Canadian Pacific Hotels, page 22, 28b
Capilano Suspension Bridge, page 142
Clipper Cruise Line, page 339
Crandall, Alissa, Alaska Stock, © 1998, page 88a,320b
Cruise West, page 14, 18
Dedman Photo page 248,
Defreitas, Michael, page 8, 9b, 26, 30b, 85,98, 100a,107 100b,193a& b, 196a & b, 200, 201a, 228a, 233, 236b,237a, 264c, 268b, 269, 272b & c, 275, 281, 297
Emily Carr painting courtesy of Vancouver Art Gallery, page 116
Hardy, Pete, page 74,
Harvey, Al, Vancouver Aquarium, page 77
Holland America Line, page 87, 149, 255, 256, 320d, 325, 327
Hyde, John, Alaska Stock, © 1998, page 6, 69, 80a
Kelley, Mark, Alaska Stock, © 1998 page 65c,
Kit Elswa, Johnnie, page 98
Klotz, Grant, Alaska Stock, © 1998 page 88b,
Kodiak Historical Society, page 67,
Nakano, Alan – photos, page 9c,76, 86, 204b, 224, 258, 260b, 287
Nakano, Alan – illustrations, page 68, 70, 71,74, 92-93, 203, 260-261
Norris-Jones, Raymond, page 35,

Norwegian Cruise Lines, page 13,
P&O Cruises - Beken & Sons, page 38,
Princess Cruises, page 21,300a
R.H. Judd Archives, page 50, 51, 271,
Royal Caribbean Int'l., page 34, 39,
Schafer, Kevin, Corbis Images, © 1998 page 84
Seattle, Port of, page 122
Seattle Tourism, page108, 121, 124,125, 127
Shinnick, John, page 135
Short, Nan, page 239, 328
U.S. National Ocean Service, page 56,
University of Washington, page 120
Vancouver, City of, Archives, page 53, 110, 130, 131, 147, 174 242, 250
Vancouver Tourism, page 100, 133, 136, 140,145c, 148, 247
Whistler Resort Association, page 23,144 ,145b
Wood River Gallery (Circa Art), page 4, 20, 25,
Yukon Tourism, page 31b, 329

All other photography by Anne Vipond.